# Metaphor Analysis

Studies in Applied Linguistics
Series Editors: Srikant Sarangi, Cardiff University, and Christopher N. Candlin, Macquarie University

This series publishes books that are innovative applications of language and communication research; it is a companion series to the Journal of Applied Linguistics.

Advisory Board:
Charles Goodwin (University of California, Los Angeles)
Jim Martin (University of Sydney)
Kari Sajavaara (University of Jyväaskyläa)
Gabriele Kasper (University of Hawai'i)
Mary McGroarty (Northern Arizona University)
Ron Scollon (Georgetown University)
Gunther Kress (Institute of Education, London)
Merrill Swain (OISE, University of Toronto)

Published in the series:
*Sociocultural Theory and the Teaching of Second Languages*
Edited by James P. Lantolf and Matthew E. Poehner

*Language, Identity and Study Abroad*
*Sociocultural Perspectives*
Jane Jackson

Forthcoming:

*Applied Linguistics*
*Towards a New Integration?*
Lars Sigfred Evensen

# Metaphor Analysis

## Research Practice in Applied Linguistics, Social Sciences and the Humanities

Edited by
Lynne Cameron and Robert Maslen

LONDON   OAKVILLE

Published by

UK: Equinox Publishing Ltd., 1 Chelsea Manor Studios, Flood Street, London SW3
    5SR
USA: DBBC, 28 Main Street, Oakville, CT 06779

www.equinoxpub.com

First published 2010

British Library Cataloguing-in-Publication Data

A catalogue record for this book is available from the British Library.

ISBN   978 184553 446 2   (hardback)
       978 184553 447 9   (paperback)


Library of Congress Cataloging-in-Publication Data

Metaphor analysis : research practice in applied linguistics, social
sciences and the humanities / edited by Lynne Cameron and Robert Maslen.
    p. cm. -- (Studies in applied linguistics)
Includes bibliographical references and index.
ISBN 978-1-84553-446-2 (hb) -- ISBN 978-1-84553-447-9 (pb) 1.
Metaphor. I. Cameron, Lynne. II. Maslen, Robert, 1970-
P301.5.M48M46115 2010
418--dc22
                            2009045389


Typeset by CA Typesetting Ltd, Sheffield, www.sheffieldtypesetting.com
Printed and bound in Great Britain by Lightning Source UK Ltd., Milton Keynes and
Lightning Source Inc., La Vergne, TN

# Contents

# Preface

Metaphor is an important way of thinking; people use metaphor in constructing analogies and to make connections between ideas. Metaphor is an important way of using language; people use metaphor in explaining ideas or to find indirect but powerful ways of conveying feelings and emotions. By investigating people's use of metaphors, we can better understand their emotions, attitudes and conceptualizations, as individuals and as participants in social life. Metaphor thus offers a tool that researchers across applied linguistics, social sciences and the humanities can use to reveal more about how people think and feel.

The core aim of this book is to explain how metaphor can be used as a research tool as well as being a research object. Central chapters describe a method of 'metaphor-led discourse analysis' that has been developed over several research projects using spoken discourse data. This method is supported by a dialogic dynamics perspective on metaphor, i.e. metaphor occurs in the flow of discourse and social interaction, and to understand its nature and use requires that we understand metaphor as a dynamic and discourse phenomenon.

Other approaches to metaphor have focused primarily on its poetic dimension or on its cognitive dimension. Until around 30 years ago, the home ground of metaphor was considered to be literature and rhetoric, where strong and deliberate metaphors would be carefully constructed and placed for maximum effect. Since then, with the rise of cognitive theories, metaphor has been considered to be located in thought and thinking processes, rather than in language. Discourse based studies of metaphor have grown in number in the last few years, partly in reaction to the neglect of language prompted by cognitive metaphor theory. Metaphor has been studied in the everyday talk of school classrooms and the doctor's surgery, in advertisements and newspapers, in large corpora of political discourse and in the smallest exchange between individuals. The move to understand and investigate metaphor in discourse opens up possibilities for using metaphor as a research tool in a wide range of discipline areas, and this book aims both to demonstrate the possibilities and to serve as an introduction to methodology.

When real world language use is taken as the site of metaphor study, researchers face a raft of methodological issues that have only recently begun to be addressed. This book began in a research methodology project funded by the UK National Centre for Research Methods, *Metaphor Analysis: Theoretical and Methodological Challenges in using Discourse Data.* A group of research- ers interested in metaphor and discourse came together to develop ideas and materials for training researchers in various social science disciplines, and several members of the group have contributed chapters to this volume. The starting point for the project workshops was the discourse dynamics approach to metaphor being developed by Cameron (Cameron, 2003, 2007a; Cameron *et al.*, 2009) and its method of metaphor analysis. Although members of the project team have their own preferred theories, approaches and methods, we were united by a concern for the quality and rigour of metaphor research. As meta- phor scholars, presenting our field across disciplines was a challenge, requiring us to put narrow divisions and arguments to one side in order to provide sound techniques that would address a range of research questions. The contributors to this volume have all found ways to resolve methodological problems in their own research projects and in contributions to the metaphor analysis project, and have contributed to developing the techniques that are brought together here.

## Acknowledgements

The editors would like to acknowledge the following for support in producing this volume: National Council for Research Methods for the initial funding of the metaphor analysis project; CREET (Centre for Research in Education and Education Technology) at the Open University for hosting the project website, which produced preliminary drafts of some of the chapters, and for funding some of the editorial work; Carol Johns-Mackenzie for assistance with putting the book together.

## Formatting conventions

The argument of the book makes it important to distinguish between metaphor in language use and metaphor in people's thinking. We have used the following formatting conventions to reflect that:

- *italics:* words or phrases extracted from real data are italicized in the text.
- underlining: metaphorically used words and phrases are underlined in data extracts, and, unless obvious, when discussed in the text.
- **bold:** is used for emphasis, or to introduce important technical terms.
- *ITALICS SMALL CAPITALS*: systematic metaphors are written in small italic capitals, to reflect their origins in real data.
- SMALL CAPITALS: conceptual metaphors are written in small capitals.

# Section 1

# Introducing metaphor analysis

The opening chapters set out to inspire readers with an enthusiasm for metaphor analysis and what it can offer to research projects in applied linguistics, the social sciences and the humanities.

The first chapter introduces metaphor as seeing one thing in terms of another, a multi-dimensional discourse phenomenon that involves language, thinking, physicality and social interaction. It then demonstrates how metaphor can be used as a research tool to open up discourse data and reveal something of people's ideas and attitudes and values. Cameron summarizes her empirical study of metaphor and reconciliation, in which metaphor analysis helped to uncover the strategies by which former enemies came to understand each other.

In the second chapter, Todd and Low present a selective survey of published studies that use some form of metaphor analysis and evaluate their methodology and outcomes. Studies are selected on the basis of being helpful to researchers reading this book in order to carry out their own empirical projects.

# 1 What is metaphor and why does it matter?

## Lynne Cameron

The first chapter introduces metaphor and aims to demonstrate the power of metaphor-led discourse analysis. After a brief review of why metaphor is important for researchers using discourse data to answer questions about people's ideas, attitudes and beliefs, a demonstration of metaphor analysis is presented, taken from the author's study of reconciliation talk between a bomber and a victim (Cameron, 2007b; 2009). The overview presented here is designed as an entry point for readers into the type of research methodology dealt with in much more detail in later chapters. By presenting a completed study first, we aim to tempt researchers with the possibilities of using metaphor in their own research.

## What is metaphor?

> Metaphor is a device for seeing something in terms of something else.
>
> (Burke, 1945: 503)

This description of metaphor is still one of my favourites, even though it is obviously inadequate as a definition of the phenomenon. I like it because it says in simple terms what lies at the heart of metaphor: that there are two distinct ideas involved and that we use one idea to better understand the other. The 'seeing... in terms of' is the process of metaphor. As a definition, this is inadequate because metaphor is described using two imprecise metaphors: *device* and *seeing*. Burke's description of metaphor is useful as a starting point, but much more technical detail is needed to be able to identify metaphor in language use or theorize about the process of metaphor. First, there are various dimensions of metaphor that need to be considered: linguistic, embodied, cognitive, affective, socio-cultural, dynamic.

### Metaphor as linguistic

In this book, we are concerned with metaphor as it is used by people engaged in specific social interactions involving language. Language use in social interaction is how, in this book, we define 'discourse'; specific instances of social interaction involving language are called 'discourse events'. In the metaphor literature, as elsewhere, the reader should be alert for other senses of discourse; for example, 'discourse' is used by some writers to refer to conventionalized ways of using language, as in 'the discourse of science' or 'racist discourse'.

Metaphor in active language use is our object of concern and what is collected as data. There may be metaphorical thinking that never shows itself in language, but that is not our concern, and cannot be while discourse is our only source of data. The term 'linguistic metaphor' here refers to metaphors that are found in language use. Again, a terminological warning to readers is needed: the term 'linguistic metaphor' is sometimes used to mean the instantiation in language of conceptual metaphor (Steen, 2008; see also Chapter 3). Our use of the term here does not restrict it in this way.[1] A linguistic metaphor is signalled to the researcher by the arrival of 'something else', as Burke put it – a word or phrase which contrasts with the meaning of the discourse at that point. This word or phrase is not itself the linguistic metaphor, but is the 'vehicle term' of the metaphor. In metaphors that are very obvious or active, the vehicle term stands out clearly as incongruous or anomalous in its discourse context. For example, in the popular song title *The Windmills of your Mind,* the word *windmills* appears incongruent against the background of the song's topic of minds and thinking. However, less striking, conventionalized metaphors can also be seen as somehow incongruent when we stop and look at them – consider, for example a pension fund which is said to be *in a healthy position*, or a person who *gets into difficulties*. The conventionalized phrases that describe finances in terms of health and physical position, or a process of bad luck in terms of movement to the inside of something, keep their potential as metaphor even though we may usually process them without consciously attending to incongruity or without 'seeing one thing in terms of something else'. Because we rely on latent potential as indicative of metaphor, what counts as linguistic metaphor includes the full range from novel through to the most conventionalized.

## Metaphor as embodied

Language is seldom, if ever, used in social interaction without gesture and other physical movements. As we see in Chapter 11, patterns of gestures can be analysed for metaphor both as a complement to language analysis and in their own right. Metaphor in use is embodied, in the sense that speaking or writing, listening or reading, are much more than mental processes; our bodies participate and interpret, eyes and head move, skin reacts and responds. On longer timescales too, metaphor is embodied, as conventionalized forms reflect, and perhaps activate, memories of physical experience. The phrase *take a deep breath*, for example, derives from the physical process of taking a deep breath in order to summon up strength to cope with a difficult situation, although it is now often used meta-phorically to refer just to the summoning up of strength (Deignan, 2005).

From the perspective of embodiment (Gibbs, 2006a), linguistic metaphor represents only a part of what is happening with metaphor in social interaction, but it happens to be the part that is most obvious, and that we have most experi-ence in analysing. In the future, software may be developed that facilitates the analysis of gesture and other physical changes in social interaction, but in the meantime researchers need to compromise between the number of embodied aspects of data they wish to analyse and the amount of data that can be analysed in the time available for a project.

## Metaphor as cognitive

The second section of the book includes a summary of cognitive approaches to metaphor, contrasting these with discourse approaches. In this introductory chapter, we should note the dramatic shift in metaphor studies that occurred from 1980 onwards as a result of Lakoff and Johnson's *Metaphors We Live by* – the 'cognitive turn' (Gibbs, 1994). This shift introduced the idea of 'concep-tual metaphor' as a mapping between two domains in the conceptual system, which may give rise to metaphorical language. Here, the focus is firmly on the cognitive processes of connecting two concepts (Lakoff, 1993). Burke's description of metaphor can fit this cognitive version, with the 'device' being conceptual rather than linguistic. There is increasing discussion and debate about the adequacy of conceptual metaphor theory (e.g. Haser, 2005; Cameron, 2007b; Chapters 4 and 5, this volume) and in focusing in this book on metaphor in language use in social interaction, we acknowledge conceptual metaphor theory as a source of inspiration but do not necessarily accept it as 'the truth' or as the only basis for theorizing.

One of the key contributions of conceptual metaphor theory has been to highlight the systematic nature of conventionalized metaphors in language usage across discourse communities. The use of HEALTH[2] metaphors to talk about finances in English, for example, can cover both *healthy* and *sick* finan-cial conditions, *ailing* and *recovering* economies, and even *emergency meas-ures to save* banks.

## Metaphor as affective

The vehicle terms of linguistic metaphors often carry evaluations, attitudes, values, perspectives or beliefs. When metaphor is used to talk about 'something in terms of something else', it seems that people choose that 'something else' so that it expresses how they feel about what they are saying. While a single linguistic metaphor may not tell us much about affect, when we look at metaphors across episodes of social interaction we may find patterns that reveal speakers' attitudes or emotions. For example, a study of teachers' use of metaphors (Cameron, 2003) showed how they often chose metaphors that reassured learners and downplayed the cognitive effort required of learners: teachers introducing lessons to students said: *I'm going to give you a little bit of information* (rather than *I'm going to present you with some difficult information*), or *We're going to look at* ... (rather than *we're going to study*). Over a period of time, the affective force of these kinds of metaphors would build up and create a climate in which students may expect teachers to make their studies comfortable and accessible.

For research purposes the affective aspect of metaphor is very promising, since it offers access to emotions and attitudes via linguistic metaphors. Section 3 of this book deals with how exactly one can collect and analyse data to do this.

## Metaphor as sociocultural

Discourse and language use defined in this book as social activities. The dialogic is taken as the norm (Bakhtin, 1981; Linnell, 1998) rather than individual language use, which hardly occurs independently of social interaction or imagined social interaction. Furthermore, the discourse dynamics approach sees metaphors as emerging from social interaction over different timescales (Cameron, 2007b, 2008a; Gibbs and Cameron, 2008; Cameron *et al.*, 2009; Chapter 5, this volume). Conventionalized metaphors in language usage can emerge over long periods of time across speech communities, while individuals engaged in conversation may come to use particular metaphors as shared ways of talking over a few turns of talk. Groups of people who spend time in the same place or talking about the same ideas will also come to share metaphors. Cooper (1986) offers the example of prisons as metaphor-generating discourse communities: prison warders come to be spoken of as *screws*; time spent in prison is referred to as *porridge*.

## Metaphor as dynamic

One further dimension of metaphor becomes important when we study language use rather than conventions of usage – metaphor dynamics. As text and talk proceed, linguistic metaphors are selected, adapted and built on with subsequent metaphors. Metaphor dynamics may result from the process of interaction, as one participant in a conversation responds to another, or from the development of ideas, as a speaker or writer builds an argument, clarifies a position, or constructs a description. Our objects of concern are not isolated linguistic metaphors but strings of connected metaphors and the patterns of meaning that they produce or reflect. Chapter 5 develops these ideas further.

Summary: Metaphor offers a tool for understanding people

Metaphor is thus a multi-faceted phenomenon, or perhaps it would be more accurate to say that the idea of metaphor encompasses multiple phenomena. The attraction of metaphor as a research tool lies in what it can tell us about the people who use it. We argue in this book that linguistic metaphors in discourse can tell us something about how people are thinking, can indicate socio-cultural conventions that people are tied into or that they may be rejecting, and can reveal something of speakers' emotions, attitudes and values.

To use metaphor as a research tool we need first to identify metaphors in relevant discourse; we need to consider why these metaphors were used at their particular points in the discourse activity, i.e. the discourse function of the metaphors; we need to find patterns in metaphor use and function; from patterns in data, we can make inferences about the people using the metaphors. Each of these stages in metaphor analysis will be described in Section 3 in some detail, and good practice will be illustrated. Meanwhile, the rest of this chapter shows how metaphor analysis was used in a study of post-conflict reconciliation.

## The discourse dynamics of metaphor in reconciliation talk

Pat Magee and Jo Berry met for the first time in 2000. Their personal histories were very different but had coincided 14 years earlier, when Jo Berry's father was killed by the bomb that Pat Magee had planted in a Brighton hotel. As a member then of the Irish Republican Army (IRA), Pat planted the bomb with the intention of killing members of the ruling Conservative party who were meeting in Brighton for their annual conference. Jo's response to her father's killing was not a desire for revenge, but to understand what had led to the event. She had long wanted to meet the bomber face-to-face and, when Pat was released from prison early under the peace agreement between the British government and the IRA, this became possible.

Jo Berry provided the author with video recordings of conversations between the two of them, recorded over two and a half years, which became data for an applied linguistic study (Cameron and Stelma, 2004; Cameron, 2007b; Cameron, 2009).[3] The study aimed to answer the research question: How does metaphor contribute to the process of reconciliation?

From the recordings it was apparent that metaphor was used by both participants in explaining their ideas and expressing their feelings; careful analysis allowed us to understand more about the types of metaphors used and about the dynamics of metaphor use, i.e. how metaphors changed over time as the participants came to know each other better, as they asked more searching questions of each other, and as they accepted the other person's ideas and feelings. The study was 'applied' in the sense that we wanted to seek out implications for assisting the process of reconciliation – might it be possible, for instance, that mediators in post-conflict situations could use metaphor in particular ways to facilitate new understandings between former enemies?

### Starting points of the participants

The participants arrived at their first meeting, not only from their very different histories, but with different motivations for agreeing to participate in the conversations. Before describing the method, extracts from a radio interview that Jo and Pat participated in two and a half years after first meeting will give readers a feel for the kind of talk that comprised the data, and the sorts of metaphors that appear. In Extract 1.1, Pat reflects on how he came to the reconciliation process, thinking back over the two years since first meeting Jo. The underlined words in extracts are the vehicle terms of linguistic metaphors.

Extract 1.1

Pat     as a republican
        … I <u>felt</u> obliged
        as a republican
        to sit down and talk about that
        and against the <u>backdrop</u> of the political reasons
        given a <u>platform</u>
        for a republican <u>message</u>
        that had been censored for decades
        so
        when <u>offered</u> an opportunity
        to sit down
        and talk about
        what motivated you
        then you should
        avail of that
        so that's the <u>way</u> I walked into it

Pat's starting point metaphors speak of his motivation to meet Jo in terms of the theatre or public speaking using metaphors of *backdrop, message, platform*. His motivation was framed by *political reasons* and the discourse he expected to participate in was delivering a political *message* rather than person-person interaction. The change from what he expected to what happened is described in Extract 1.2.

Extract 1.2

> Pat    but as I said
> when you meet somebody
> who's so <u>open</u>
> to understanding your <u>perspective</u>
> then you're obliged to somehow reciprocate

The audience receiving the *message* changed from non-specific mass to a particular individual whose personality influenced his participation. Instead of the monologic *platform* of his expectations, Jo created in the conversations an atmosphere of *open*-ness that encouraged reciprocation.

Jo, in the same radio interview, described her starting point as in Extract 1.3. An immediate reaction to the death of her father was to want to *bring something positive out of* the event. She was thinking metaphorically of her reaction in terms of a journey with a purpose. As with Pat above, the reconciliation process eventually becomes a more mutual and interpersonal experience, described metaphorically as *hearing each other's stories*.

Extract 1.3

> Jo    <u>in</u> er,
> the first few days after the bomb
> just thinking
> if only I could <u>bring</u> <u>something</u> positive <u>out of</u> this
> and <u>feeling</u> very <u>strongly</u>
> that my father was killed
> because he was <u>part</u> of a conflict
> and it was a conflict which I was suddenly emotionally
> involved <u>in</u>
> and I realized
> I wanted to <u>hear</u> Pat's <u>story</u>
> because I believe that
> if anyone <u>opens up</u> and <u>shares</u> their <u>story</u>
> ehm
> it's very hard to hate
> and my idea of Pat
> was of someone
> without much humanity
> and I wanted to meet him
> and <u>hear</u> his <u>story</u>
> and <u>discover</u> his humanity
> later on also <u>came</u> the idea that I wanted him
> to <u>hear</u> my <u>story</u>

## Research Question

One of the sub-questions that contributed to answering the central research question, and which is addressed in this chapter, was:

- How is metaphor used to describe the reconciliation process?

## Method: The process of metaphor analysis

### Overview

The study worked within a discourse dynamics approach (more in Chapter 5) to track metaphors as they appeared and shifted across the conversations, looking for how the two participants reacted to metaphor: Did they reject the other's metaphors? Did they offer alternatives? Did they come to share metaphors? and what did the different metaphors contribute to the process of reconciliation through talking together? In a process of metaphor-led discourse analysis, a search for patterns of metaphor use across the discourse events was combined with close investigation of the negotiation of metaphors between speakers at the moment of use.

Figure 1.1 tries to capture the interaction across the various levels and types of analyses carried out. We are always working with metaphor in discourse, even though some initial steps of the metaphor analysis (on the left side of the diagram) are carried out separately from the discourse analysis (the right side of the diagram). This means that we must find ways to keep the discourse context active when working with metaphors, and not consider them in a decontextualized manner.

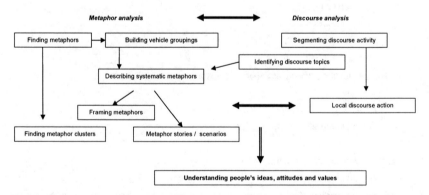

Figure 1.1.

The discourse function of metaphor is examined on several interconnecting timescales. At the level of local discourse action, we examine the negotiation of metaphors across speakers; at the level of episodes of talk and the discourse event, we track the evolution of metaphors as an outcome of negotiation, and check whether changes on the local level lead to longer-term changes in the metaphors used by the participants. On the longer timescale of the two and half years covered by the data, we search for emerging patterns of metaphor use. One kind of pattern, 'systematic metaphors' (Chapter 7, this volume) is semantic, and found by identifying connections between individual linguistic metaphors. These systematic metaphors may map on to discourse themes in telling ways. Another kind of pattern is distributional: heavy use of metaphors clustering at certain points in the discourse, or absence of metaphors at certain points (Chapter 10, this volume). Metaphor clusters often occurred at highly charged moments in the conversations. Sometimes participants' metaphors fit into a narrative, construct a metaphorical story, or connect into a larger, coherent 'metaphor scenario' (Musolff, 2004). The importance of metaphor stories and scenarios is their power to suggest what is *not* made explicit – because of our cognitive tendency to construct explanatory stories for our experiences, a partial story or scenario may invoke a larger story or scenario in hearers' minds.

## Finding metaphors

Analysis begins with finding metaphors in the data. Linguistic metaphor vehicles were identified in the transcribed conversations and radio interview (a total of 27,375 words of transcribed talk), using the method that will be described in detail in Chapter 6. The reconciliation conversations had a high density of metaphors, with an average of around 90 per 1000 words of transcribed talk.

The reliability of metaphor identification is important for consistency across studies and across researchers. Chapter 6 includes details of how reliability can be maximized.

## Building metaphor groupings

With over 2000 metaphors identified from several hours of talk, it was necessary to reduce the data by constructing larger groups or categories. These groupings can then be more efficiently manipulated or mapped on to discourse analysis to answer the research questions. Any process of data reduction or condensation carries risks – one may lose sight of some aspect of the data that really mattered; one may push the data into categories that are an inaccurate reflection of the reality they came from; one may choose labels for the groupings that influence interpretation of the condensed data. Good quality research attempts to minimize these risks, and throughout the method chapters of Section 3, we try to be as explicit as possible about how this can be done. We use the term 'trustworthiness' (Lincoln and Guba, 2000) to describe the goal of rigour in qualitative research. Trustworthiness includes (and adapts) more familiar research goals of validity and reliability. Chapter 7 shows how trustworthiness in building metaphor groups can be maximized.

After the linguistic metaphors were gathered together in a list, they were grouped and organized according to the basic meanings of the vehicle terms. For example, a grouping labelled *JOURNEY*[1] included *bring...out of* as in Extract 1.3, together with explicit metaphorical descriptions of Jo's coming to terms with her father's death such as *my healing journey, the end of that journey, come along that long journey*, and terms relating to movement on journeys such as *reached some conclusion, came the idea, one step at a time*. A grouping labelled *CONNECTION/SEPARATION* brought together various forms of *open*, along with related vehicle terms such as *detached, separate, bridges can be built, breaking down barriers*.

Creating groupings of metaphor vehicles is an interpretive process that works recursively between the data and the emerging categories. Labels for groupings are drawn from participants' words and placed at a level of generality/specificity just sufficiently above that of the vehicles in the group to include them all. Because our concern is with the language and thinking of these specific participants, we do not generalize higher, as would happen in an analysis based on conceptual metaphor theory (see Chapter 3, this volume). Nineteen groupings emerged from this stage of the metaphor analysis and are shown in Table 1.1.

Table 1.1. Vehicle groupings for reconciliation metaphors

| |
| --- |
| *JOURNEY* |
| *SEA/WATER* |
| *DIMENSION* |
| *SEEING* |
| *CONNECTION/SEPARATION* |
| *VIOLENT OR NEGATIVE ACTION* |
| *PHYSICAL ACTION* |
| *FICTION/PLAY/THEATRE* |
| *MONEY/VALUE* |
| *WORKING* |
| *TEXTILES* |
| *SCIENCE* |
| *PARTS OF THE BODY* |
| *LIVING WITH* |
| *HEARING/SAYING* |
| *COMPONENT PARTS* |
| *THING* |
| Prepositions |
| Other |

## Finding systematic metaphors

Systematic metaphors generalize by describing a pattern of metaphor use across the data. Systematic metaphors are found by searching within a vehicle grouping for a set of vehicles that are connected to the same topic. For example, in the *JOURNEY* grouping, a subset of vehicles which were used to talk about the first meeting between Jo and Pat were grouped together as the systematic metaphor:

*THE FIRST RECONCILIATION MEETING IS A STAGE ON A JOURNEY*

This systematic metaphor groups together a chain of related metaphors from both participants, including Jo's description of meeting the bomber, Extract 1.4:

Extract 1.4

    Jo    ... the end of that journey,

            would be,

            ... sitting down and,

            ... talking to the people who did it.

Another example of a systematic *JOURNEY* metaphor concerns Pat's process of accepting responsibility:

*COMING TO TERMS WITH RESPONSIBILITY IS A JOURNEY*

        something I have to go through.

        ... and how you ... come to terms with that,

While compiling systematic metaphors, we also noted who uses them, whether the metaphors moved across participants or whether they remained as preferred by just one speaker. Systematic metaphors are another condensation or reduction of the data that help us describe the actions of participants. They are a convenient shorthand, with each systematic metaphor standing for a set of connected linguistic metaphors which were each used at a particular time, by a particular speaker and in a particular discourse context. It is the researcher's task and duty not to lose sight of these particulars when interpreting systematic patterns.

## Findings: Systematic metaphors

To answer the research question, 'How is metaphor used to describe the reconciliation process?' the most relevant systematic metaphors about this topic were extracted. Four major systematic metaphors were found to be used in relation to the reconciliation process (Cameron, 2007b):

> *RECONCILIATION IS A JOURNEY*
> *UNDERSTANDING THE OTHER REQUIRES CONNECTION*
> *RECONCILIATION HAPPENS THROUGH LISTENING TO THE OTHER'S STORY*
> *RECONCILIATION IS CHANGING A DISTORTED IMAGE OF THE OTHER*

By examining how each of these was used in the discourse action, i.e. working across the two sides of Figure 1.1, we can answer the research question in more detail.

### RECONCILIATION IS A JOURNEY

*JOURNEY* metaphors are highly conventionalized and frequently occurring in English, and over 300 instances were used in the data. Very early in the first recorded conversation, Pat alludes to Jo's explicit metaphorical analogy with a *journey*:

Extract 1.5

Pat     I was aware from speaking to certain people,

          … (1.0) how… y-you –

          … saw this as a journey et cetera

Jo applies *JOURNEY* metaphors to two interconnected topics: her *inner JOURNEY* of moving on from her grief at the death of her father, and a second *JOURNEY* to understand the roots of violence and the motivation of those who caused the death, which she calls *walking in the footsteps of the bombers*. The second, metaphorical, *JOURNEY* resulted from (non-metaphorical) physical journeys to Northern Ireland to meet other victims and eventually members of the IRA. Alongside metaphors that explicitly mention *journeys*, Jo uses related metaphors to focus on the manner of moving – often long and difficult, as in: *there's another mountain to climb now* – and on the various stages on her *JOURNEYS*, the most important of which is her meeting with Pat.

As Extract 1.5 shows, Pat attributes the *JOURNEY* metaphor to Jo, although he uses such metaphors himself to talk about his own experience, including his decision to join the IRA as *the start of my journey*, his meeting with Jo, and the difficult process of accepting responsibility for Jo's father's death. It is often the case that particular metaphors are used more by one speaker than by another, and looking closely at the local discourse action can show whether these metaphors stay as the property of one person, or whether they come to be shared, and if so, what discourse work goes on to make this happen.

### UNDERSTANDING THE OTHER REQUIRES CONNECTION

When Jo Berry and Pat Magee talk about the processes of understanding each other through their meetings, they use metaphors of *CONNECTION/SEPARATION*, which include three, more specific, systematic metaphors. Two are ways of making connections: BUILDING BRIDGES and BREAKING DOWN BARRIERS. The third is a pre-condition to connection: being OPEN.

The metaphor vehicle *open* was used 45 times across the discourse events, mainly as an adjective – *I find you very open* (Pat to Jo) – and with a positive evaluation, being *open* is a good way to be. Early on people are described just as being *open,* but in the later conversation they are also *open* to *each other; you; me; the other person's story; to the other's humanity.* Extract 1.6 illustrates the phenomenon of contrasting metaphors, which was frequently observed with these data. Here, several metaphors that contrast with *open* are used to paint a negative picture of a hypothetical situation, thereby justifying Jo's choices and decisions:

Extract 1.6

| Jo | ... if I was – |
| | ... was still angry. |
| | --- |
| | ... (1.0) I would be <u>stuck</u> |
| | my heart would be <u>shut</u>. |
| | ... and I [would've] <u>lost out</u>. |

The BUILDING BRIDGES metaphor entered the talk as a theme of a poem that Jo Berry had written before meeting Pat Magee, which conceptualizes reconciliation as *building bridges* and asserts the possibility of this process. As a metaphor, it emphasizes the gap between self and other as what is in need of *bridging*; understanding is metaphorized as the *bridge*, and the reconciliation process is the act of *building the bridge.* In the talk outside of this poem, the metaphor was used 21 times. It is not much extended, remaining close to the form in which it was first used: *build* is only used once without being accompanied by *bridges; bridge* occurs in singular and plural form but other aspects of *bridges* are not found in the talk. Although the BUILDING BRIDGES metaphor starts as the 'property' of Jo in her poem, Pat also comes to use it over the course of the conversations. In one of his first uses in a response to the poem (Extract 1.7), Pat elaborates the vehicle term *bridge* to emphasize their different starting points:

Extract 1.7

| Pat | ... (1.0) <u>in</u> the er -- |
| | <u>the journey,</u> |
| | ... (1.0) <u>coming ... to a bridge,</u>/ |
| | ... you [know]. |
| Jo | [hmh] |
| Pat | ... with <u>two ends.</u> |

By elaborating the *bridge* metaphor to emphasize its *two ends*, Pat distances himself slightly from Jo, while at the same time maintaining alignment by repeating her *bridge* metaphor.

Six months later, in the second recorded conversation, Pat uses and extends Jo's metaphor to talk about wider conciliation processes between other people caught up in violence:

Pat     all those <u>bridges</u> are there to be <u>built.</u>

Metaphors of SEPARATION are often lexicalized as *loss* or parts of the verb *lose* (31 uses in total). As the metaphor used to speak of the killing of Jo's father, *loss* is the starting point for the talk and for the reconciliation process, for both speakers:

Pat     ... (2.0) you who've <u>lost</u> your father

For Jo, a consequence of the loss of her father is, paradoxically perhaps, a *connection* to others who had suffered in similar ways and to the Irish conflict:

Extract 1.8

Jo          ... and it <u>felt</u> like my heart was <u>broken,</u>
            ... <u>through</u> the conflict.
            ... (1.0) and,
            ... the suffering was ... my suffering.
            I couldn't <u>separate</u> it.
            I couldn't be <u>detached</u> anymore.
Pat         hmh
Jo          from ... and that --
            ... (1.0) that um,
            ... that <u>pain,</u>
            that <u>loss,</u>
            ... was <u>shared</u> by,
            ... by everyone.

The metaphor of BREAKING DOWN BARRIERS, with 13 uses across the talk, can be seen as more violent alternative to BUILDING BRIDGES, enabling connection through removal of a *barrier* rather than through making contact across a gap. There is a strong resonance between the metaphor and the physical barriers constructed during the conflict on the streets of Irish cities, both the barriers of burning cars and of army road blocks. Extract 1.9 shows the metaphor of *breaking down barriers* being used alongside the metaphor of *hearing stories* in talk about wider reconciliation processes, leading to a positive state of *closeness*:

Extract 1.9

| Jo | &lt;X where X&gt; victims of all <u>sides</u> have been meeting, |
| | … and -- |
| | er, |
| | … (1.0) that is just about, |
| | … er, |
| | … br- <u>breaking down barriers</u>, |
| | <u>sharing</u> stories, |
| | and -- |
| Pat | hmh |
| Jo | … and <u>through</u> .. experiencing each other's <u>stories</u>, |
| Pat | hmh |
| Jo | … there's a real <u>feeling</u> of, |
| | … <u>closeness</u> and humanity of everyone, |

**RECONCILIATION HAPPENS THROUGH LISTENING TO THE OTHER'S STORY**

The listening to the other person's story metaphor appeared in the first conversation in the dataset (21 uses) but became more important throughout the second conversation (67 uses). In the later radio interview (13 uses, as in Extract 1.2), this is Jo's preferred way of describing what she and Pat have done and what they hope to do for other people. Since to have a story is a mark of being human, in a reconciliation context merely allowing that the Other has a story is in itself an act of re-humanization (Extract 1.10). Being prepared to listen to that story is a gesture of empathy.

Extract 1.10

| Pat | but you are also, |
| | and I <u>find</u> you very <u>open</u>. |
| | … to my <u>story</u>. |
| | <u>where</u> I -- |
| | … er, |
| | … I feel there is more to me than just a perpetrator. |
| | … (1.0) and er, |
| | … (1.0) I suppose, |
| | … (1.0) what we're doing here. |
| | … is, |
| | … <u>exchanging</u> our <u>stories</u>. |

The power of the metaphor of LISTENING TO THE OTHER'S STORY comes not particularly from flexibility and productivity, which characterized the JOURNEY metaphor, but from its varied lexicalizations, its collocations, and its redeployment from the topic of reconciliation processes to the topic of accounting for political violence. A significant moment occurs in Extract 1.11 where Jo uses the *story* metaphor, in negative forms *not listening…not hearing their story*, as she accepts some responsibility for the Irish situation:

Extract 1.11

> Jo    … as a daughter of a conservative MP,
>
> I … can sort of <u>take</u> responsibility for the --
>
> … (1.0) what the government … didn't do.
>
> and,
>
> … the not <u>listening</u>,
>
> not <u>hearing</u> [<u>their story</u>].

It is important, however, that allowing the Other to 'tell their story' remains distinct from giving validity to that story as 'truth', since it is likely that participants in post-conflict reconciliation need to retain this distinction. Victims in particular may need to be able to listen and hear, and thereby understand better, without necessarily accepting the Other's justification for violence.

### RECONCILIATION IS CHANGING A DISTORTED IMAGE OF THE OTHER

English (and many other languages) conventionally uses metaphors of *SEEING* to talk about *UNDERSTANDING*, as in: *you <u>saw</u> this is a journey*. In addition to its conventional use in this way, a significant use of *SEEING* metaphors in the reconciliation conversations occurred when speakers used negative forms to create a contrast between the limited understanding of the other person before meeting and the fuller understanding that results from talking together (29 instances). For example, the de-humanization of other people that accompanies violent conflict was talked about in terms of *losing sight of the whole picture*. Re-humanization and understanding was metaphorized as a move from a distorted image to one that was correct and complete, as in Extract 1.12:

Extract 1.12

> Pat    you present yourself
>
> in --
>
> in order
>
> you hope
>
> to <u>break down</u> misrepresentations
>
> because I --
>
> until we do <u>see</u>
>
> each other

in our true light

---

we're always going to be dealing with some reduction
or a caricature

## Findings: Metaphor clusters

Linguistic metaphors are not evenly spread across talk and text, but seem to cluster at certain points, some of which are critical moments and all of which are worth looking at when carrying out discourse-based studies. Chapter 10 explains in more detail the method of finding metaphor clusters that can then be examined more closely.

The reconciliation data was explored for clusters of metaphors (Cameron and Stelma, 2004), and these were found to occur at two timescales: there were clusters of metaphors in discourse episodes that lasted between one and two minutes and, often inside these, smaller clusters in about five seconds of talk. The rate of metaphor use increased on average by 50% inside clusters from its rate in non-cluster talk. Many of the extracts used in this chapter include smaller clusters, Extract 1.12 being a good example. The first conversation contained 21 longer and 31 shorter metaphor clusters. All but six of the shorter clusters were also part of a longer cluster. The second conversation, which was twice as long, had 22 longer clusters and 68 shorter clusters.

Clusters in the conversations were analysed for discourse purpose, perspective (whose point of view is presented), interaction between speakers, topic, and connections between the metaphors in the cluster. Participants used metaphors in clusters mostly to present their own point of view to the other. There were 22 instances in clusters where a speaker presented his or her own point of view, six where they offered the other's point of view, and just two where a joint perspective was presented.

Clusters in the reconciliation talk most often included metaphor vehicles from several different groupings, rather than a single metaphor that was extended and elaborated. Two particular types of talk in clusters were found in interaction around reconciliation which have not been noted in other kinds of talk: appropriation of the other speaker's metaphors and the metaphorical exploration of alternative possibilities.

## Metaphor appropriation
Within metaphor clusters at several key points in their conversations, a participant began to use a metaphor that had, until that point, been the discourse

'property' of the other speaker. Appropriating the other person's metaphor, and being allowed to appropriate it, could be seen as a significant step towards acknowledging the other's perspective through language. In Extract 1.13, Pat Magee, the bomber, makes first use of the metaphor of *healing* in reference to himself. Before this, *healing* had been Jo's metaphor, used to talk about recovering from grief. The appropriation of the metaphor is accompanied by hesitation, pausing and permission seeking.

Extract 1.13: Appropriation of *healing* as metaphor

| | |
|---|---|
| Pat | how do you <u>put</u> it, er, |
| | … (2.0) maybe that's <u>part</u> of <u>healing</u> too, |
| | … my <u>healing</u> |
| Jo | your <u>healing</u>. |
| | … [yeah] |
| Pat | [yeah] |
| | … (1.0) you know, |
| | er, |
| | … (2.0) it's — |
| | <u>something</u> I have to <u>go through</u> |
| Jo | … hmh |
| Pat | … if I'm going to sort of |
| | er, |
| | … (1.0) really <u>retain</u> my humanity |

The topic of the *healing* metaphor shifts with this new use: Pat's *healing* is to do with accepting the consequences of his decision to plant the bomb, rather than Jo's recovering from grief. The re-use of the vehicle term with *part of, my, your* as it is passed from one speaker to the other, contributes to the formation of a cluster. What is happening in the cluster is an important contribution to the reconciliation process.

### Metaphorical exploration of hypothetical possibilities

A further type of discourse move found within clusters in the reconciliation talk is from what actually happened to what might have happened, with exploration of alternative actions that could have been taken. For Jo, the alternative to seeking conciliation would have been to give into anger and revenge. Pat several times contrasts acting from hatred with acting from political conviction. In Extract 1.14, Pat considers what motivated him and the IRA members that he knew, and how this was in most cases something other than *hatred*.

Extract 1.14

| | |
|---|---|
| Pat | I know very very few people, |
| | ... (1.0) that hatred was a <u>big part</u> of it. |
| | ... and those you could <u>say</u> to it, |
| | ... <u>say</u> that it was, |
| | ... wouldn't have lasted. |
| | ... it's -- |
| Jo | [hmh] |
| Pat | [it's] not enough to <u>sustain</u>, |
| | ... during a <u>struggle</u> like this. |
| Jo | hmh |
| Pat | ... I don't think so. |
| | ... you -- |
| | you couldn't <u>keep up with</u> it, |
| | if it was just <u>driven</u> by that sort of -- |
| | ... (1.0) hatred that <u>gnaws away at</u> you. |
| Jo | ... [hmh] |
| Pat | [you would] soon be a <u>casualty</u> of it. |

The dense mixture of strong metaphors in Extract 1.14 helps Pat to explore the alternative possibility and reject it. There were several instances of this type of discourse activity from both speakers across the conversations, and they seemed to be a significant and successful way of explaining to each other the choices made over the years, and how these choices affected their respective lives. While enabling participants to verbalize what were often very negative 'might have been' scenarios, they at the same time revealed to the other person the strength of their feelings.

## Findings presented as a metaphor synthesis

The metaphors used in the reconciliation talk were sometimes vivid, but more often were conventionalized ways of talking. Once all metaphors were identified, grouped systematically, and examined in their discourse contexts, through clusters where relevant, the researcher comes to know their patterns of use in sufficient depth to attempt to put together a synthesis that covers the range of metaphors and connects them together as coherently as possible. The scenario below is 'an interpretive synthesis' constructed by the researcher and staying as close as possible to the words of the participants (Cameron, 2007b: 206). The coherence of the synthesis is negotiated, sometimes contested, and interim, presenting a stabilization that has emerged from the dynamics of the talk covered in the study, but that may change further.

After the bombing, Jo Berry and Pat Magee complete separate journeys, long and on foot, until they meet face-to-face and try to connect across the gap between their experiences. Jo's journey has the aim of understanding the roots of violence and is a long, uphill journey on foot, sometimes following the path of journeys made by the bombers, sometimes stopping to meet other victims. The journey out of grief becomes a healing process. Pat does not talk much about his life between the bombing and the meeting, but speaks of an earlier journey when, as a young man, he joined the IRA and agreed to use violence.

When Jo and Pat meet and sit down to talk to each other, it is, for both and in different ways, a momentous point in their journeys. It is not, however, where the journeys end, rather it is a new starting point. For Pat, meeting Jo is a confrontation with an unavoidable obstacle, the consequences of his actions. He has to face this and cannot walk away from it. He can however come through this dark phase of his journey.

When Jo and Pat meet, they need to open channels of communication between them. For Jo, and then also for Pat, connection comes through being open, which may require the breaking down of barriers. Jo wants to build bridges to cross the gap between them. Through careful listening to the story that the Other tells, each comes to know and understand the Other better – they can see the Other more clearly and more completely.

The metaphor synthesis provides a general answer to the research question to complement answers already provided by establishing the four key systematic metaphors that framed participants' understanding of the reconciliation process and by the metaphor cluster analysis that highlighted the use of metaphor to present and understand perspectives on issues, metaphor appropriation and using the exploration of hypothetical possibilities to justify decisions made.

### Metaphor in the discourse dynamics of reconciliation talk: Conclusions

The research study showed how metaphor offered participants ways to explore alternatives to violence and revenge; it allowed victim and perpetrator to explain their feelings to each other, and to make gestures of empathy; it allowed them to control and adjust the affective 'climate' of the talk. Through metaphor, small acts of reconciliation, such as allowing the appropriation of metaphor, contributed to the larger process.

The above report of this first study gives an overview of metaphor used as a research tool to investigate discourse data. The discourse data in this study came from spoken interaction, transcribed and then analysed for the use of linguistic metaphor. Answers to the research question, 'How is metaphor used to describe the reconciliation process?', were found through a process of metaphor analysis that began with identification of metaphors, grouped metaphors together semantically and by topic to find important 'systematic metaphors' or patterns of meaning, tracked clusters of metaphors across the discourse and examined what happened inside them, and produced an interpretive metaphor synthesis to reflect participants' thinking and emotions. Attention was paid throughout to changes in metaphor use, i.e. the discourse dynamics of metaphor. We introduced the idea of trustworthiness as vital at each analytic stage to ensure quality.

The study findings offer several applications to mediators engaging people in reconciliation through talk. For example, participants might be encouraged to discuss alternative decisions and outcomes that would have been negative, then reverse and explore the metaphors. Mediators might listen for metaphors preferred by one of the participants and offer them to the other speaker in questions to see if they will be appropriated.

## Conclusions: Questions for critiquing methods that use metaphor as a research tool

In summarizing the points made about metaphor analysis in this first chapter, a set of questions emerge, below in italics, that will help readers engage in critical reading of the methodology of other people's published studies and in devising their own.

*How do the researchers understand the nature of metaphor and which dimensions of metaphor do they include?*

We have introduced metaphor as a multi-dimensional phenomenon: linguistic, embodied, cognitive, affective, sociocultural. Any of these dimensions can be identified in data and used in analysis, depending on the stance of the researchers.

In the reconciliation, metaphor was seen as linguistic, cognitive, affective and sociocultural.

*What is identified as metaphor? e.g. vehicle terms, manifestations in language of conceptual metaphor.*

In the above study, linguistic metaphor vehicle terms were identified in the transcribed talk and used as the primary 'unit of analysis'. It was these vehicle terms that were grouped and organized, prior to making generalizations and inferences.

*How tightly are the connections between metaphors and their discourse context maintained?*

The reconciliation study illustrated a discourse approach to linguistic metaphor that tried at all times to keep connections between metaphors and how they were used in the discourse action. The degree of connection that studies maintain between metaphors and their context of use can vary, and the feasibility of connection relates to the amount of data.

*What do the researchers do with the metaphors they identify? How do they generalize upwards from instances of metaphor; downwards from discourse to metaphor; across stretches of discourse?*

The metaphor analysis worked on the data from several directions: upwards from individual linguistic metaphors to systematic patterns of meaning; downwards from finding metaphor clusters to analysing the discourse work being done inside a cluster; across the metaphors and patterns to the construction of a metaphor synthesis.

The discourse dynamics approach that we develop in this book, with its focus on linguistic metaphor rather than conceptual metaphor, adopts a principle of staying close to participants' own words when labelling categories or patterns of meaning.

*How do the researchers describe the patterns of metaphor that they infer from the data?*

Patterns of metaphor were described through systematic metaphors, through metaphor clusters and discourse action inside them, and through the production of an interpretive metaphor synthesis which reflects participants' thinking and emotions.

The next chapter will apply these questions to evaluate a selection of published research studies in the social sciences and humanities.

## Notes

1. Steen, and some other cognitive linguists, assume a separation of system and use (or 'grammar' and 'usage' in cognitive linguistics terminology) that those of us who work with a dynamics approach resist. System and use are not separable in a dynamic systems theory perspective; instead use is seen as giving rise to system through self-organization and emergence (Larsen-Freeman and Cameron, 2008).
2. Conceptual metaphors are conventionally written with SMALL CAPITALS.
3. The author would like to thank Jo Berry and Pat Magee for allowing their conversations to be used as data. The Arts and Humanities Research Board (now Council) supported the original

research project with an Innovation Award. Juup Stelma provided research assistance on this project. This section of the chapter draws on Cameron (2007b).

4.  Larger groupings of metaphors found in discourse data (called systematic metaphors) are labelled in SMALL CAPITALS AND ITALICS. The use of italics is to emphasize a contrast with conceptual metaphors, assumed in conceptual metaphor theory to be pre-existing rather than found in the discourse (see Chapters 5 and 7, this volume).

# 2 A selective survey of research practice in published studies using metaphor analysis

## Zazie Todd and Graham Low

This chapter surveys the use of metaphor analysis in the social sciences and humanities, paying particular attention to the methods that are used and the methodological issues that arise. Metaphor analysis is increasingly being used across a diverse range of disciplines beyond linguistics. The lack of established guidelines for research practice, and the need for researchers to follow conventions within their home discipline, means that there is a lot of variability in research practice. In this chapter, we aim to illustrate the diversity of work that is being carried out, and some of the different ways in which researchers are tackling these difficult issues. We begin with detailed summaries of six articles from the fields of health and education that illustrate some of the exciting work that has been done, before moving on to a discussion of the details of how research practice is evolving.

It is useful to consider initially some of the reasons researchers give on the question of why they have chosen to study metaphor. Here are a few examples:

> The purpose of this analysis is to highlight the subtle ways that metaphors (and with them, values) creep into the environmental science lexicon. (Carolan, 2006: 922)

> We ask why research on the human genome has not led to widespread negative reactions comparable to those provoked by cloning and GM food. Part of the answer lies in the metaphors, images, literary and cultural references used in the announcement of this development. (Nerlich et al., 2002: 445)

> the construction of metaphoric models can help social researchers better understand how individuals conceptualize and construct student doctor/ patient relationships. (Rees et al, 2007: 725)

One thing to note about many of these explanations is the claim that metaphor *does* something in the discourse, that it has an effect on the reader or listener. In Carolan's (2006) example, the metaphors have values which *creep* in; for Nerlich *et al.* (2002) they provide an explanation for a fairly positive reaction to scientific advances that throw up many ethical concerns; and for Rees *et al.* (2007) they relate to how people think about the medical relationship. In just three studies, we have different understandings of the nature of metaphor as carrying values, reducing anxiety, and shaping thought processes. This is something we will return to when we consider the questions posed at the end of Chapter 1, but first we will look in detail at six studies that have used metaphor analysis. We have tried to pick papers that are interesting methodologically as well as for their substantive findings, and which illustrate the range of approaches taken by researchers.

## Summaries of published studies

**Nerlich, B. and Halliday, C. (2007) Avian flu: The creation of expectations in the interplay between science and the media. *Sociology of Health and Illness* 29 (1): 46–65.**

The aim of this study was to discover which linguistic devices were being used by experts and the media in talking about bird flu (H5N1) in the first half of 2005, and to investigate the function of the devices used. The data comprised a set of newspaper articles that were retrieved from a database by searching for words and phrases such as 'avian flu', with a particularly detailed analysis of a subset of 51 words and phrases that appeared during a flurry of media reporting in February and March of 2005. The method that was used to identify and categorize metaphors is unfortunately not described, but two experienced coders worked on the full corpus (rather than just a sample), and the quoted reliability was very high. The metaphor analysis was conducted alongside a content analysis which searched for pragmatic markers such as *warn* or *frighten* that would indicate the illocutionary or perlocutionary force, respectively, of the text (the intended or the actual effect on readers). The combination of these two methods enabled Nerlich and Halliday (2007) to focus on what metaphor was being used for – in other words, to answer the question, what is metaphor doing?

Two main metaphors contributed to a general 'discourse of uncertainty'. Metaphors of fear drew on links to other kinds of disaster, such as earthquake or flood, e.g., pandemics *hit world populations like a flash flood* (Stöhr, in a January 2005 editorial for the *New England Journal of Medicine*, cited by Nerlich and Halliday, 2007: 60) or *Flu season comes every year as reliably as hurricane season* (in a 2005 editorial for *Scientific American*, cited by Nerlich and Halliday, 2007: 59). The other kind of metaphor described by Nerlich and Halliday related to a discourse of blame. Although they provided one example of a direct accusation, most of the accusations were, as one would expect, indirect. Given the rich illustrations of fear metaphors, it is disappointing that the same level of detail was not included in this section. However, it did make the valuable point that the media appeared to be more interested in apportioning blame than focusing on possible solutions.

One of the interesting findings of this article is that the media was not solely responsible for the climate of fear around bird flu. Contrary to stereotypes of scaremongering by the media, some of the more frightening metaphors came from scientists and were merely reported. For example one scientist, Professor Pennington, is quoted as saying,

> this is the biggest threat to the human race. It far outweighs bioterrorism, this is natural bio-terrorism. It won't spare anybody (quoted in *The Express*, 4 March 2005). (Nerlich and Halliday, 2007: 58)

Alongside the metaphors of size and weight used to describe the threat is the frightening metaphor THE VIRUS IS A NATURAL BIOTERRORIST. Another example came from John Oxford, reported in *The Guardian* (20 March 2005):

> Forget Al Qaeda, the biggest terrorist threat we face today is Mother Nature. (Nerlich and Halliday, 2007: 59)

In fact, a number of the quotes from experts reported in the media were what Nerlich and Halliday term 'scare quotes'. Novel metaphors were used almost exclusively by the experts who were quoted, and not by the journalists. This raises the question of whether scientists' better understanding of bird flu enabled them to produce novel metaphors, and whether journalists' lesser scientific knowledge led them to be more literal. Future research could investigate the role of expertise in metaphor production.

This paper provides a nice illustration of the problems faced by those whose job it is to communicate professionally about risk. In the context of frightening warnings and predictions from scientists, policy makers had to decide how to allocate resources to tackle a devastating situation that might or might not have been going to happen. The metaphors found in the media reports were considered as risk signals within the Social Amplification of Risk Framework (Kasperson, 1992; Kasperson *et al.*, 2003), that could either attenuate or amplify the perception of risk. This study provides an excellent example of risk signals as they appear in the media, but further work is needed to address the question of the effects they actually have on readers. In the case of terrorism, some work is beginning to look at the metaphors that people use to talk about risk (Harrison *et al.*, 2008; Cameron *et al.*, 2009; Chapter 14, this volume). Future research needs to investigate both the metaphors used by the media and those used by the general public in order to study how risk signals presented by the media are picked up, interpreted, and perhaps subverted, by the general public.

One of the innovative features of this paper is the way that metaphor was considered alongside a content analysis that focused on pragmatic markers of illocutionary and perlocutionary force. The metaphors (and similes) were studied in the context in which they appeared, and in terms of what they actually did. This provides a useful framework for investigating how metaphor is used to warn, frighten, and sell newspapers. Indeed we would further propose that receiver-and-producer oriented research designs (above) will need to include the linguistic context and the devices used to foreground or background parts of the message.[1] For a general review of work on language used to talk about risk and disease, see Brown *et al.* (2009).

**Low, G., Littlemore, J. and Koester, A. (2008) Metaphor use in three UK university lectures. *Applied Linguistics* 29 (3): 428–455.**

Low *et al.* (2008) explored how British university lecturers used metaphor in three UK social science lectures from the BASE corpus held at the University of Warwick.[2] The motivation underlying the study was that although international (L2) students were known to often find metaphoric statements difficult (Littlemore, 2001, 2003, 2005), it was unclear how much metaphor lectures contained, what sort of metaphor was involved and what functions it had. Did metaphor serve to frame sections of the lecture, as Low (1997) had found for written academic discourse? Or did it appear in tight clusters as, Corts and colleagues (Corts and Pollio, 1999; Corts and Meyers, 2002; Chapter 10, this volume) had found? Was it used in an overarching way, as Ponterotto's (2003) work had suggested? Or was it used for more 'local' ad hoc effects?

Answering these questions required a metaphor analysis to be overlaid on one or more functional analyses. Initial metaphor identification was carried out by using the MIP (Metaphor Identification Procedure) suggested by the Pragglejaz group (Pragglejaz group, 2007), as it is reasonably systematic – in the sense that a series of clearly defined steps is suggested for isolating lexical units whose contextual meaning differs from their basic sense. The result isolates examples of polysemy based metaphor, but not 'direct' metaphor like similes (where no polysemy is involved); for this a different procedure, like that in Cameron (2003) is required. For the 2008 paper, Low *et al.* excluded simile, but did have a second pass over the data to establish metaphoric groups (phrases and sayings).

Finding an appropriate functional framework was surprisingly hard. The notion of 'episode' which is often applied to lesson analysis (e.g. Lemke, 1990; Gibbons, 2002) only works where there are obvious changes of topic or of discourse rules; episodes thus work well with task-based classes, but less well with monologues, especially where there are few questions, or where the lecturer is questioned on an earlier topic and then uses the question as a springboard for the next topic. Low *et al.* used intonation and topic marker verbal cues where possible to indicate boundaries that the lecturer seemed to be trying to communicate to the listeners. At times this resulted in a clear set of higher and lower units, where each unit that was started had a discoverable end. However, for the most conversational of the three lectures this did not happen, and as a result it was not at all clear at times which unit the listener was in.

The interest in this study on the positioning of metaphor meant that it was important to be able to examine where metaphor occurred in utterances and turns, and not just in topic units. Therefore the discourse was broken into intonation units. However, there remained the usual thorny questions of how, for example, to treat relatively level intonation and filled pauses. Ultimately there can be no intonation analyses that do not involve a degree of subjectivity.

This is not the place to discuss the results at length, but the method, with its reliability checks, did make it clear that most of the less conventional metaphors in the three lectures was used on a one-off basis, and was not used to create overarching metaphors or clusters which kept recurring throughout the discourse – which perhaps made it harder for students using English as a second or foreign language to set up patterns of figurative use in their minds. However, one of the three lectures, the most conversational one, did have a metaphor cluster towards the end where the lecturer brought together, possibly quite unwittingly, several of the metaphoric words and phrases used earlier. Establishing how far final clustering and lecture style correlate requires, as the authors admitted, a much larger study.

**Zapata, G. C. and Lacorte, M. (2007) Preservice and inservice instructors' metaphorical conceptions of second language teachers.** *Foreign Language Annals*, **40 (3): 521–534.**

The last 15 years have seen the publication of a series of studies examining the relationship between metaphor selection and professional practice. Quite a high proportion of these papers have involved participants in language learning: whether teachers (e.g. Block, 1992; Cortazzi and Jin, 1999; de Guerrero and Villamil, 2000, 2002), learners (e.g. Block, 1992; Oxford *et al.*, 1998; Wan, 2007; Nikitina and Furuoka, 2008) or other stakeholders such as parents (e.g., Bialostok, 2008). The precise focus of interest varies from conceptualizations of the processes of language teaching/learning, to conceptualizations of the roles involved. Zapata and Lacorte (2007) started out as a combination of both. Their working assumption was fairly typical of such studies, namely that the researcher can accurately reconstruct opinions, affiliations and beliefs about education and professional practice from the metaphors people use. Serious errors of inference can easily occur where observational, naturalistic data are used. One can, for example, in many cases infer very little about a teacher (or even a psycholinguist) who uses conventional examples of the conduit meta-phor, singly or repeatedly, when referring to communication in 'natural' dis-course situations, beyond the fact that s/he knows how to speak (say) English. The conduit metaphor describes a message as a series of objects (words) that the speaker has filled with meaning moving along a pipe or line to be unpacked by the listener (Reddy, 1979) and is pervasive in the English language. Saying *There's a lot in that question* or *Fire away* does not commit the speaker to a belief that the conduit metaphor accurately represents how people communi-cate, or that the speaker somehow needs professional retraining; that is simply how communication is expressed in English and there are few conventional phrases representing recent scientific conceptualizations. Zapata and Lacorte, wisely perhaps, preferred to guide their respondents; they assumed that teach-ers faced with a *Teaching is like/is X* task would actively select answers that best reflected their personal perspectives. They accordingly designed four *is like/is* completion prompts: for *An L2 language teacher*, *An L2 student*, *An L2 classroom* and the slightly differently worded *Learning a second language entails/ can be defined as*. The prompts were given to 69 teachers and teaching assistants in American, Argentinian and Spanish language institutions (or uni-versities). Metaphors selected were assigned to teaching/learning philosophies using the 'four theory' model developed in Oxford *et al.* (1998). The aim was to examine how metaphor choice (and implied learning theories) varied with type of teaching undertaken (pre vs in service), extent of teacher training received and cultural background.

This study is of interest here in three ways. First, Zapata and Lacorte are one of the few research groups (with Wan, 2007) to recognize that decontextualized 'complete a metaphor/simile' tasks are not unproblematic or methodologically transparent, and to report failure rates. Both the L2 classroom and L2 learning questions were dropped from the analysis because *c.* 20% of respondents did not or could not answer appropriately (the precise figure comes from personal communication[3]). This immediately suggests the possibility of a hierarchy of 'complete a metaphor' task difficulty, such that it is easier to find metaphors for people (teachers or learners) than for non-personal classrooms or abstract (and/or very broad) processes like learning. Having eliminated two of the four questions, Zapata and Lacorte found that 5/69 (7%) of respondents had not answered the first two either and had to be eliminated (2007: 525). Zapata and Lacorte are not able to offer an explanation for the failures, but clearly some people do have serious problems with the task and more research is needed.

One way to begin to establish why failure occurred would be to have follow up interviews and classroom observations, and Zapata and Lacorte did do both with 'some' respondents, though the results were not reported in the study and the interviews preceded the task, rather than followed it (p.c.). Perhaps the ideal solution would be to have both pre- and post-task interviews. These could establish not only why some found the task hard, but also the extent to which the choices made by 'successful' respondents (a) genuinely reflected their beliefs and/or (b) were an adequate reflection of their views (as apart from being one of several ways in which they regarded teachers and learners). These latter data are crucial in constraining unilateral allocations of people to educational philosophies on the basis of metaphor use.

Second, Zapata and Lacorte are again rare in that they discussed coding problems at some length when it came to applying the Oxford *et al.* (1998) model, which is something that the original paper does not do.

Third, Zapata and Lacorte repeatedly found, when they matched the metaphors to Oxford *et al.*'s four educational philosophies/theories, discrepancies between metaphors about teachers and metaphors about learning. On the one hand, this strongly validated the fact of using more than one completion task. It also appears to validate the use of more than one investigative method; one could use post-task interviews to ask respondents directly whether they held multiple perspectives. If they did, which seems quite plausible, inasmuch as a good learner is doing something different from a good teacher and is in a quite different social context, the next question would be to query the accuracy of the Oxford *et al.* model, or at least the way metaphors are interpreted and fitted to it.

In short, Zapata and Lacorte may not have reported all their data in the (2007) paper and may not have carried out interviews and observations to quite the degree of rigour we are suggesting, but their honest reporting and their championing of a multi-method approach means we can begin to think seriously about how to answer the methodological and analytic questions that bedevil metaphoric belief-reconstruction exercises.

**Bialostok, S. (2008) Using critical metaphor analysis to extract parents' cultural models of how their children learn to read.** *Critical Inquiry in Language Studies* **5 (2): 109–147.**

Over the last ten years or so, as we have noted above, numerous books and papers have explored how teachers, learners or other stakeholders use metaphor to describe aspects of teaching and/or learning. Research on teachers and learners often draws on sociocultural theory to suggest that learning can be generated by manipulating symbolic objects (including metaphors) and to this end the metaphors should be brought into learners' conscious awareness.

Bialostok (2008) is particularly interesting because it related to parents rather than teachers or learners. It also adopted an appropriate theoretical framework;

parents neither learn nor teach reading, so sociocultural approaches to learning would not be relevant; Bialostok therefore used the notion of cultural models (i.e. mental models of concepts, such as family, or of events, such as marriage, that are shared by members of the same culture), which are often partly metaphoric and which can be hypothesized by the researcher from observed language use (Quinn, 1991, 2005). Bialostok's desire for a 'critical metaphor analysis' led him to hunt for a further layer: moral or ideological models connected to the cultural models.[4] The danger with identifying or reconstructing models lies, as with the example of the conduit metaphor (above), in failing to limit subjective, vague, or biased decisions about whether language use validly reflects: (a) an underlying metaphor; (b) a cultural model; or (c) a moral model. Clearly the safest position to adopt is to require explicit mention of a link by a reasonable proportion of participants before general inferences are drawn that such a link exists. There is thus a need, not just for criteria, but for procedures for checking reliability and validity.

Methodologically, the data consisted of 45 hours of interviews with 15 white, graduate American parents in the same town, about the learning to read of 11 'kindergarteners'. Bialostok reported the use of repeated interviews, a conversational style and an attempt to avoid mentioning cultural models explicitly (Bialostok, 2008: 115), all of which represent good practice. He also presents a detailed argument for the role of metaphors in cultural and moral understanding. Although a Lakoffian approach to conceptual metaphor was adopted, no criteria were reported for identifying metaphoric expressions, for matching them to conceptual metaphors, or for establishing deliberate use (or going beyond conventionality). The lack of such criteria seems to have affected the analysis at times, as for example with *learning to read requires mastering a lot of skills* (2008: 137). Bialostok sees the verb *master* as having clear overtones of power, domination and conflict, providing evidence for both a major metaphoric dimension of the cultural model of reading and for a moral model of self-improvement. However, the fact that (to) *master* is not normally applied literally to people or peoples, and is, unlike the noun (a) *master*, only applied in standard usage to ideas, data or skills means that for some analysts it is not an example of metaphor in discourse (e.g. Steen, in press), but even if it is deemed metaphorical, the overtones that can legitimately be inferred from someone saying *mastering a skill* are seriously limited.

The presentation of results includes multiple examples of each metaphor, sometimes within large chunks of text. Sometimes the quotes include the researcher's questions, enabling the reader to see how he followed up participants' use of metaphors like *rusty* (2008: 124) or *resisting* (2008: 139). The cultural model of reading is identified at the topmost level as the schema 'Reading is a set of skills'. The fact that parents describe the latter in terms of ontological metaphors (*to have skills*) is seen as significant, as 'it evokes the discourse of the market place and labor market' (2008: 117) such that skills can be traded, developed and instructed. As reading self-evidently does require more than one activity, it is hard to see parents' emphasis on the plural form *skills* as metaphoric or not true. And it is at the same time hard to find evidence for the metonymic evoking of market places every time a parent says *has skills*: there are few other conventional ways of describing the situation in English. As with the use of the conduit metaphor above, the analyst needs to be careful about imbuing uses of conventional phrases and metaphors with deeper cultural meanings; it is easy to over-interpret such data.

The skill schema comprises at least five metaphors (2008: 117), including READING SKILLS ARE MANUFACTURED PRODUCTS, LEARNING READING SKILLS IS A JOURNEY, LEARNING READING SKILLS 'MOVES UPWARDS', and READING SKILLS REQUIRE INDIVIDUAL CONTROL. As the latter is clearly not a metaphor, it might have been preferable to coin a label such as 'metaphor related components'. These overlap with a moral model of individual success in life achieved through self-discipline and effort. Thus reading is held to be both an intellectual and a moral journey in the parents' minds. While the two models in general seem unsurprising and uncontroversial, one difficulty is that it is unclear how much explicit linguistic mention of a moral journey is needed in order to infer more than a link by certain individuals. Thus while Pamela asserted how *reading is the access road. Seth's not going to be a construction worker* (2008: 130), the quotes by parents such as Eleanor (2008: 128, 129) seem to imply no such moral journey. Simply being consistent with a moral model, like Marilyn's ambiguous *she wasn't going anywhere for the longest time* (2008: 131), is not per se evidence that one is committed to it. The issue of what can be inferred about cognitive structure from linguistic evidence is one that besets many metaphor analysts, as well as other qualitative researchers.

Metaphor researchers like Steen (2007) and Deignan (2005) have argued that one needs to be clear how and why conceptual domains are identified and labelled. While there is clear linguistic evidence in the data cited that the parents did treat reading as 'putting together a whole, a variety of components', that the fit between the parts needed to be good and the result should be *a solid reader*, it is much less clear that the various metaphors reflect a neatly coherent single domain of an assembly line involving a 'gradual construction from something simple to something elaborate' (Bialostok, 2008: 125). The references to *clues* and *detective work* (2008: 120), or fitting the *pieces of the puzzle* together (2008: 121) do not seem compatible with the predictability of an assembly line. Even the idea of using *the tools of phonics* and *working with clay* (2008: 122) is as compatible with a skilled artisan model as it is with a factory assembly line. The only semantically close connection with an assembly line that the reader is given is when Gwen talked of mechanistic aspects of reading (*the mechanics of it*) (2008: 121), but even this is not direct evidence for as specific a concept as an assembly line. The fact that parents argued that reading skills need to be *connected*, or that exercising skills leads to *strong* readers, may be consistent with an assembly line, but is not direct evidence of it. (Further discussion of the problems of relying on consistency as an identification criterion can be found in Low (2003) and Low and Todd (Chapter 12, this volume).)

Despite these methodologically problematic points, the use of multiple quotes to support each metaphor point made and the inclusion of a summary table of conceptual metaphors with frequencies and variations both represent yet more good practice. To bring the argument full circle, it might be wondered, given the problem with over-interpreting uses of the conduit metaphor, whether Bialostok sees the need to argue for change and re-education. He does, but the request is restricted to the last few lines, and is laudably muted. Teachers could usefully reduce the inference that if a child has reading or learning problems, the child is a problem, by having failed. Educationally, the position seems morally unchallengeable; how far the parents' discourse allows one to make legitimate inferences about teachers' practices is another matter.

**Skelton, J. R., Wearn, A. M. and Hobbs, F. D. R. (2002) A concordance-based study of metaphoric expressions used by general practitioners and patients in consultation. *The British Journal of General Practice* 52 (475): 114–118.**

Experts and ordinary people may use metaphor in different ways, or use different metaphors to talk about the same thing. Skelton *et al.* (2002) studied the metaphors used in general practice consultations. They studied a database of doctor-patient interactions and analysed the metaphors used by doctors and their patients. In this study, the metaphor coding was computer-assisted, using lexical concordancing software called Cobuild (see Chapter 9, this volume). The researchers identified a set of three types of search terms that would potentially signify a metaphor. Considering simile as a class of metaphor, the first search terms were for *like* and *as*; they searched for feeling and describing verbs, such as *look*; and finally, since they assumed many metaphors to be of the form *X is Y*, they searched for the verb *to be*, recognizing that this would also throw up many instances that were not metaphorical. The search was iterative; once an initial search had shown words to be metaphorical, those words then became search terms in their own right. As an example, they say that both *pregnant* and *hit* were found to be used metaphorically after a first pass of the data, and further searching on these words revealed other cases of *hit* being used metaphorically, but not *pregnant*. The researchers are to be commended for describing the iterative search process in detail and for explaining how they decided whether or not the items thrown up by the search were meta-phorical. This kind of coding process could clearly save time for researchers, but could also potentially miss some examples. It is probably better suited to studies in which the data are restricted in some way, as this makes it easier to identify suitable search terms. An interesting future study would consider the relative effectiveness of concordance based versus human coding (though we should stress that in this case the concordancing process still required human judgement).

Skelton *et al.* found that although some metaphors were used by both patients and GPs (general practitioners), other metaphors were used by only one of the two groups. Both groups used the metaphors ILLNESS IS AN ATTACK and ILLNESS IS FIRE, though even here the doctors used *burning* in a much more specific way than the patients when talking about pain. Some of the linguistic and con-ceptual metaphors used by patients were idiosyncratic and were grouped into a higher level hyperbole category given the (non-metaphoric) title AN ILLNESS IS BEYOND DESCRIPTION. Examples of this kind of utterance were: *My arms feel they should be in a collection of slings to hold them up they just ache so much* and *It's like if you've looked into the sun* (Skelton *et al.*, 2002: 117). There were also some metaphors that were used much more by the doctors, including A DOCTOR IS SOMEONE WHO CONTROLS (not cures) DISEASE (though arguably one might see this as a literal or even metonymic label, rather than a metaphoric one). Even so, if doctors and patients are using different metaphors, and some-times using the same metaphor in different ways, there is clearly potential for misunderstanding.

In this paper, the metaphors were presented as individual items, out of context of the conversation in which they occurred, so it is not known how often mis-understandings actually happened, although it is easy to see that some of the patient metaphors might be difficult to understand precisely. The reader is left wondering just what a GP says in response to a complaint that *I was like a wet leaf* (2002: 117), for example. One also wonders whether many of the metaphors that were categorized as ILLNESS IS BEYOND DESCRIPTION are in fact functioning as intensifiers, since many of the linguistic examples given seem to stress that the patient is in some distress. Taken out of context, it is hard to know how these are functioning. A sequential analysis of how these metaphors are produced and the questions with which GPs respond to them would show how understanding between doctor and patient is achieved. To be fair, this was not the purpose of the research, which set out to describe and compare the metaphors used by doctors and patients. In short, Skelton *et al.*'s paper provides a valuable demonstration of how misunderstandings might occur, but further research could investigate how this happens in the context of doctor/patient interaction.

**Rees, C. E., Knight, L. V. and Wilkinson, C. E. (2007) Doctors being up there and we being down here: A metaphorical analysis of talk about student/ doctor-patient relationships.** *Social Science and Medicine* **65 (4): 725–737.**

Sometimes researchers set out to study a particular topic and only later discover that metaphor is one of the most interesting things in their results. One paper on the use of metaphor that arose from an initially different qualitative analysis is that of Rees *et al.* (2007). They studied views about the doctor-patient relationship in medical education, collecting data from focus groups with medical students, medical educators and patients who were involved in the medical education process. The data were initially analysed using Framework Analysis (Ritchie and Spencer, 1994) which looked at both the content of what people said, and at how they said it. Since the 'how' turned out to include metaphor, this became a focus of the study, and a metaphor analysis was conducted following the original framework analysis. Understandably, since their focus was doctor-patient relationships, the researchers restricted the coding to metaphors which were about these domains, and did not identify metaphors on other topics which were not relevant to the research topic. After identifying the metaphoric expressions (linguistic metaphors), the researchers worked to group them into conceptual metaphors, first independently, and then together. This is typical of the approach found in many qualitative methods, where rather than using independent coders to check the reliability of the coding framework, discussion is used to produce final agreement.

Rees *et al.* found a number of metaphors that were used to talk about the doctor-patient relationship. One of the interesting aspects of their findings actually relates to a metaphor that was not used: they did not find participants talking about it as a partnership. Moreover, one of the metaphors that they did find was rather surprising: STUDENT/ DOCTOR-PATIENT RELATIONSHIPS ARE WAR. Participants talked as if there was a barrier between patients and student/ doctors, and sometimes even talked of patients as *troops* who were *armed with knowledge* (Rees *et al.*, 2007: 730). This is surprising because one might expect instead a view of the relationship between doctors and patients as one of help and support, not war. Other metaphors related to the hierarchy of relationships between patients, student doctors and consultants. Of course, since the doctor participants were students or educators, these results may reflect the importance of the local context and not generalize to qualified doctors in a non-educational setting; they are quite likely to reflect the anxieties of student trainees.

One of the controversial aspects of this paper is a reference to differences between conscious and unconscious use of metaphors. The authors stated that 'it was clear from listening to our audiotaped data that participants employed MLEs [metaphoric linguistic expressions] both implicitly (unconsciously) and rhetorically (consciously)' (Rees *et al.* 2007: 734). This is problematic, since it is not clear how one is supposed to tell if a metaphor is used consciously or not, and no information was given about how the distinction was made. In fact, many qualitative researchers would be unhappy with the suggestion that we can infer unconscious use of language. Leaving this aside, the paper is nevertheless a fascinating description of the metaphors used within a medical school setting.

## Methodological approaches

The studies outlined above illustrate a range of approaches to the study of metaphor, and to the analysis of metaphor for the purposes of studying other topics. We will now consider the approaches taken in the light of questions introduced at the end of Chapter 1.

*How do the researchers understand the nature of metaphor and which dimensions of metaphor do they include?*

Researchers generally begin with an understanding of what linguistic metaphor is, although they may come from different backgrounds such as cognitive linguistics, critical discourse analysis or cultural studies. The focus varies from all metaphors used, to metaphors used to talk about the research topic, or use of a specific framing metaphor (as with Lu and Ahrens's (2008) study of BUILD-ING metaphors in Taiwanese presidential speeches). There is often a trade-off between the amount of data studied and the detail of the analysis, since it can be extremely time-consuming to identify all of the metaphors in a large corpus of texts. For this reason, some researchers decide to focus metaphor analysis on a subset of their data, as with Nerlich and Halliday's (2007) paper on bird flu (above), which concentrated the more detailed analysis on a period that was of particular interest for the amount and type of reporting.

*What is identified as metaphor? e.g. vehicle terms, manifestations in language of conceptual metaphor.*

While not all papers state how the authors identified and analysed the metaphors, earlier papers tend to refer to either Cameron (1999) or Schmitt (2005), whereas more recent papers are just as likely to refer to the Pragglejaz group (2007). Different approaches are also taken to the use of multiple coders. In some cases, agreement between coders is calculated using the statistic Cohen's kappa; high agreement gives confidence that other researchers would find the same thing. In other cases, no agreement statistic is calculated; instead, researchers discuss their codes so as to reach agreement on each item. To some extent, these differences are likely to reflect the norms of the sub-discipline in which the researchers work, and whether they are more interested in a qualitative or quantitative stance. The use of multiple coders is a topic that we will return to in Low and Todd (Chapter 12, this volume). It is inevitable that sometimes there will be disagreements about whether something is a metaphor or not, and there is one rule on which researchers are in agreement: if in doubt, use a dictionary. To this we would simply add that it is important to say which dictionary was used and how precisely it was used.

*How tightly are the connections between metaphors and their discourse context maintained?*

In general, the aims of the papers dictate the extent to which the connections between metaphor and discourse context are maintained. We saw that since Skelton *et al.* wanted to find out which metaphors were used, and to compare their use by patients and doctors, they had no reason to pay attention to the discourse context in which they were produced. In contrast, because of his interest in cultural models, Bialostok (2008) provided numerous quotes from his interviews to illustrate each type of metaphor, as well as a summary table with both frequencies and salient examples.

Another example of a paper in which metaphors were largely taken out of their discourse context is that of Carolan (2006). He studied the metaphors that are used in environmental science journals, and one of his aims was simply to show that metaphor is used in this domain, which indeed it was. This may not come as a surprise to a metaphor scholar, but of course, the extent to which it occurs may well be a surprise to environmental scientists, since the ubiquity of metaphor is often not appreciated outside the metaphor community. Like Bialostok, Carolan was also interested in the moral values that might be associated with the metaphors he found, and so he considered, at a conceptual level, what it means to describe a species as alien or invasive, for example. He did this by describing the possible consequences of this viewpoint in terms of a potential scenario, rather than in terms of actual examples from the journal articles that were used as data.

Sometimes the combination of metaphor analysis with another kind of analysis, quantitative or qualitative, influences the ways in which metaphor and discourse context are considered (see also Chapters 8 and 11, this volume). In the summaries above, we noted the combination of metaphor analysis with both Framework Analysis (Rees *et al.*, 2007), and with content analysis (Nerlich and Halliday, 2007). Other examples from the literature include combining metaphor analysis with critical discourse analysis, as with Holmgreen's (2008) study of the metaphors used by Danish newspapers to write about biotechnology.

This combination of methods is sometimes planned and sometimes not. In some cases, the metaphor analysis might be termed accidental, particularly in the case of qualitative studies from which metaphors have emerged from the data, as something important in answering the research question. The paper by Rees *et al.* (2007) on metaphors in medical education was one such example, in which the authors conducted a thorough metaphor analysis following an earlier analysis which had revealed metaphor to be important. In other cases, however, researchers stay within the framework of their original qualitative analysis, and highlight metaphors as part of the findings.

*What do the researchers do with the metaphors they identify? How do they generalize upwards from instances of metaphor; downwards from discourse to metaphor; across stretches of discourse?*

Unfortunately, Method sections do not always make it clear how researchers have done what they did with the metaphors that they identified, but again it depends in part on the focus of the article. In most cases, researchers group metaphors into similar kinds, and the analysis usually focuses on the higher level groupings rather than the individual metaphors. The higher level metaphors are usually the feature of most interest to researchers, particularly when the investigation is on the use of metaphor as a framing device.

*How do the researchers describe the patterns of metaphor that they infer from the data?*

Patterns of metaphor are usually described in detail, with supporting quotes to illustrate the metaphor. This means that results sections usually make entertaining reading, and are full of the kind of rich description that qualitative researchers have come to expect (e.g., Elliott *et al.*, 1999). Regrettably, frequency counts are often not included, and we would urge researchers to include them where feasible, as they are a valuable aid to interpreting overall patterns of metaphor use. The creative nature of metaphor also means that researchers sometimes adopt creative ways of explaining and describing their data, such as through diagrams that show conceptually how metaphors are thought to link together.

## Conclusions

In this brief review we have welcomed the fact that metaphor research now takes place in a broad range of academic disciplines, often with fascinating results. We have also noted how studies involving decontextualized metaphors could sometimes be usefully extended by the adoption of multi-method, and/or multi-perspective approaches, where the metaphor use of different participants or stakeholders is studied as the people interact. Although we have repeatedly urged caution in identifying and classifying metaphors derived from discourse data, especially where mental models, beliefs or just higher level categories are involved, our primary aim has been to highlight examples of good practice and to suggest future developments which we hope other researchers find both useful and stimulating.

## Notes

1. Just a cursory examination of part of the rhetoric of John Oxford's utterance illustrates neatly why readers or listeners might end up so frightened. Oxford uses front and final position to contrast *Al Qaeda* (extreme, destructive) with *Mother Nature* (loving, fruitful). However, the normal emphasis on the final item is subverted by the use of a second extreme-case term near the start, *the biggest terrorist threat. We* is placed rhetorically and possibly symbolically in the middle.
2. The transcriptions and recordings used in Low *et al.* (2008) come from the British Academic Spoken English (BASE) corpus project. The corpus was developed at the Universities of Warwick and Reading under the directorship of Hilary Nesi and Paul Thompson. Corpus development was assisted by funding from BALEAP, EURALEX, the British Academy and the Arts and Humanities Research Council.
3. Our thanks to Gabriela Zapata for email correspondence about the study and the 2007 paper.
4. It may be felt that moral models of why one should read are unlikely to be easy to separate from cultural models of what reading involves in a culture. However, there is no necessary reason why having reading difficulties should be treated as something immoral, and Bialostok is right to consider the two separately before examining their interaction.

# Section 2

# Contemporary theories of metaphor

Applying metaphor analysis requires some familiarity with the various theoretical positions on the nature of metaphor, and this is what the following section aims to provide.

Deignan begins in Chapter 3 with an overview and critique of conceptual metaphor theory. Conceptual metaphor theory takes a cognitive view of metaphor, and, when it first came on the scene in the 1980s, offered a striking new way of understanding metaphor. For a while, cognitive theory reigned supreme, generating the new field of cognitive linguistics but also leading to a neglect of the role of language in metaphor. More recently, scholars have been trying to bring language and discourse back into the picture, combining this with important cognitive developments in, and beyond, metaphor theory. Ritchie, in Chapter 4, brings together recent developments in perceptual simulation theory, ideas about embodiment, and a concern for the details of metaphorically used language to suggest a more adequate theory of metaphor in discourse. In Chapter 5, Cameron sets out her discourse dynamics theoretical framework for metaphor in interaction. Using another recent development – complex dynamic systems theory – the framework ties together metaphor in the moment of talk with the emergence of conventionalized metaphor across social groups. While conceptual metaphor theory assumes the pre-existence of metaphorical mappings in the mind, and thus approaches metaphor in language as straightforward instantiation, the approaches of both Ritchie and Cameron require attention to the nuances of metaphorical meaning constructed in discourse context. The discourse dynamics framework will provide the theoretical background for the approach to metaphor analysis adopted in Section 3.

# 3   The cognitive view of metaphor: Conceptual metaphor theory

## Alice Deignan

Conceptual metaphor theory, sometimes called cognitive metaphor theory, was developed by researchers within the field of cognitive linguists. It became widely known with the publication of *Metaphors We Live By* by Lakoff and Johnson, in 1980. Conceptual metaphor theory has since been developed and elaborated (see, for example, Lakoff, 1993; Lakoff and Johnson, 1999). This chapter describes the central points of the theory, attempts to evaluate it within its historical context, and outlines implications for researchers in the social sciences and humanities.

## Central claims

The fundamental tenet of conceptual metaphor theory is that metaphor operates at the level of thinking. It is argued that metaphors link two conceptual 'domains'. A domain is an area of meaning, such as the ideas associated with CLEANLINESS AND DIRT (in the literature on conceptual metaphors, small capital letters are used to show that a domain is being described). Domains consist of sets of linked entities, attributes, processes and relationships, which are apparently stored together in the mind. The elements comprising a domain are lexicalized, that is, expressed in language, through words and expressions. These sets of words and expressions resemble the sets termed 'lexical sets' or 'lexical fields' by linguists. The domain of cleanliness and dirt is lexicalized through words and expressions such as *clean, dirty, spotless, cleanse, filthy, tarnish* and *smear*.

### Metaphor as linking two mental domains

Conceptual metaphor theory proposes that a metaphor is a link between two domains, termed the 'source' domain and the 'target' domain. The source domain is usually concrete, consisting of entities, attributes, processes and relationships that are directly, usually physically, experienced. The literal meanings associated with CLEANLINESS AND DIRT form an example of a source domain.

The 'target' domain tends to be abstract, and it takes its structure from the source domain, through the metaphorical link, or 'conceptual metaphor'. Entities, attributes, processes and relationships associated with the source domain CLEANLINESS AND DIRT include the following:

> Entities: dirt, dust, cleaning materials;
> Attributes: cleanliness, dirtiness;
> Processes: cleaning, cleansing, dirtying, muddying, smearing;
> Relationships: opposition between cleanliness and dirtiness, causal relationship between cleaning and the resulting cleanliness.

The source domain is lexicalized in English using the above words and many others. Conceptual metaphor theorists would argue that in conceptual metaphors such as AMORAL IS DIRTY, MORAL/ETHICAL IS CLEAN (Kövecses, 2002: 210) the source domain CLEANLINESS AND DIRT is 'mapped' on to the target domain of human moral behaviour. (Like domains, conceptual metaphors are conventionally depicted in small capital letters.) This connection between two domains, through a 'conceptual metaphor', is sometimes referred to as a 'mapping'. The target domain of MORALITY or ETHICS is thought and talked about using many of the entities, attributes and processes from the source domain CLEANLINESS AND DIRT. At the linguistic level, this means that many words and expressions from the source domain – but not all – are used to talk about the target domain. These words and expressions would include *spotless*, in *a spotless reputation*, *dirty*, in *dirty tricks* and *clean*, in *clean up one's act*; such expressions are sometimes called 'linguistic metaphors' or 'metaphorical expressions' to distinguish them from conceptual metaphors.

## Metaphor as structuring ideas

Conceptual metaphor theory also claims that the target domain takes its structure from the source domain, meaning that the way we mentally organize the target domain is partly determined by the organization of the source domain. For CLEANLINESS AND DIRT metaphors, that would mean that metaphorical dirt, or immorality, is, through the metaphor, opposed to metaphorical cleanliness, or virtue. Importing relationships from the source domain of literal cleanliness and dirt also leads to the implication that metaphorical *dirt* is something that can be removed through a deliberate *cleaning* process. Many other relationships of sameness, opposition, inclusion and causation are structured by the metaphor; for example, the same term, *dirty* is used to mean 'unfair and underhand' in *dirty tricks*, and 'mildly pornographic' in *dirty jokes*, implying that these qualities both belong in the same category. A person's name or reputation is an entity that can be damaged, made metaphorically *dirty*, by deliberate *smearing*, *blackening* or even *mud slinging*. Some of these relationships might be thought to be intrinsic to the target domain regardless of the metaphorical link with the source domain – for instance, a *clean* election campaign seems self-evidently the opposite of a *dirty* one. Other relationships, such as near synonymy between dishonesty and talk that refers to sexual matters, suggested by the use of *dirty* to describe both, are less neutral, perhaps even constructed by the metaphor.

Proponents of conceptual metaphor theory argue that few or even no abstract notions can be talked about without metaphor: there is no direct way of perceiving them and we can only understand them through the filter of directly experienced, concrete notions. For instance, the conceptual metaphor A PURPOSEFUL LIFE IS A JOURNEY is cited widely in the literature (for example, Lakoff, 1993), and it is pointed out that there are few or no ways of talking about life without metaphors. The conceptual metaphor is realized linguistically through expressions such as:

> He got <u>a head start</u> in life.
> He's without <u>direction</u> in life.
> I'm <u>where</u> I want to be in life. (Lakoff, 1993: 223)

Many, perhaps the majority, of linguistic expressions about the development of an individual's life are also used to talk about literal journeys. We talk about people who are starting out in life, who have to choose which path or direction to follow, and who sometimes look back on their lives.

Other metaphors are used to talk about different abstract aspects of life; Lakoff cites A PURPOSEFUL LIFE IS A BUSINESS, realized through expressions such as:

> He has a <u>rich</u> life.
> It's an <u>enriching</u> experience.
> I want to <u>get a lot out of</u> life. (Lakoff, 1993: 227)

Researchers within the conceptual metaphor school have gathered a mass of linguistic evidence to support their contention that abstract subjects are generally talked about using metaphor. However, the ways in which they have collected and analysed these data are sometimes questioned; these criticisms are summarized below. If their central contention is true, or even partly true, despite the weakness of some of their evidence, a close examination of the metaphors used to talk about a particular abstract domain might be an important key to the way in which that domain is structured in the minds of language users.

## Metaphor as hiding and highlighting

Conceptual metaphor theorists claim that all metaphors both hide and highlight aspects of the target domain. For instance, the conceptual metaphor UNDER-STANDING IS SEIZING, discussed by Lakoff and Turner (1989) suggests that an idea is a concrete object which can be metaphorically *grasped* and then *held*. This highlights a familiar aspect of understanding new ideas but it hides the important point that in some cases understanding comes slowly, and only with effort. The metaphor also suggests that an idea has an identity separable from people, and that this identity is permanent and fixed, as the shape and appearance of a concrete object would be. In fact, individual language users reinterpret ideas as part of the process of understanding them, but the use of metaphor to concretize ideas hides this and may lead to us forgetting it.

This aspect of conceptual metaphor theory suggests an ideological significance to metaphor use. In slightly overemphasizing the intuitive ways of understanding new ideas and down-playing different processes, the metaphor *grasp [an idea]* distorts the target domain a little. The capacity of metaphor to distort can be exploited by speakers who wish to present their message with their own spin. For example, to describe an entity as metaphorically *dirty* highlights a strongly negative evaluation, because the word carries over the negative connotations of its literal meaning from the source domain, where dirt is undesirable. The DIRT metaphor is notoriously exploited in the expression *ethnic cleansing*, originally used to suggest that racist and sometimes murderous practices were acceptable, even beneficial.

In their original exposition of conceptual metaphor theory, Lakoff and Johnson (1980) contended that metaphor is intrinsically ideological. In subsequent years, Lakoff and his co-researchers have applied conceptual metaphor analysis to many texts with the aim of making explicit their ideological bias. These include speeches, newspaper articles and other texts used to justify the 1991 and 2003 wars in the Persian Gulf. For instance, Lakoff (1991) argued that source domains such as SPORT, FAIRY TALES and SURGERY were used to manipulate the picture of war presented to soldiers and to the general public before and during the first Persian Gulf War, in 1991. Lakoff and Frisch (2006) argued that the characterization of the response to 9/11 as WAR rather than as a response to a 'crime' was a critical choice of metaphor, with far-reaching international consequences. Other applications of conceptual metaphor theory to the study of ideology in texts are discussed below.

### Conceptual metaphor theory in its historical context

For most of the twentieth century, metaphor research was largely undertaken by scholars of literature and philosophy, and was not of mainstream interest. There was a strong tendency to regard literal language as the default means of communication, meaning that metaphors were analysed in terms of their relationship to literal language. Philosophers of language such as Searle worked within this tradition, positing questions such as:

> Why do we use expressions metaphorically instead of saying exactly
> and literally what we mean? ... How is it possible for speakers to com-
> municate to hearers when speaking metaphorically inasmuch as they do
> not say what they mean? (Searle, 1979: 83)

At this time, scholars tended to use poetic and other deliberate, highly marked
metaphors as their data. For instance, Searle tackled his questions through the
discussion of metaphors such as *Sally is a block of ice* and *Richard is a gorilla*.
He concluded, perhaps inevitably given his starting assumptions, that hearers
arrive at the intended meaning of a metaphor via its literal meaning, using a
series of inferences. This view was later to be termed the 'Standard Pragmatic
Model' (Gibbs, 1994: 83), and violently contested by conceptual metaphor
theorists.

However, even as work by Searle and other scholars within this tradition
was published in 1979, the ideas that were to be developed into conceptual
metaphor theory were beginning to appear alongside it. Within the same collection as Searle's paper, Reddy (1979) put forward arguments that metaphor
is intrinsic to thought rather than a purely linguistic device. He argued that we
think about communication using the 'conduit' metaphor, discussed above, in
which communication is talked about as if it were the transference of concrete
objects. He claimed that if we could conceptualize communication using a different metaphor, the way we perceive it would be different. In contrast to the
innovative metaphors used by Searle and others, Reddy's data were the many
everyday, unmarked metaphorical expressions that we use to talk about communication such as *absorb [ideas]*, *[concepts] float around*, and *put [thoughts]
down on paper*. In 1993, Lakoff wrote of this work:

> Reddy showed, for a single, very significant case, that the locus of meta-
> phor is thought, not language, that metaphor is a major and indispensable
> part of our ordinary and conventional way of conceptualizing the world,
> and that our everyday behavior reflects our metaphorical understanding
> of experience. (Lakoff, 1993: 204)

Related ideas were being put forward at this time; for instance, also in 1979
and in the same collection of papers, Schön argued that metaphors are used to
tell stories. He showed that metaphorical stories can have entailments that may
come to be seen as logical, even inevitable, thus articulating the argument that
has underlain all subsequent work on metaphor and ideology within the conceptual metaphor tradition. Like Reddy, he had moved away from the practice
of drawing on literary or invented and highly marked metaphors; his data were
taken from naturally occurring texts on the topic of urban housing development. In this respect, he was a forerunner of more recent, post-conceptual meta-

phor theory trends in metaphor research, which now develop and apply theory to texts from many real world genres.

Lakoff and Johnson's book *Metaphors We Live By* (1980) drew together and built substantially on these strands, developing a full blown theory, albeit one that was still in need of fleshing out with detail, and for which there was, at that point, relatively little hard evidence that would meet the usual academic requirements of rigour and reliability. Seen in its historical context, the book presented a strong reaction to the assumptions prevalent at the time that saw metaphor as extraneous to real language use, and mainly concerned with marked and innovative language use. The work revolutionized the study of metaphor, as well as making a central contribution to the developing discipline of cognitive linguistics. It took metaphor to new audiences, including applied linguists, and, a little later, social scientists. Everyday language became the object of mainstream metaphor study, while the proposed relationship between metaphor and thought has been studied from many perspectives. The implications for related disciplines are still being explored and this book is an example; metaphorically speaking, the ripples continue to spread. While few scholars now accept conceptual metaphor theory uncritically, it changed the field irreversibly.

## Developments of conceptual metaphor theory

In the years since the publication of *Metaphors We Live By*, a number of researchers, particularly within the field of cognitive linguistics, have built on the theory and suggested modifications and developments. Those that seem to have the most importance for the analysis of naturally occurring data are briefly reviewed in this section.

### Primary metaphors

A widely discussed problem for conceptual metaphor theory is that conceptual metaphors seem to work at various levels of specificity: for instance, Lakoff and Johnson (1980) cite some very general mappings such as MORE IS UP, and some which are much more specific, such as WEALTH IS A HIDDEN OBJECT. Further, most, if not all metaphors only apply partially; for example, Grady (1999) discusses Lakoff and Johnson's conceptual metaphor THEORIES ARE BUILDINGS, noting correspondences between source and target domain such as *foundations*, *support*, *design* and *solidity* or *weakness*, but noting that 'some of the most important elements of buildings [...] do not figure in our conventional understanding of theories: doors, windows, floors and even the occupants themselves' (1997: 270). A further problem for THEORIES ARE BUILDINGS as a conceptual metaphor is that the basis for the mapping is unclear. Lakoff and Johnson

(1980) had claimed that conceptual metaphors are grounded in our concrete, physical experience but it is difficult to see how this works for this metaphor.

Grady explains these problems by arguing that THEORIES ARE BUILDINGS is not a conceptual metaphor at the most basic level. It is a compound of two more basic levels, 'primary' metaphors: ORGANIZATION IS PHYSICAL STRUCTURE and PERSISTING IS REMAINING ERECT. These interact to give us a compound mapping that can be expressed as ABSTRACT ORGANIZATIONS ARE ERECT PHYSICAL STRUC-TURES, which generates the linguistic metaphors linking theories to buildings. This mapping can account for related linguistic metaphors, such as when a marriage is described as having *foundations*, which are not accounted for by THEORIES ARE BUILDINGS and would require the existence of another conceptual metaphor, such as MARRIAGES ARE BUILDINGS. Grady's argument for basic meta-phors is widely accepted by scholars working in theoretical metaphor studies who may be trying to make statements about the conceptual system or language as a whole. However, in applied metaphor studies, most researchers analyse individual texts or genres, and continue to identify mappings at a more detailed level, which has proved to be a productive approach for this purpose.

## Metonymy

Metonymy is the relationship between an entity and an aspect or part of it, such as the relationship between a physical location and the people who live or work there. Metonymy is used in the utterance:

*The whole town turned out to welcome the team back*

since *town* refers, not to the physical structures of the town, but to the people who live in it.

Metonymy was mentioned in early expositions of conceptual metaphor theory, but was not given prominence. However, in recent years, it has been seen as increasingly important theoretically, with researchers such as Barcelona (2000) going so far as to suggest that all metaphor is grounded in metonymy. This is a logical extension of the claim that all metaphor is grounded in experi-ence. For instance, it is claimed that the conceptual metaphors HAPPY IS UP, SAD IS DOWN (realized through expressions such as *My spirits rose* or *I'm feeling down*) are grounded in our physical behaviour when happy or sad. Lakoff and Johnson (1980: 15) write: 'drooping posture typically goes along with sadness and depression, erect posture with a positive emotional state'. If an erect posture, and, in children, literally jumping, are an aspect of feeling happy, then alluding to posture to refer to the associated emotion can be seen as a metonymy.

Goossens (1995) argued that many linguistic expressions are the result of a combination of metaphor and metonymy. The argument can be applied to HAPPY

IS UP as follows. A happy child who is literally jumping might be described as being *in high spirits*. This is a metonymy because the literal action, being *up* or *high*, is an aspect of the associated emotion. Metonymy is usually considered a within domain mapping, and here the mapping is from the child's feeling to a physical consequence of the feeling, which is, arguably, within the same domain. However, if the child is happy but sitting down, he or she is no longer literally *high* or *up*, and using these words to describe him or her as happy now involves a crossing of domains from physical to abstract. This is therefore a metaphor, albeit one that is based on a metonymy. This argument means that a decontextualized linguistic expression cannot be described as either a metaphor or a metonym; context is needed to determine which it is.

The notion that all metaphors are ultimately derived metonymically from our direct, physical experience of the world is an offshoot of a central theme for cognitive linguists in recent years, that all thinking is embodied, that we experience the world in the way that we do because of the nature of our physical selves and physical interaction with our environment. Gibbs (2006a) gathers evidence from a range of sources to support this contention. The argument is not explored further here because though an important development within cognitive linguistics, it is of less relevance to the analysis of naturally occurring data.

## Blending

Another recent development in metaphor theory is the notion of conceptual 'blending' (Fauconnier and Turner, 2002). For blending theorists, the mind works with fluid areas of meaning, named 'mental spaces', rather than with the semi-permanent domains of meaning described in conceptual metaphor theory. Mental spaces are a way of describing an area in the mind in which we construct mental representations of the world, as we process information. 'Blending' takes place when a thought or utterance uses more than one mental space. This happens in metaphor, where a word or image with a literal meaning (one mental space) is juxtaposed with a different, usually abstract, context (a second mental space). The blend of input from the two different mental spaces creates a third mental space. It can be seen that this is related to – but not the same as – the conceptual metaphorists' notion of mapping two domains. The notion of blending has been used to explain utterances that are difficult to account for in the standard reading of conceptual metaphor theory. For instance, Kövecses took the example of the linguistic metaphor *Steam was coming out of his ears* (2002). He argues that the metaphor creates an image, of a person with steam literally pouring from each ear, which does not exist in either the source domain of heat or the target domain of anger, and claims that the existence of the conceptual metaphor ANGER IS HOT FLUID IN A CONTAINER does not account for this image. He claims that the image can only exist in a third mental space, a space in which elements of the source and target domains are fused. Although it provides explanations for such problematic examples, blending theory is of limited use for applied metaphor analysis. Work has largely concentrated on the possibilities of the theory for exploring mental structures, and to date, it has not been developed as a tool for linguistic analysis. The explanations that are offered tend to be post hoc (Gibbs, 2000), and, for applied purposes, do not seem to offer insights additional to conceptual metaphor theory.

## Implications of conceptual metaphor theory for research methodology

### Text analysis: Methodological issues

If conceptual metaphors help people to understand abstract subjects of such central importance as life and communication, then studying metaphor could help researchers to identify the conceptual structures that both reflect and shape the thought patterns of the community. By their nature, conceptual metaphors are not directly accessible, and the main way of identifying them has been through their linguistic realizations. A common technique is to identify the linguistic metaphors used to talk about a topic, and from these, to postulate the underlying conceptual metaphors that are presumed to motivate them. The researcher might then consider which aspects of the target domain are high-lighted and hidden by the metaphor. There are a number of issues that this process raises; these, and possible solutions, are discussed in detail by Steen (2007). Briefly, the researcher needs to choose representative texts to search; he or she needs to have a reliable procedure for identifying linguistic metaphors. Ideally the researcher would need to be able to carry their procedure on large amounts of text, with appropriate co-rating procedures. The researcher would then need to develop a reliable way of grouping linguistic metaphors semantically and deciding which source and target domains they realize. None of these issues is trivial, and in the early days of applied metaphor research much work was less than rigorous because of an over-reliance on individual intuition in addressing them.

### Metaphor and speaker meaning

Several research projects have used conceptual metaphor theory to shed light on how people think about their lives and experiences. Metaphors can help people to talk about difficult, emotionally intense or uncommon experiences, and thus, according to conceptual metaphor theory, to think about them. Illness is an area that has been investigated in a number of studies, of which I describe two here. In a relatively early study, Gwyn (1999) analysed the metaphors that seriously ill people used to talk about their experience, and drew conclusions about their thoughts and feelings on the basis of these. An analysis of metaphors in his data convinced him that his participants viewed their mental and spiritual health as closely entwined in their physical conditions. As well as speech data, Gwyn analysed behaviour more widely, seeing metaphors in a patient's physical reaction to their illness as well as in their words. For instance, he cites a participant who having suffered a heart attack became a compulsive walker; Gwyn notes:

> we walk 'the road to recovery', we get 'back on the right track', we 'get better one step at a time'. [The patient] lived the ambulatory metaphor to its full. (Gwyn, 1999: 216)

Semino *et al.* (2004) analysed the metaphors they found in a corpus of conversation about cancer. They show alternative analyses of the data to demonstrate the difficulty of making decisions about assigning linguistic metaphors to conceptual metaphor. The writers find that cancer is variously described as *galloping, travelling, dormant* and *erupting* among other expressions. They show that the different linguistic metaphors imply different conceptualizations of cancer for example, as an ANIMAL, or as a VOLCANO, each of which has different entailments.

## Analysing ideology

The utterances analysed in the above two studies were probably produced with little or no conscious thought about how metaphor would present one interpretation rather than another. Sometimes however, it seems that speakers or writers may have deliberately chosen particular ways of expressing ideas metaphorically in order to convey an ideological or persuasive point. Some of Lakoff's work in this area was briefly mentioned above.

Genres that have been investigated include political texts and advertising. In particular, some analysts have used conceptual metaphor theory to try to identify the ideological stance underlying a text or corpus of texts. For instance, Sandikcioglu studied metaphors from the magazines *Time* and *Newsweek* from around the period of the 1991 Gulf War, and argued that these demonstrated a racist agenda, in which the world is polarized into 'the Orient vs the West, Us vs Them' (2000: 300).

Santa Ana (1999) analysed metaphors in articles from the *Los Angeles Times* reporting on anti-immigrant legislation, and found that they constructed

immigrants negatively, as animals, plants and commodities. The nation was metaphorically constructed as a *house*, and immigrants talked of as metaphorical
threats such *floods* or *invasion*. While many valid and important points are made,
in this and similar studies, a difficulty is the possibility of over-interpretation.
For instance, Santa Ana analysed linguistic metaphors such as *curb* and *hunt*
as realizations of a conceptual metaphor IMMIGRANTS ARE ANIMALS. While this
interpretation cannot be ruled out, analysis of *curb* in a wide range of contexts
shows that the word is only very rarely, if ever, used in its literal sense of restrain-
ing animals, so it is possible that for current speakers there is no metaphorical
mapping. Analysis of *hunt* shows that things that are hunted are often considered
very desirable; in Santa Ana's example, immigrant labour is presented as much
sought after, suggesting that if there is an underlying ANIMAL metaphor, it is not
completely negative.

Metaphor analysis seems to have a good deal to offer researchers who are
interested in the ideological bias of texts, but caution is needed, especially as
topics such as race are already emotive and potentially divisive.

## Criticisms of conceptual metaphor theory

The conceptual metaphor approach is potentially very enlightening as a tool for
identifying underlying meaning, but it has been criticized. Some of those criticisms are briefly summarized in this section.

### The need for reliable data collection

Steen (2007) has explored the implications and applications of contemporary
metaphor theories in detail, from a methodological perspective, and he shows
that proponents of conceptual metaphor theory have not considered other possible explanations for their data. He describes how the theory could be applied
to identify metaphor and identifies a number of points in the process where
researchers have omitted to explain or question their assumptions, or have
offered unreliable data, analysed in methodologically unsound ways.

### The domain problem

One of the major problems for conceptual metaphor theory is delimiting
domains; although the notion of a domain is intuitively strong, it is difficult
to operationalize. For instance, if cancer is described as *galloping*, should the
researcher postulate the domain ANIMAL? Intuition, and language analysis, tells
us that only horses and a few similar animals gallop, so it might seem appropri-

ate to describe the metaphor as a mapping from horses on to cancer. However, as Semino *et al.* (2004) argued, the domain shift from the movement to an animal may be an over-interpretation. The difficulty arises frequently; temperature metaphors for emotions are described variously as EMOTIONS ARE TEMPERATURES, ANGER IS HEAT, and ANGER IS HEATED FLUID IN A CONTAINER – that is, the source domain is described at increasing levels of specificity. Steen (2007) reviews and critiques researchers' attempts to define domains, and shows that a rigorous, reliable definition is difficult or perhaps impossible to achieve.

## Prioritizing thought over language

For proponents of conceptual metaphor theory, thought has primacy over language. The theory was not intended to account for language in use, which is seen as merely the surface manifestation of more important phenomena. Nonetheless, patterns of word usage are the main evidence presented for the theory. These linguistic data have tended to be generated intuitively, either by the researcher or by informants, but in recent years some researchers have started to analyse naturally occurring language data. The reliability and validity of introspective language data have been questioned by corpus linguists (for example, Deignan, 2005), and most researchers concerned with linguistic metaphor now use naturally occurring language data.

## Methodological issues in inferring conceptual metaphor from language data

From the perspective of using the theory to explore underlying metaphors in text, researchers need to be alert to the dangers of overgeneralizing on limited linguistic evidence, and to the need to establish consistent procedures for identifying metaphors (Deignan, 2005). Metaphorical expressions in discourse are not necessarily instantiations of conceptual metaphors; an over-simplistic approach is to identify conceptual metaphors on limited language data. For instance, Kövecses (2002: 123) takes the naturally occurring citation *Vincent met his father's icy stare evenly* as the evidence for a conceptual metaphor UNFRIENDLY IS ICY. In this case the problem may be that the proposed conceptual metaphor is over-specific; a conceptual metaphor such as FEELINGS ARE TEMPERATURES would describe the data satisfactorily and more evidence would be available. Gibbs, *et al.* (1997) cited the idiom *a shot in the arm* as an instance of a conceptual metaphor ENCOURAGEMENT IS GIVING SOMEONE A DRUG, without providing further evidence for this conceptual metaphor, and *burst her bubble* as an instance of PRIDE IS INFLATION. Other examples they offer are much more convincing, such as OPTIMISM IS LIGHT. For this conceptual metaphor, many linguistic realizations are readily found, such as *a bright smile, a sunny disposition,*

and *light at the end of the tunnel*. It is therefore important for applied researchers to be very cautious of inferring conceptual patterns on the basis of a small
number of linguistic examples.

### Finding an appropriate and adequate theory for research

For the significant and developing group of language scholars who are concerned with language as discourse, an approach which relies completely on
conceptual metaphor theory is inadequate. Researchers such as Cameron (for
example, 2003) regard context and speaker meaning as central factors to the
analysis of metaphors in discourse, and the theory does not appear to take these
into account. Further, for applied linguists, the early work on conceptual metaphor theory lacked credibility because it did not customarily give sources for
language citations. In more recent work within the tradition, some sources are
given, but context and speaker meaning are not generally discussed.

For applied linguists and social scientists there is little acceptable evidence
that conceptual metaphors are actually ways of thinking. They work quite well
as generalizations about language, often enabling a systematic approach to
word meaning, for example. Further, the notion that a linguistic metaphor might
suggest an entailment seems reasonable, and does not have to imply that all our
thinking is structured by metaphors. For this reason, some current scholars are
avoiding the term 'conceptual metaphor' and, as we do in this book, seeking
instead metaphorical systems.

## Conclusion

The importance of conceptual metaphor theory for current research in metaphor cannot be underestimated. It is difficult for contemporary researchers to
imagine the field without the contributions of figures such as Reddy, Lakoff and
Johnson. The excitement of their early ideas led many researchers to apply them
uncritically and without rigour though, and the claim that all metaphor should
be seen as conceptual was taken to extremes. Metaphor research is increasingly
influenced by developments in fields such as applied linguistics, which have
contributed methodologies such as the study of language using corpora and as
discourse, and new ways of thinking about the relationship between language
and thought. Conversely, metaphor theory is increasingly being applied to analysis across disparate fields. Despite the reservations expressed in the latter half
of this chapter, the approach has much to offer any discipline in which texts can
be used to attempt to infer people's beliefs and meanings.

# 4 Between mind and language: 'A journey worth taking'

## L. David Ritchie

After her father was killed by an IRA-planted bomb, Jo Berry decided that she wanted to understand the experience of the people who had committed this crime, to *walk in the footsteps of the bombers* and *bring something positive out of it* (Cameron, 2007b; Chapter 1, this volume). Later in the same conversation comes Extract 4.1, spoken by Pat Magee who planted the bomb (metaphor vehicles underlined):

Extract 4.1 (from Cameron, 2007b: 205)

> ... but certainly you --
> ... (1.0) ha- --
> ... (1.0) you know,
> totally <u>come along</u> that <u>long journey</u>,
> you know,
> you --
> you'd <u>reached</u> some conclusion.
> <u>put a line under</u> the past.

In an essay about the grieving process, Obst (2003: 1) reminds readers that

> There are some journeys that we get excited about going on. The journey of a cross-country vacation, so invigorating and full of adventure. The *journey through* college *toward the goal* of a career. The *journey* of a new relationship with a *significant other filled with all of its discoveries* of one another.

She then tells us that grief is also a *journey*, not *into a cave* but *through a dark tunnel*.

In a conversation among a group of college students about homelessness (Ritchie, 2009), one participant suggests that homeless people eventually

> <u>get to that point</u> where they just wander
> the streets and talk to themselves.

In relation to the difficulty poor people experience in securing steady employment, participants note that:

> you have to have <u>somewhere to start from</u>

and criticize the harshness of the capitalist system because

> you really have <u>nowhere to start from</u>.

Describing a typical sequence of events in the life of a homeless person, one participant observes that

> it <u>goes from</u> ... drugs <u>to</u> uh ... you know,
> like, mental illness

and another participant says

> you get so deep into it you can't you can't get back out.
> [eh heh]
> You're <u>on the streets</u> talking to yourself
> [yep!]
> yah know ... starts with something small and builds up.

Throughout this conversation, *on the streets* is sometimes used literally, sometimes metonymically, sometimes metaphorically, and sometimes, as seems to be the case here, both literally and metaphorically – just as *journey of reconciliation* in Cameron (2007b) can be understood as simultaneously literal and metaphorical. *Starts with something small and builds up* exemplifies another common phenomenon, the combination of a metaphor based on JOURNEY (*starts with*) with a metaphor based on CONSTRUCTION (*builds up*).

For the 2005 parliamentary election, Britain's Labour party campaigned on the slogan, '*Forward, not back*'. In a speech to the 2005 Labour party conference (see Appendix), further analysed in later chapters of this book, Tony Blair declared, *I'm <u>back</u>*. Other excerpts from the same speech include:

> *Events have sometimes taken me far from home.*
> (paragraph 14)
>
> ...
>
> *Where we have lost old friends,*
> *we try to persuade them to come back to the fold.*
> (paragraph 23)

> *And now you, the British people, have to sit down*
> *and decide whether you want the relationship to continue*
> (paragraph 38)

In these examples, expressions are clearly drawn from, or at least related to, the JOURNEY conceptual metaphor described by Lakoff and Johnson (1980; Chapter 3, this volume). As in the example from the conversation about homelessness, the JOURNEY metaphor is also combined with other metaphors, as in *come back to the fold*, in which JOURNEY is combined with a SHEPHERD-ING metaphor. Moreover, the JOURNEY metaphor often seems to have different meanings in different passages, and literal journeys are mentioned alongside metaphorical journeys. In each case, it seems that the metaphors can best be understood by considering the context in which they appear, including not only the immediate passage, the surrounding words and phrases, but also the cultural and relational context, the situation of the writer or speaker with respect to readers or hearers, and the apparent relational and interactive objectives of the writer or speaker.

Until recently, metaphor was usually treated at best as a kind of decorative embellishment on language. Lakoff and Johnson (1980) inverted the traditional view by placing metaphor at the core of language, arguing that concepts are themselves primarily metaphorical, and that verbal metaphors are but expressions of underlying conceptual metaphors. It follows that analysis of metaphorical language can lead to insights about the conceptual structure that underlies thought as well as language. However, Lakoff and Johnson continued the tradition of examining metaphors independent of any communicative context, often relying on metaphorical expressions invented to illustrate particular principles.

In the past decade or two, researchers have begun to investigate metaphors from a cognitive perspective in the context of actual discourse (e.g. Charteris-Black, 2005; Musolff, 2004). Notably, Cameron (2007b; Chapter 5, this volume) demonstrates how the pattern of metaphor use, re-use, and modification can contribute to understanding the cultural and social as well as the cognitive and emotional processes in an emotionally intense conversation (or series of conversations). Cameron's work directly challenges previous approaches to metaphor theory, including conceptual metaphor theory, by emphasizing the interconnection of linguistic with other crucial dimensions in metaphor use and interpretation, and by insisting on the need to analyse metaphors in their communicative context. In this approach, metaphors are neither merely decorative nor merely manifestations of underlying conceptual systems. Rather, as Cameron's work illustrates, metaphorical expressions can themselves become resources in the negotiation of a shared social reality, and the use or adaptation of a particular metaphor can become meaningful in itself, independently of the meaning or interpretation of the metaphor.

Gibbs (2006b) has proposed an extension of conceptual metaphor theory in which readers or hearers experience a more or less detailed conceptual simulation of the state or action described by the conceptual metaphor associated with a particular metaphor vehicle. Gibbs argues that metaphors partially activate neuron groups associated with related schemas so that the described object or event is experienced in connection with the topic. When one of the participants describing drug use by the homeless says *you get so deep into it you can't you can't get back out,* the hearer will experience a simulation of a person going into deep water (or perhaps a cave) and becoming trapped; the experience may include visceral as well as visual sensations. When Tony Blair speaks of trying to persuade old friends to *come back to the fold,* the hearer will experience a simulation of a flock of sheep walking into a shelter. In a somewhat similar approach, Barsalou (1999, 2008) has proposed that thinking in general is accomplished at least primarily through the activation of simulations of perception (including perceptions of mental states such as recognition or agreement as well as of emotional and internal bodily states). The most important difference is that Barsalou's approach recognizes that simulations can be activated and experienced either as part of an inclusive and multimodal schema or independently. In this chapter, I propose a model of metaphor use and interpretation that builds on and merges Gibbs's and Barsalou's approaches to perceptual simulation, and explicitly incorporates the communicative context in which a metaphor appears, including the cultural and relational context as well as the extended context of the conversation or text as a whole.

I begin with a brief summary and critique of the most relevant aspects of conceptual metaphor theory, building on Deignan's more detailed discussion in Chapter 3. I then discuss Gibbs's extension of conceptual metaphor theory, and his idea that metaphor interpretation involves a kind of mental simulation of the situation or action designated by the metaphor vehicle. Following that, I review a theory of cognition as perceptual simulation proposed by Barsalou (1999, 2008), discuss how perceptual simulation theory can contribute to our understanding of how people use and interpret metaphor, and suggest a way to synthesize Gibbs's extension of conceptual metaphor theory with perceptual simulation theory. Finally, I return to the questions that motivate this volume: How do people use metaphorical language to accomplish relational and task objectives in everyday talk? How can researchers use metaphorical language to understand the cognitive, relational, and cultural processes that produce and inform everyday talk?

## Conceptual metaphor theory

Lakoff and Johnson (1980) argue that correlations between perceptual experiences provide the basis for conceptual metaphors in the form of neural connections, and these in turn provide the basis for almost all abstract conceptual thought. Commonplace expressions such as *a warm relationship*, *a close friend*, or *a big problem* all originate in and provide evidence of correlations between physical sensations (physical warmth and proximity, perceived size) and more abstract concepts (love, friendship, problem solving). Thus, metaphor is primarily conceptual, and the linguistic expressions we usually think of as 'metaphors' are but expressions or manifestations of underlying conceptual metaphors. Conceptual metaphors are expressed in coherent *systems* of linguistic metaphors; to use one of Lakoff and Johnson's primary examples, expressions such as *win* or *lose* a debate, *attack* or *defend* a position, and *undermine* an opponent's argument all manifest a single underlying metaphor, ARGUMENT IS WAR. According to conceptual metaphor theory, when we use or encounter these expressions, we actually experience argument as war. Similarly, in the previously quoted example from the homelessness conversation (Ritchie, 2009), *you have to have somewhere to start from* expresses LIFE IS A JOURNEY and *homeless people eventually get to that point* expresses HOMELESSNESS IS A JOURNEY.

Vervaeke and Kennedy (1996) object to Lakoff and Johnson's broader claim that everyday expressions necessarily demonstrate the existence of an underlying conceptual metaphor that is experienced as a unified gestalt. Continuing with the *argument* example, Vervaeke and Kennedy point out that expressions such as *win* or *lose* an argument, *defend* an argument, and *develop a strategy* can all be interpreted in terms of 'a process undertaken in a certain order' and that various such processes can be mapped on to each other with none having precedence over any of the others (Vervaeke and Kennedy, 1996: 276). Since many of the expressions Lakoff and Johnson list as elements of war also pertain to competitive games, Vervaeke and Kennedy conclude that ARGUMENT IS BRIDGE or ARGUMENT IS CHESS would be equally defensible as ARGUMENT IS WAR (for a more detailed discussion, see Ritchie, 2003a, 2006).

Pursuing this line of reasoning further leads to the conclusion that a broad array of contentious activities, with varying degrees of violence, competitiveness and other characteristics, may be organized, both cognitively and culturally, into a 'field of meaning', such that metaphor vehicles may be chosen from various elements within the field, according to the intensity of perception or feeling that is to be expressed (Ritchie, 2003a, 2006). Thus we have BUSINESS IS WAR (*invade the competitor's territory*) but we also have WAR IS BUSINESS (*an unprofitable manoeuvre*) and ARGUMENT IS BUSINESS (*exchange opinions, an unprofitable line of reasoning*).

Based on experimental evidence, Keysar and Bly (1999) report that participants often give idiosyncratic explanations for metaphors, even when the metaphor vehicle is so obscure that the metaphor is apparently uninterpretable, for example *the goose hangs high*. Metaphors of another type, in which the vehicle at least seems to make sense, were also given a wide variety of interpretations, many of them mutually contradictory. For example, *warm his britches* was interpreted as a reference to punishment by some subjects, but others interpreted it in terms of praise. Gibbs (1998, personal communication) points out that most of the idioms studied by Keysar and Bly are metonymic rather than metaphorical in origin: to continue with the same example, *warm his britches* originally referred to the once-common practice of punishing disobedient children with a willow switch or a leather belt or strap, which brings blood to the surface of the skin and creates a literal, physical sensation of warmth.

However, other, more clearly metaphorical, expressions are also frequently interpreted in quite diverse ways, for example *toe the line*, often understood and spelled as *tow the line* (Ritchie, 2006). These alternative spellings imply very distinct underlying conceptual metaphor source domains, something like IMAGINARY LINE ON A MILITARY PARADE GROUND and A BARGE TOWED BY A TUGBOAT. (Informants have also produced THE STARTING LINE FOR A FOOT-RACE and A GAME OF TUG-O'-WAR, respectively.) Although the two spellings have somewhat different implications (*toe* suggests a more passive compliance; *tow* suggests more active compliance), the implied acquiescence to authority is sufficiently similar in quality that participants in a conversation might never realize that they interpret the metaphor in entirely different ways. In another familiar example, *the grass is greener on the other side of the fence* is interpreted in terms of a suburban home-owner looking at the neighbour's lawn as readily as in terms of the original agrarian reference of a cow reaching through a fence to the adjacent pasture (Ritchie, 2006).

## Metaphor and simulation

Perception of external objects and events as well as internal (bodily and mental) states and processes occurs through the activation of neuron groups (Barsalou, 2008); the raw experiences are filtered and aggregated in a series of steps up to the conscious experience of an object, event, or sequence of events as a whole. These experiences are stored in memory as schemas, aggregates of objects, features, etc. that tend to occur together and have been abstracted from our experience of the world (Gibbs, 2006b). Bodily action is accomplished by a sequence that occurs in more or less the reverse order, starting with higher-order action schemas and disaggregating to actions of specific muscle groups. As used in this chapter, simulation refers to a neural process in which either the same neural groups that would be activated during direct experience (or parallel groups) are partially activated: in most cases the actual performance of simulated muscular actions and the interpretation of simulated perceptions as 'real' are inhibited. (This inhibition can be weakened or eliminated by conditions such as extreme exhaustion or very strong emotion, as when a distraught person involuntarily cries out or slams a fist into a wall.)

Gibbs (2006b) argues that language interpretation in general involves simulation in at least two interrelated senses. First, language automatically activates 'construction of a simulation whereby we imagine performing the bodily actions referred to in the language' (Gibbs 2006b: 434). Second, Gibbs claims that understanding language requires listeners to draw inferences about the speaker's communicative intentions, which in turn can be accomplished by simulating the speaker's experience and thoughts at the moment of the utterance. These two ideas are implicitly related inasmuch as simulating the performance of bodily actions implied by a speaker's utterance is one way to simulate the speaker's thoughts and experience.

The claim that listeners must consider and draw inferences about speakers' communicative intentions is defensible on logical grounds, if we assume that speakers and listeners actively use and maintain something like 'common ground' (Clark, 1996). However, an experiment by Barr and Keysar (2005), in which participants who were not visible to each other attempted to communicate about the shape and orientation of visual images, yielded evidence that communicators do not necessarily consider differences in common ground even when these differences are apparent (in their experiment, for example, when one member of a team has been replaced by a new member who was not privy to preceding exchanges). Barr and Keysar conclude that people are cognitively lazy, and tend to assume that others have the same knowledge they have. A clear implication is that listeners are likely to consider speakers' specific knowledge *or* speakers' specific intentions only when something about the exchange is problematic, or perhaps when the outcome is of particular importance.

The assumption that listeners always consider speakers' communicative intentions, however, is not necessary to Gibbs's overall argument. There is ample evidence that humans, like other primates, are neurally capable of mirroring others' actions, and that humans *do* tend to mirror or echo others' communicative behaviour during conversation (Feldman, 2006). Moreover, Gibbs produces extensive experimental evidence in support of the claim that inconsistencies between subjects' actions and words they are asked to process interfere with (and consistencies facilitate) language processing and comprehension. As only one among many examples, a subject required to signal comprehension by *pushing* a lever will react more slowly to a verb that implies movement *towards* the subject than to one that implies movement *away*, strongly suggesting that motor control neurons consistent with the action of a word or phrase are at least partially activated during processing. It seems reasonable to conclude that simulating the action (or state) associated with a word or phrase plays at least *some* role in everyday language processing.

## Perceptual simulation theory

Barsalou (1999, 2008) has proposed a theory of cognition that is embodied in a slightly different sense. Barsalou notes that the perceptual neural system aggregates perceptual experience at ever higher levels of abstraction, up to the conscious experience of objects and action sequences as coherent entities. He suggests that a *conceptual* neural system parallels the perceptual neural system at every level, and is capable of partially simulating any aspect of perceptual experience on the basis of schemas (densely interconnected sets of perceptions/simulations that tend to be experienced together) stored in memory. Again, as in Gibbs's model, *simulation* in Barsalou's theory takes the form of *partial* activation of the neural circuits that would become fully activated in actual physical perception or action.

In Barsalou's theory, perceptions (and associated simulations) include not merely the standard 'five senses' but also introspective awareness of one's own thoughts and emotions and proprioceptive awareness of one's internal bodily states (e.g., pain, pressure, exertion, fatigue). Just as we are able to experience a partial simulation of a visual phenomenon, such as the deep blue of a mountain lake or the sound of a cat purring, we are also able to experience a partial simulation of a cognitive state, such as recognizing that 2 + 2 is equivalent to 4, or a bodily state, such as feeling hot and out of breath after climbing several flights of stairs. Barsalou claims that cognition occurs primarily through the interaction of perceptual simulations, including the introspective simulation of mental states such as agreement or disagreement, recognition, etc. Although Barsalou (2008) recognizes that language is sometimes processed primarily or even entirely in terms of connections with other language, he claims that language is capable of activating perceptual simulations and, when it is processed deeply, language comprehension is largely accomplished through the partial activation of associated simulations. (For a review of research consistent with this claim see Gibbs, 2006b; Gibbs and Matlock, 2008.) Conversely, language is itself activated more or less automatically by perceptual experience.

For example, consider the word, *cat*. According to Barsalou's theory, for most English-speakers, *cat* activates primary simulations of certain perceptions (size, shape, fur texture, purring), and other features that would be considered part of the definition of what it means to be a *cat*. Activation of the concept, *cat*, either by seeing the neighbour's cat run across my lawn or by encountering the word, will also at least partially activate semantic links to other words such as *pet, feline* and *predator*. That favourite example of metaphor discussions, s*hark*, activates its own set of primary simulations of certain perceptions, primarily visual, and its own set of related words (*cartilaginous skeleton, predator, sharp teeth,* etc.).

Both of these concepts, *cat*, and *shark*, are frequently encountered in our culture, and each also activates a large set of secondary simulations, simulations of perceptions that are frequently associated with the animal in question, even though they are not defining. *Cat* may activate simulations of a certain kind of independent behaviour, the comfort of a cat snuggled up on one's lap, the sight of hair on a black wool skirt, emotions associated with home and hearth. *Shark* may activate memories of scuba diving, scenes from old B movies, emotions such as awe, terror, dread, and even respect. The primary simulations and words considered part of the 'definition' of a concept such as *cat* or *shark* can be thought of as similar to the conventional notion of 'denotation' or dictionary meaning. Secondary simulations and words, not part of the 'definition' but often experienced in connection with the concept (emotions such as fear, dread and awe), are similar to the conventional notion of 'connotation'. These secondary simulations and words may be connected with a range of evocative concepts independently of the hierarchy of conceptual categories. Thus, the emotional and bodily simulations of *fear*, *dread* and *awe* associated with *shark* may be connected, along with those associated with *avalanche, tsunami,* and perhaps even *oral examination*, in a 'field of meaning' that can be activated by very different conceptual metaphors associated with entirely different conceptual categories.

When a word or phrase is encountered, many, perhaps all, of the simulations associated with it, both primary and secondary, are at least fleetingly activated (Gernsbacher *et al.*, 2001). Simulations that are not relevant in the present context, that cannot be readily connected with ideas already activated in working memory, are suppressed, usually before reaching conscious awareness, and those that are relevant in the present context become more highly activated (Gernsbacher *et al.*, 2001; Kintsch, 1998). The connections between current contents of working memory and the context-relevant simulations activated by a phrase become the 'meaning' of the phrase in the present context. If the word or phrase is metaphorical, the primary or definitional perceptual simulations are suppressed and the secondary simulations that are relevant in the current context (Sperber and Wilson, 1986), the nuances of experience associated with the concept, remain activated and are connected with the topic of the metaphor. This will happen at least to some extent whether or not the underlying metaphor is actively processed. Thus, a phrase such as *attack her argument* may activate perceptual simulations associated with emotional nuances such as hostility and anger, even if it does not activate any of the other simulations associated with WAR or any other CONTENTIOUS ENCOUNTER schema.

## Context-limited simulation theory

Ritchie (2006) emphasizes the nuances of perceptual simulations, especially the emotional, introspective and interoceptive (perceptions of internal bodily states) simulations that may potentially be activated by highly expressive language such as metaphor, narrative or playful language. A metaphor may activate an entire conceptual schema as a unified *gestalt*, as posited by conceptual metaphor theory (Gibbs, 2006b; Lakoff and Johnson, 1980), it may also activate only a small subset of simulations associated with the underlying conceptual schema; non-relevant simulations may be actively inhibited by accompanying metaphors as well as by other elements in the context. Since the simulations activated by a particularly expressive metaphor may remain activated for some time, if subsequent metaphors activate similar or compatible simulations the cumulative effect may be distinct from what could be accomplished by any one metaphor on its own, and may also be more enduring. Conversely, and consistent with Cameron's approach (2007b; Chapter 5, this volume), the simulations activated by a previously used metaphor may be expanded and connected with entirely different topics through the artful repetition and transformation of a metaphor or narrative. Thus, through a sequence of metaphors, a speaker or an interacting dyad or group may build, alter and sustain a backdrop of emotional, perceptual, and conceptual ideas that become part of the participants' overall experience of the communicative event, separate from but interacting with the overt informative content of the words and phrases themselves. As Cameron (2007b) shows, this background can have profound effects on the development of the conversation and of the relationships within which the conversation takes place.

The entailments of conceptual metaphors, discussed in conceptual metaphor theory, refer approximately to the perceptual simulations that are activated when words, phrases, or other stimuli associated with the vehicle or source domain term are encountered. Thus, a 'field of meaning' (Ritchie, 2003a, 2006) can be thought of as linking together an array of concepts, which may belong to entirely different conceptual categories (Lakoff and Johnson, 1980) or systems of metaphor (Cameron, 2007b), by the perceptual simulations they evoke to varying degrees of intensity. To continue with the WAR example discussed by Lakoff and Johnson (1980), Vervaeke and Kennedy (1996) and Ritchie (2003a), interoceptive (emotional and visceral) simulations of physical violence and anger are strongly activated by phrases closely associated with war, such as *demolish* and *attack* but only weakly activated (and may be actively suppressed) by phrases more closely associated with games, such as *score one* and *strategy*. Conversely, introspective simulations of rules and orderliness are weakly (if at all) activated by *demolish* and *attack* but more strongly activated by *score one* and *strategy*. Consistent with Vervaeke and Kennedy's argument, the speaker or writer will choose the phrases that activate the simulations that most closely match the experience to be expressed, and suppress inapplicable simulations. The relationship between verbal metaphors and experience is two-way: experience activates schemas that activate words, including metaphors; words, including metaphors, activate schemas that regulate (activate and/or suppress) simulations that enter into experience.

This account is consistent with Lakoff and Johnson's (1980) discussion of fundamental embodied metaphors (MORE IS UP; AFFECTION IS WARMTH) – the conceptual metaphors they posit, in effect, anchor certain positions in one or more extended fields of meaning. But the assertion that we somehow experience argument *as* war can itself probably best be viewed as figurative – it is more accurate to say that we experience simulations of some perceptions (emotional, introspective, and visceral) associated with an argument by activating a few of the contextually relevant perceptual simulations associated with and activated by allusion to war and warlike behaviour – or perhaps to other contentious activities such as bridge or chess (Vervaeke and Kennedy, 1996). At the same time other, non-relevant simulations associated with war are likely to be suppressed.

This account is also consistent, up to a point, with Gibbs's (2006b) claim that a metaphor activates a simulation of the complete action or perception identified by the metaphor vehicle. Where the context-limited simulation theory approach differs from Gibbs's approach is that Gibbs emphasizes metaphor induced simulations of the perception or action as a unified *gestalt*, but context-limited simulation theory emphasizes the potential of metaphors to activate simulations of context-relevant perceptions independently of the less relevant elements of the underlying conceptual category. This emphasis on partial, context-relevant simulation is more consistent with Barsalou's (2008) theory but, as Gibbs points out, metaphor is a complex cognitive and linguistic phenomenon, unlikely to be explained by any one theory.

## X IS A JOURNEY and other metaphors

According to conceptual metaphor theory, each of the passages quoted at the beginning of this chapter includes a JOURNEY metaphor. Jo Berry and Pat Magee both express versions of RECONCILIATION IS A JOURNEY; according to conceptual metaphor theory, these phrases lead the reader or listener to experience reconciliation *as* a journey. The Obst essay includes several journey metaphors; in the passage quoted, we find COLLEGE IS A JOURNEY and RELATIONSHIP IS A

JOURNEY as well as GRIEF IS A JOURNEY, the central theme of the piece; according to conceptual metaphor theory, these lead us, respectively, to experience college, relationship formation, and grief as journeys. The passage from the homelessness conversation includes LIFE IS A JOURNEY and HOMELESSNESS IS A JOURNEY, and arguably DRUG ADDICTION IS A JOURNEY. Each of these passages also presents other conceptual metaphors, including a MORAL ACCOUNTING metaphor in Pat Magee's response to Jo Berry (*put a line under the past*), RELATIONSHIP IS A CONTAINER in the passage from Obst, ADDICTION IS A CONTAINER (or A CAVE, perhaps) in the homelessness excerpt, and LEADER IS SHEPHERD from the Blair excerpt (*we try to persuade them to come back to the fold*).

Following Gibbs's account, *walk in the footsteps of the bombers* could activate a simulation of Jo, walking the same route as the bombers, placing her feet where their feet were placed. This simulation might include a visual image of a woman stepping in a sequence of footprints as well as simulations of actual muscle movements associated with walking, and with the kind of attentiveness required to place one's feet precisely in someone else's footprints. In Gibbs's theory, the phrase also activates a simulation of what Jo must have intended for the hearer to experience when hearing this phrase.

When Pat says Jo has *come along that long journey* and *reached some conclusion*, the relevant aspects of movement are quite different – *walking in the footsteps* is specifically embodied, at the level of legs and feet in motion, whereas *come along*, that *long journey*, and *reached* have more to do with a more general concept (and experience) of travel. Here, the perceptual simulations account seems more useful than the conceptual metaphor approach. Phrases like *long journey* and *reach a destination* or *a conclusion* may activate simulations of bodily motion, but they also activate emotions and introspective thoughts associated with travel, such as weariness (with respect to *long journey*) and satisfaction and relief (*reach...*). *Walk in the footsteps* also activates emotional and introspective simulations – and these may be the most important feature of Jo's metaphor. Thus, with respect to these phrases, a combination of the more global schema simulation suggested by Gibbs and the more limited simulation of particular perceptions suggested by perceptual simulation theory seems more promising than either, taken on its own.

The second part of Jo's utterance, *bring something positive out of it*, also activates a motion schema, but it is primarily *carrying* rather than simple movement, and the movement is explicitly *out of* some *container*. Here, the kind of detailed simulation suggested by Gibbs seems less useful than the simpler and more straightforward perceptual simulation account. *Walking in the footsteps* is not the sort of journey that would ordinarily involve retrieving an object – it seems likely that the vivid imagery of the *footsteps* schema would inhibit full realization of the *bringing something out* schema.

Pat Magee's second phrase, *put a line under the past* activates a very different sort of schema, and may activate a detailed schema of drawing a line under a column of numbers to signify the completion of an accounting period, consistent with Gibbs, or it may activate only a simulation of the sense of completion and relief associated with finishing up a set of accounts. Given that all of these phrases are familiar idioms, it seems all the more likely that a listener might process only the emotional and introspective simulations associated with the idiomatic use of the phrases, without activating the full schema as a *gestalt*, although the participants' high levels of emotional involvement in the conversation could render them more than usually attentive to the full underlying schemas.

As Cameron (2007b) points out, there is an implicit ambiguity in the use of the JOURNEY metaphor with respect to Jo, since her *journey* of discovery and reconciliation has involved a literal *journey* to various parts of Ireland and the United Kingdom. This ambiguity is explicit in the Obst (2003) essay, which begins with reference to the literal *journey of a cross-country vacation, so invigorating and full of adventure*. Obst then lists two metaphorical *journeys*, college and a relationship, before introducing the more unpleasant metaphorical *journey* of grief. Mention of the literal vacation journey seems likely to reinforce activation of a more complete JOURNEY schema by the metaphorical uses. However, in the context of the essay, what seems most important is the activation of *pleasant* emotion simulations by *vacation*, and the activation of simulations of both satisfaction and accomplishment by *college. New relationship* builds on these positive emotion and introspective simulations by activating additional simulations of affection and hope, and provides both a transition to and a contrast with the immediately relevant simulations of sorrow and misery activated by *grief.*

Obst's essay also includes a series of striking metaphors, like *discoveries* of one another in the relationship *journey* and a *cave* that is replaced with a *dark tunnel* through which the griever must *journey*. These may be intended to activate and may activate full simulations of the associated schemas – or they may activate only simulations of associated emotions. Here again, a combination of Gibbs's approach with the more limited perceptual simulations approach seems to be most useful.

The homelessness discussion also includes a mixture of literal and metaphorical uses. The claim that homeless people eventually *get to that point where they just wander the streets and talk to themselves* invokes a metaphorical *journey* that leads to a *destination*, but the metaphorical *destination* reached by the homeless person is a state in which he or she is engaged in a literal journey that has no destination or purpose. The metaphorical usage activates emotional and introspective simulations of completion that are directly contradicted by the emotional and introspective simulations associated with and activated by *just wander the streets and talk to themselves*. This illustrates another important implication of the simulations account: many words and phrases activate strong secondary simulations (perceptual and emotional associations) whether they are used literally or figuratively. In many cases, it may matter very little whether the phrase was intended metaphorically. As in *get to that point where they just wander the streets and talk to themselves*, the meaning is in the contradiction between simulations activated by the two phrases, one of which is metaphorical and one literal, or perhaps metonymic.

Even *somewhere to start from* may have this ambiguous duality, affording interpretation as simultaneously literal (a home) and metaphorical (a social situation, family, or friendship group). It may activate the full JOURNEY schema but it seems likely that it activates only the introspective and emotional simulations associated with *having* a social base (happiness) or *not having* one (sadness or despair). The description of addiction, *you get so deep into it you can't get back out*, seems even less readily susceptible to an interpretation in terms of conceptual metaphors or associated *gestalt*-based schemas. ADDICTION IS A CONTAINER, ADDICTION IS A CAVE, and ADDICTION IS A LAKE seem equally improbable. ADDICTION IS DEBT may contribute something, even though it is a secondary metaphor. Like *dig your own grave* (Fauconnier and Turner, 2002; Ritchie, 2006), *get so deep* and *can't get back out* activate simulations of entrapment, danger and hopelessness that may be based on any or all of a number of conceptual metaphors, all within an extended field of meaning. It is the simulated thoughts and emotions that seem most important here; attempting to identify a specific underlying conceptual metaphor is simply a distraction and may lead the analyst farther from, rather than closer to, the intended and experienced meanings.

Tony Blair's speech (Appendix) also combines literal with metaphorical, beginning with his early declaration that *I'm back*, which seems to refer both to the physical location of the conference in his home district and to his figurative *return* to the foundational concerns of the Labour Party. *Events have sometimes taken me far from home* is also simultaneously literal (in connection with the Afghan and Iraq wars he visited numerous other world capitals) and figurative (his preoccupation with world politics was *remote* from Labour's typical emphasis on issues like employment, wages and opportunity (Ritchie, 2008)). Inviting *old friends* to *come back to the fold* and inviting the British people to decide *whether you want the relationship to continue* are both purely metaphorical – but it seems unlikely in either instance that a detailed JOURNEY schema is activated. It seems sufficient to posit activation of a very limited set of introspective simulations associated with these idioms (Ritchie, 2008).

## Extending the analysis

The four examples briefly analysed in the foregoing call attention to several interesting implications of the simulations approach. Lakoff and Johnson's

(1980) conceptual metaphor theory implies that concepts are formed through direct sensory experience and, at least during early language acquisition, vocabulary is associated with these directly embodied concepts. Landauer and Dumais (1997) have produced convincing evidence that a large proportion of the typical adult's vocabulary was initially acquired and continues to be at least partially understood by way of connections to other words. In many cases, including many of the concepts that figure strongly in Lakoff and Johnson's argument, such as WAR and JOURNEY, richly embodied associations are developed. Even if these words and their associated concepts were first acquired through association with other words, they quickly come to be associated with rich sensory schemas. But in other cases, the association with other words may continue to provide most of a concept's meaning. For most of us, *algorithm*, *capitalization* and *antimatter* are probably understood primarily in terms of their associations with other words and have little if any meaning in terms of embodied perceptual simulations – other than the 'introspective' simulations posited by Barsalou as an explanation for abstract logic.

If the above is true, then many (but probably not all) words have both primary and secondary associations with perceptual simulations, and words differ (within as well as between individuals) in the richness of the simulations they potentially activate. For example, compare the metaphorical phrases, *his theory is <u>divorced</u> from reality* and *<u>dead</u> metaphor* with the literal phrases, *his parents are recently divorced* and *dead princess*. The metaphorical uses activate few if any of the emotional simulations associated by the literal uses.

Another implication of the foregoing analysis is that words and phrases are often used in a way that is ambiguous with respect to metaphorical intention, and sometimes may be used in a way that invites simultaneous literal and metaphorical usage. Words and phrases differ across communicative contexts in the degree to which they should be considered 'metaphorical'. Moreover, it may be less important to classify words as 'metaphorical' or 'not metaphorical' than to identify the simulations that are likely to be activated by their use in a particular context. As seen in the examples, all associated with JOURNEY, semantically related metaphors may activate very different simulations and have very different meanings in different contexts.

## Stories and metaphor

The examples discussed in the foregoing also call attention to a close and often reciprocal relationship between metaphors and stories. (Here I use 'stories' in a general and non-technical sense to refer to accounts, sometimes quite brief or merely implied, of persons performing actions and experiencing events.) Tony Blair's *I'm back* comes at the end of a recounting of his literal return to

Gateshead, but it also comes against the background of an unspoken but highly salient story about his metaphorical journey *away from the central concerns* of the Labour Party. Obst's entire essay (2003) takes the form of an extended story about the grieving process, a story that is advanced through her series of evocative metaphors.

Stories themselves often have a metaphorical quality. In his speech, Blair relates a domestic soap opera story in which disagreements about some of his policies are expressed as a domestic fight in which *before you know it you raise your voice. And I raise mine. Some of you throw a bit of crockery.* In the homelessness discussion, one of the participants tells a (possibly apocryphal) tale about homeless people relieving themselves in people's cars, and others tell about seeing homeless people relieve themselves in parks, behind bushes, etc. All of these activate a combination of emotions including disgust, pity and horror in a way that seems both metonymic and metaphorical. Over half of the homelessness conversation consists of explicit stories, and in many places stories are implied by brief phrases (*I've been homeless myself,* for example). With stories as with metaphors, what may be most important is the capacity of the language, whether recalled or invented, literal or metaphorical, to activate the simulation of emotions, perceptions, and in some cases complete schemas in the minds of the listeners or readers.

## Playful metaphors

Until recently there has been a tendency to undervalue the play element in language use and communication generally. Theorists have tended to treat play as an activity restricted to juveniles, and indulged primarily for utilitarian purposes such as rehearsal for adult activities and roles (Sutton-Smith, 1995; Sherzer, 2002; Bateson, 2005). However, Cook (2000) and Carter (2004), among others, have pointed to the importance of language play in the acquisition of language, and more generally the enjoyment of language play among adults. Ritchie and Dyhouse (2008) show that metaphors are often used primarily for their playful quality, and advocate more deliberate attention to language play in metaphor research. Norrick (1993) shows how even overtly aggressive forms of language play such as mocking and teasing, within an intimate social group such as a family or circle of friends, can often enhance rather than undermine affection and group solidarity. Among other things, by showing that the relationship need not be constrained with the formalities of ordinary politeness they demonstrate a higher level of mutual trust and solidarity. Joking and language play generally help to demonstrate common ground, and provide a means to amuse – that is to say, to provide pleasure for – others in the group (Norrick, 1993; Ritchie and Dyhouse, 2008).

There is no evidence in Cameron (2007b) of playfulness in the interaction between Jo Berry and Pat Magee, but each of the other examples analysed in the foregoing incorporates many elements of playfulness. Blair's *throwing crockery* metaphor is a prime example, in which the seriousness of the policy differences within the Labour Party is diminished, perhaps even trivialized; there is also a decided playful element in his multiple uses of *back* in a positive sense that seems to contradict the negative implications of its use in the party campaign slogan (Ritchie, 2008). The participants in the homelessness discussion (Ritchie, 2009) repeatedly change from serious to playful and back again, and the conversation ends with a playful comparison of the vulgarisms in their conversation to George Carlin's (1972) *Seven Words You Can Never Say on Television*. Even Obst's essay on the very serious subject of grief (2003) has a playful quality in her skilful repetition and modification of metaphors and images.

Metaphors are inherently playful at least in the general sense of flexibility and looseness – they are often created, altered, and used in a sense that is more specifically playful, done for the mutual amusement of speaker and audience. An interesting example of playful modification comes in the homelessness conversation, when one of the participants refers to an episode from a popular TV series, *South Park*, in which homeless beggars invade a neighbourhood, as *night of the living bums*, a metaphorical reference to a classic horror movie. In another example from the same conversation, one participant talks at length about the apparent social *collapse* in Africa, then predicts *that's where we are headed.* Another participant deliberately misinterprets the intended metaphor as literal and responds *Africa? Jumping on a ship – let's go.* Playful use and transformation of metaphors and narratives, as Norrick (1993) shows, can contribute both to the development of social relationships and to the development and expression of ideas and feelings.

## Implications for metaphor theory and for metaphor analysis

These examples illustrate the value of identifying the simulations that are potentially activated by a series of metaphorical expressions and assessing how they can be used to accumulate and activate a range of schemas and concepts that, again, have the potential to alter the shared cognitive environment of the participants and consequently reshape the social reality (Ritchie, 2006). The perceptual simulations approach suggests that cognitive interpretation of a metaphor may often involve, not the full activation of an underlying conceptual schema associated with the vehicle as a unified gestalt, but merely a small subset of context-relevant simulations associated with that schema. Thus, *come back to the fold* (in the Blair speech) need not necessarily lead the hearer to experience disillusioned party members as STRAY SHEEP (or in the intermediate metaphorical reference, ERRANT PARISHIONERS); a mere activation of a few of the introspective and emotional simulations associated with the underlying narrative will suffice, so that the idea of reunion and the associated emotions of comfort, welcoming, and safety become linked to the topic, *party solidarity* – all within a single field of meaning.

As the foregoing analysis shows, the perceptual simulations approach provides at the very least a useful supplement to existing analytic approaches such as that suggested by Cameron (2007b). Identifying potential simulations activated by figurative language focuses analytic attention directly on the subtle nuances of meaning that often motivate metaphor use in the first place, and connects these nuances of meaning with a coherent account of how language itself is used and interpreted (Ritchie, 2006; Barsalou, 2008).

## Methodological Issues: Researching perceptual simulations

The proposed view that metaphors accomplish their effects by activating secondary (non-defining) perceptual simulations, nuances of perception and feeling associated with an object, concept, or experience, poses a challenge for research: How does one determine the subtle shadings of another person's cognitive response to either a direct experience or a linguistically described experience? How can the researcher identify activated perceptual simulations, organize them into fields of meaning, and show how these may be activated by or instantiated in figurative and otherwise expressive language? Metaphors are often used because conventional language does not fully express the nuances of meaning and feeling in a particular experience or idea. If a speaker is unable to find direct linguistic labels to express the nuances of experience, and relies on figurative language to activate simulations that more or less accurately match these nuances of experience, then it is hard to see how the analyst would be able to find linguistic labels for these same simulations. Accordingly, it may often be the case that the best the analyst can do is to point to the apparent accumulation of simulations, to consult actual participants in conversations as well as other members of relevant speech communities, and draw on shared cultural knowledge to show how a sequence of figurative expressions seems to or has the potential to invoke a consistent underlying field of meaning.

A degree of validation can be accomplished by looking for convergent evidence elsewhere in a text, in other interpretive accounts of the same text, and, if available, accounts of other readers or hearers' responses. In some cases it may be possible to validate an interpretation by interviewing participants, although this procedure is too cumbersome and expensive to be used in every case, and it leads to well known methodological problems of its own, such as biased recall and demand effects. But primarily, the 'nuances' problem crops up again – if neither the speaker nor the analyst can put a label on a subtle visceral simulation activated by, say, *buried alive* or, from Blair's (2005) speech, *throwing crockery*, how is a listener to do any better during a subsequent interview?

The approach I have taken (Ritchie, 2008) is to accept the limitations of intuitive interpretation and consistently label the results in terms such as 'potential simulations'. This approach is theoretically consistent in any event, since there is no reason to expect that all hearers or readers will process a figurative expression sufficiently to experience more than a few (or indeed, any at all) of the potential simulations, and there is good reason to expect that many hearers or readers may interpret even common expressions in quite idiosyncratic ways, experience few of the usual simulations but experience several unique simulations.

The problem of identifying and classifying metaphors is much less important in simulations based research than in some other approaches to metaphor research. The emphasis is on the simulations that are potentially activated by a word or phrase in a particular context, and not on whether hearers understand or speakers intend a phrase as metaphorical. For example, Vervaeke and Kennedy (1996) contend that *attack* is ordinarily understood not as a metaphor but as a lexicalized synonym for *attempt to refute*. Even if Vervaeke and Kennedy are right about this, it seems likely that the word *attack* will activate visceral and emotional simulations associated with violence and hostility, simulations that are connected with the word itself as well as with the underlying conceptual schema (Ritchie, 2003a). Whether or not it is explicitly identified as metaphorical, a particularly evocative expression may have the potential to activate several perceptual simulations at once, some rather weakly but, as the *divorce* and *dead princess* examples illustrate, some quite strongly. These potential simulations will interact with the pre-existing cognitive contexts of various individuals in various ways, with effects that can be estimated from subsequent interactions and reactions. The purpose of identifying potential perceptual simulations associated with a phrase is to provide a basis for understanding these overall contextual (e.g. dialogical and relational) effects.

## Summary

Analysis of four very different discourse samples has been used to illustrate the utility of identifying perceptual simulations that may potentially be activated by figurative language, and observing the way these simulations interact with those activated by other words and phrases and with the overall context. Simulation comes into play at different levels, depending on the metaphor and the context in which it is used. It appears that the imaginative simulation of the object or action named by a metaphor vehicle, proposed by Gibbs, incorporates a partial but coherent subset of detail-level perceptual simulations associated with the vehicle. The kind of underlying conceptual metaphors posited by Lakoff and Johnson (1980) may be but are not necessarily always activated – and at least in some instances, seeking to identify underlying conceptual metaphors may distract the analyst and make it more difficult to identify the pattern of perceptual and emotional simulations that create central meaning in an interaction. Implications of this view include downplaying the importance of classifying language as either metaphoric or not, and increasing the importance of studying narrative and playful use of language along with metaphors.

# 5 The discourse dynamics framework for metaphor

## Lynne Cameron

The role of theory is to describe and explain the phenomena under consideration. A good theory describes carefully and logically, checking descriptions for
adequacy against empirical evidence, and offers explanation of how the phenomena come to be as they appear to be and to function as they do.[1]

In this book, the phenomena of interest centre around metaphor, or, more
precisely, metaphor in discourse as social interaction, as distinct from metaphor in isolation. As we started to argue in Chapter 1, when we take discourse
as the site of metaphor use, we produce a need for theory and methods that
are suited to working with discourse. In this chapter, we continue developing
such a theory. The theoretical section began in Chapter 3 with a description
of conceptual metaphor theory because this ground-breaking work shifted our
views of what metaphor is and what it does. As we saw in both Chapters 3
and 4, however, when metaphor is at work in discourse, conceptual metaphor
theory is not adequate to explain what is happening. Deignan in Chapter 3
commented on the lack of empirical discourse evidence used in the process of
constructing conceptual metaphor theory and the lack of concern for language
that came with the shift in focus to concepts and cognition. Ritchie in Chapter
4 reviewed more detailed arguments against the assumptions and methods
of conceptual metaphor theory, and suggested that attending to perceptual
simulations produced by metaphors is necessary if we are to understand how
metaphors affect, and are affected by, the people who use them. This chapter
introduces an alternative, discourse-based, theoretical framework for thinking
about how metaphor works. The 'discourse dynamics' framework is inspired
and informed by conceptual metaphor theory, but rejects its formulation of
metaphor in terms of highly generalized and abstract conceptual domains
that pre-exist actual uses of metaphors in language. Instead, the framework
is designed to apply to metaphor in language use in social interaction, and
builds explanatory theory that accounts for what we know about actual discourse. It draws on both contemporary cognitive psychology and Vygotskyan
sociocultural theory, as well as discourse analysis of various types. The

pulling together of compatible understandings from a range of fields is what makes this a 'theoretical framework' rather than a 'theory'. It also means that researchers can slot in their own preferred theories, as long as the requisite theoretical work is done to ensure compatibility.

To introduce this chapter we return to the set of questions that ended Chapter 1 about the nature of metaphor, and answer these for the discourse dynamics approach in order to give readers an overview of what the chapter will contain.

## How does the discourse dynamics framework understand the nature of metaphor and which dimensions of metaphor are included?

Underpinning the discourse dynamics framework is the assumption of **interconnectedness** of the dimensions of metaphor in use (linguistic, cognitive, affective, physical, cultural). To state that language, thought and culture are interconnected might appear uncontroversial, and yet conceptual metaphor theory has emphasized an artificial separation, downplaying language in order to focus on the cognitive, and disputing the role of culture (Lakoff and Johnson, 1980; Quinn, 1991; Lakoff, 1993). In a series of cross-linguistic studies, Slobin (e.g. 1996) convincingly demonstrates that structural aspects of a given language can influence how speakers think and conceptualize. Quinn has shown how cultural influences offer an alternative explanation for the nature of metaphor in language use (Quinn, 1991), while Gibbs and others have long argued that a theory of metaphor needs to include culture (e.g. Gibbs, 1999; Kövecses, 2005). As we saw in Chapter 1, the physical, or embodied, and the affective dimensions of metaphor also need to be considered. The connections between metaphor and people's physical bodies and their interaction with the material world has been persuasively argued by Gibbs (2006a), used by Lakoff and Johnson (1999) and is integral to primary metaphor theory (Grady, 1999; Chapter 3, this volume). The affective, i.e. the emotions and feelings that influence human activity (Damasio, 2003), has often been neglected in metaphor studies, although perceptual simulation theory (Chapter 4, this volume) offers one way of examining the affective force of metaphors that people use. Cameron (2003) introduced the term 'talking-and-thinking' to refer to the connected linguistic, cognitive and affective processes of people engaged in discourse. The phrase is used again in this chapter to act as a reminder that these processes cannot be separated.

In order to work adequately with the interconnectedness of metaphor dimensions, the discourse dynamics framework draws on the theory of complex dynamic systems.

## What is identified as metaphor? e.g. vehicle terms, manifestations in language of conceptual metaphor

The manifestation of metaphor in discourse is metaphorically used words or phrases, i.e. **metaphor vehicles**, produced in the flow of the talk or text. Metaphor vehicles are central to the various metaphor phenomena covered by the framework, and can be connected theoretically to other aspects of metaphor at other timescales.

Metaphor vehicles appear at the level of language use, and, in the discourse dynamics theoretical framework, are not necessarily considered to be manifestations of underlying conceptual metaphors. By taking this view, the discourse dynamics approach departs theoretically from conceptual metaphor theory. I remain agnostic about the existence or whereabouts of conceptual metaphor – as will be seen later in the chapter, I do not rule out the possibility of conceptual metaphor altogether, although I do not require these to be a mental store of static and fixed mappings with their attached linguistic expressions.

## How tightly are the connections between metaphors and their discourse context maintained?

In Chapter 1, I contended that, in order to usefully infer information about people's ideas, attitudes and values, we need to identify patterns of metaphor use across single or multiple discourse events,[2] and beyond. The discourse dynamics approach works with the assumption that metaphor **cannot** be separated from its discourse context without becoming something different.[3] The theoretical framework therefore needs to describe and explain the connections between discourse context and metaphor use. A methodological challenge, addressed in later sections of the book, then becomes how to find ways of holding on to these discourse connections while also analysing and isolating units of language use.

## How are generalizations made upwards from instances of metaphor? And how are connections made between metaphors occurring across stretches of discourse?

Because linguistic metaphors are not, in the discourse dynamics framework, seen as manifestations 'downwards' of conceptual metaphor expressed in language, there is no requirement to describe sets of metaphor with the highly generalized labels used by conceptual metaphor theory, and furthermore, doing so would be to lose valuable information. However, we *are* interested in patterns of metaphor vehicles used across a discourse event, or particular bounded episode of discourse. This chapter shows how ideas from complexity/dynamic systems theory can help describe and account for emergent systematic patterns. These ideas also address the interconnectedness of metaphors used in a particular discourse event with metaphors used more widely in society and over time.

To summarize, this chapter explains the discourse dynamics theoretical framework with its emphasis on interconnectedness:

- connections across and between the linguistic, embodied, cognitive, affective and sociocultural dimensions of metaphor;
- connections between metaphors and the discourse contexts where they are used;
- connections across metaphors in a particular discourse event;
- connections between metaphors used in a particular discourse event and metaphors more broadly across society and over time.

## Empirical imperatives on theory construction: What are we trying to explain and describe?

The theoretical framework needs to describe and explain the nature of metaphor in use in discourse, and its connection to ideas and attitudes and values. Before we begin to develop a framework, an example will help illustrate the nature of metaphor in discourse. Extract 5.1 is a short section of transcribed talk that occurred during a focus group discussion that was part of a dataset collected for a social sciences project about people's perception of the risk of terrorism (details can be found in the Appendix). The focus group discussion is used in some detail from Chapter 6 on. At this point, we can note that the research questions were:

- How do people use metaphor in discussion about topics related to terrorism?
- What do people's metaphors reveal about their ideas, attitudes and values?

Over a period of about 90 minutes, eight non-Muslim men, who had been recruited on the basis of their ethnicity, socioeconomic status and religion, responded to a set of questions posed by a moderator. The questions were designed to elicit talking-and-thinking about how participants feel and act in response to the threat of terrorism in their everyday lives. The extract comes from near the beginning of the discussion, at which point participants were still strangers to each other, having shared only their names (here replaced with pseudonyms) and where they come from. The moderator opens this exchange by asking for initial reactions to the idea of terrorism (lines 76–77). The under-lined words and phrases in the extract have been identified as being used meta-phorically. (In Chapter 6, we explain in detail how the transcript was made and how metaphors were identified; here we are interested in how metaphor appears in spoken discourse.)

Extract 5.1

| 74 | Mod | okay. |
|---|---|---|
| 75 | Mod | … Terry, |
| 76 | Mod | … what is the first <u>thing</u>, |
| 77 | Mod | that <u>comes into</u> your mind? |
| 78 | Terry | it -- |
| 79 | Terry | terrorism to me, |
| 80 | Terry | it's -- |
| 81 | Terry | … it's a <u>sneaky way</u> -- |
| 82 | Terry | … it's almost <u>like bullying</u>, |
| 83 | Terry | … 'cos you don't know when it's going to happen, |
| 84 | Terry | you can't … legislate for it, |
| 85 | Terry | … you can't <u>control</u> -- |
| 86 | Terry | it's <u>not like war</u>, |
| 87 | Terry | … <u>where</u> you've got two .. <u>opposing sides</u>. |
| 88 | Terry | … terrorism … is just a -- |
| 89 | Terry | an <u>invisible enemy</u>. |
| 90 | Terry | … almost. |
| 91 | Terry | … I mean you don't know when it's going to happen, |
| 92 | Terry | … where it's going to happen, |
| 93 | Terry | … but you do know, |
| 94 | Terry | that people are going to get, |
| 95 | Terry | … killed. |
| 96 | Terry | maimed. |
| 97 | Terry | whatever. |
| 98 | Mod | … and, |
| 99 | Mod | … Phil? |
| 100 | Phil | hiya. |
| 101 | Phil | .. er, |
| 102 | Phil | it's -- |
| 103 | Phil | well a lot of er, |
| 104 | Phil | a lot of bloodshed, |
| 105 | Phil | erm, |
| 106 | Phil | you'd get <u>from</u> it. |
| 107 | Phil | … erm, |

| 108 | Phil | ... I would also say it's a <u>flaw in the system</u>, |
| 109 | Phil | as well. |
| 110 | Phil | someone's not doing their job right. |
| 111 | Phil | ... 'cos if somebody were doing their job right, |
| 112 | Phil | it wouldn't happen <u>in the first place</u>. |

In this extract from the stream of spoken discourse, participants Terry and Phil respond to a question from the moderator about what comes into their minds when they think about terrorism. Both Terry and Phil use metaphors in their responses, as they extend and expand their ideas. Phil picks up some of Terry's ideas and offers a further metaphorical way of thinking about terrorism. The participants' metaphors show themselves in the words of the transcribed talk, sometimes as part of longer phrases. Sometimes the metaphors appear to be original, while at other times they are familiar and conventionalized. Sometimes speakers seem to have new ideas, whereas at other times they seem to be reproducing ideas that they have thought about before.

The theoretical conceptualization and description of metaphor needs to account for its appearance and its development in this spontaneous ebb and flow of ideas, and for connections between the moment of talk, as in Extract 5.1, and ways of thinking and talking that have conventionalized over time and across speech communities.

## Discourse and metaphor as complex, dynamic systems

At the heart of the discourse dynamics framework lies an understanding of linguistic and cognitive phenomena as processes, flows or movement, rather than as objects (Cameron, 2003, 2007a; Cameron and Deignan, 2006; Gibbs and Cameron, 2008; Larsen-Freeman and Cameron, 2008; Cameron *et al.*, 2009). Drawing on complexity theory and dynamic systems theory, discourse is seen as a dynamic system that is in continual flux and working on various interconnected dimensions and timescales.

A transcription like Extract 5.1 is then seen as a 'trace' of the talking-and-thinking, or discourse activity, which took place in real time. The discourse event is understood as the unfolding of the complex dynamic system[4] of the group of people engaged in interaction. The dynamic system of discourse develops, adapts and flows as speakers' contributions build on each other, and as people develop their own or others' ideas. We can also understand the discourse activity of each participant as emerging from multiple interacting subsystems within each individual: complex dynamic language systems, complex dynamic cognitive systems, complex dynamic physical systems. Local discourse activity connects outwards into wider networks of environmental, social and cultural systems. So, any system that we focus on, such as a particular discourse event, is massively connected into larger and smaller systems.

The systems and subsystems of a discourse event can be identified and described on (at least) two scales that are helpful to our framework: of time and of social organization. The focus group discussion is a discourse event that takes place on the timescale of hours and minutes; episodes of talk around particular questions, like the one that begins in Extract 5.1, occur on the timescale of minutes and seconds; utterances take place on a timescale of seconds; and all these timescales are themselves influenced by brain activity occurring on the timescale of milliseconds. When we look to larger timescales than the discourse event, we acknowledge that what people say in the moment of a discourse event can be influenced by what has happened to them recently or much earlier in their lives, on a timescale of days, months and years.

Scales of social organization (or 'levels', as we will call them here to avoid conflating the social with the temporal) range from the tiniest biological system inside the individual outwards to the ad hoc focus group, to friendship, family and other social groups, to communities and nations.

The episode of talking-and-thinking in Extract 5.1 can then be recast in terms of complex dynamic systems, with different kinds of subsystems activated at various levels of social organization and timescales, and interacting as the discussion moves on. In order to theorize these changing systems, we use a striking and useful way of thinking about the activity of a dynamic system as a path across an abstract landscape. Each point on this system landscape represents one of the possible states that the system could occupy. At each moment of time, the system occupies just one of its many possible states, i.e. is at one point on the landscape. As the system changes and moves through successive states, the successive points that the system has occupied form a 'path' or 'trajectory' of states in the system's 'landscape of possibilities' (Thelen and Smith, 1994). The surrounding landscape represents possible states that the system might have occupied, but did not – words that might have been spoken or ideas that might have been talked about, but were not. The trajectory or path, representing the actual states that the system moves through, remains as a trace of the system activity after the event, just as the shiny trail left behind by a snail is a trace of its movement or the white trail left in the sky by a speeding jet is a trace of its flight. A recording of the discourse event is a physical trace of the trajectory, but can only ever be partial. A video recording would be a more detailed than an audio recording, but still only partial. A transcription of a recording becomes therefore a trace of a trace, useful data to work with but several versions away from the actual activity.

The metaphors that people use contribute to the trajectory of the discourse system. Although the metaphors are inseparable from the surrounding discourse, in metaphor analysis we identify and pick out these metaphors as if they were occasional lights or signals along the trajectory of the discourse system. We then look for connections between metaphors, constructing a 'metaphor trajectory' inside the discourse trajectory.

### Visualizing the levels and scales of the system of discourse

The view of discourse that we are building up is of an interconnected collection of complex dynamic systems and subsystems, operating at various different timescales and levels of social organization. The trajectory of the talking-and-thinking, a trace of which we see in the transcript, emerges from the interaction of these various systems. Figure 5.1 (adapted from Larsen-Freeman and Cameron, 2008: 168) aims to show the different kinds of systems that might contribute to the discourse event on various timescales and levels of social organization, and thus to the use of metaphor.

The figure uses the convention of representing continuous events as a sequence of discrete, overlapping frames. Social change appears as overlapping circular frames across the top of the diagram; changes in the individual life course are shown as overlapping small circles through the middle of the diagram; and the discourse event (conversation, focus group discussion, etc.), with its face-to-face interaction, is represented as a series of square frames coming towards the reader in the bottom half of the diagram, with individual

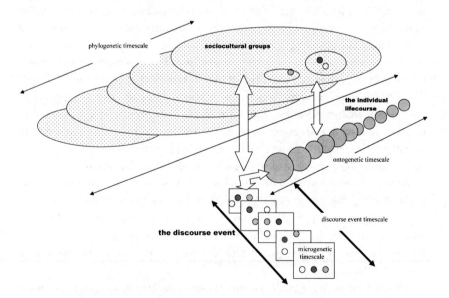

Figure 5.1. The dynamics of metaphor in face-to-face spoken interaction

contributions to the interaction shown as dots inside the frames. Black arrows on the diagram indicate time, with the phylogenetic (or social life) timescale encompassing years, decades and centuries, while the ontogenetic (or human lifespan) timescale reflects the years and months of an individual's life, and the discourse event works on a timescale of hours and minutes, incorporating the microgenetic timescale of utterances and episodes over seconds and minutes. Extract 5.1 would thus occupy several discourse event frames in Figure 5.1.

Large double headed arrows indicate influences and connections: between the discourse event and individual lives up to this point, between the discourse event and individuals' membership of various social groups, between individual lives and membership of social groups. Each participant brings with them to the discussion their own personal histories on the ontogenetic timescale. Participants also bring with them influences from their membership of multiple sociocultural groups, such as their families, peer groups and religious or political organizations (for simplicity, only one group and one subgroup are represented in the diagram). Each sociocultural group has its own history and influence on the phylogenetic timescale.

The levels and scales as illustrated in Figure 5.1 become part of the discourse dynamics explanatory and descriptive framework, enabling us to trace out connections across metaphors and outwards from metaphors. When a metaphor is spoken in the discourse event, there are connecting influences with individual lives and social groups, as well as across the emerging discourse event.

## The discourse dynamics of linguistic metaphor

The dynamics of talking-and-thinking include responding to comments, opening topics, asking questions and answering, agreeing and disagreeing, and so on (hence the need for discourse analysis to accompany metaphor analysis, Chapter 8). As we have seen, metaphors appear in the microgenetic moment as vehicle words or phrases, such as those underlined in Extract 5.1. These metaphor vehicles, together with their explicit or implied referent or 'topic', comprise what we describe as **linguistic metaphors**. Taking an example from Extract 5.1, line 76, the moderator uses the linguistic metaphor: *thing* as meaning (something like)[5] 'ideas'. In the next line, she uses the linguistic metaphor *comes into* as meaning (something like) 'is mentally activated'.

The occurrence of a linguistic metaphor would be explained by conceptual metaphor theory as the putting into words of an underlying and pre-existing mapping. The speaker would be held to possess a conceptual metaphor IDEAS ARE OBJECTS which produces the word *thing* in his talk. The discourse dynamics framework does not rule out this as a possible process, but holds that there are multiple ways in which linguistic metaphors may come to be used in discourse, beyond this kind of top-down instantiation from thought to language (e.g. Lakoff and Johnson, 1980; Kövecses, 2005; Chapter 3, this volume). As in Figure 5.1, ideas and attitudes are influenced by the circumstances of the discourse that speakers are involved in, including other participants, and by the language being used (Slobin, 1996; Cameron, 2003; Spivey, 2007). Different kinds of cognitive processes may be involved (Gibbs and Cameron, 2008). In spontaneous conversation, the words that people speak may be fluid, tentative verbalizations of 'ideas', or may be reiteration of ideas that have become fixed for the person concerned, perhaps even employing the same words that have been used many times before. Metaphors may, for example, be produced as learnt formulae that the situation activates in memory as appropriate to say, or as conventionalized expressions that are produced from memory in connection with certain ideas, or through active processing that introduces a vehicle term and idea to compare with what is being spoken about. Most of the time it is not possible to know, from discourse data, what prompts the production of a particular metaphor.

Extract 5.1 illustrates how other systems at other timescales and different levels of social organization can also contribute to discourse activity in the moment. In describing terrorism as *a sneaky way* in line 81, Terry uses a conventionalized movement metaphor, *way*, to say something about the method or manner of terrorism. The conventionalization of the metaphorical meaning of *way* as 'manner' from its original meaning of road or path occurred several hundred years ago, and so is likely to have been learnt by Terry as he grew up, becoming part of his everyday language repertoire. When Terry pre-modifies *way* with the adjective *sneaky*, he does something more creative with metaphor (Cameron, in press a). The collocation of *sneaky* and *way* evokes a sense of metaphorical movement that is somehow suspicious and concealed, trying to avoid being noticed. As a metaphor about terrorism, *sneaky* is not conventionalized, although Terry may have encountered its use before coming to the focus group. He uses it to express an attitude towards terrorism as negative, underhand and deceptive. Terry immediately afterwards reinforces this affective force with a comparison between terrorism and *bullying*, as his specific example of *sneaky* behaviour. *Bullying* (in current British English usage) relates to a cultural schema in which a larger or older child oppresses a smaller or younger victim, usually in a school scenario. The unfair exertion of power in *bullying* is considered by the broader sociocultural group of contemporary British society, to be both cowardly and socially unacceptable. Terry, in using the connected linguistic metaphors *sneaky* and *bullying*, builds up a negative perspective on terrorism while also appealing to social and cultural knowledge that people in the group are likely to share. In lines 83–5, he justifies his evaluation of terrorism as *sneaky* and like *bullying* by elaborating the particular aspects of unpredictability (*you don't know when it's going to happen*) and uncontrollability (*you can't control*).

The discourse moves in a slightly different direction with the negative comparison, or contrast, in line 86 between terrorism and *war*[6] which appeals to shared knowledge in the group and probably also connects outwards to the global sociocultural arena; the idea of a metaphorical *war on terror* is attributed to former US president George W. Bush and was used widely in the media and by politicians between 2001 and 2009 (Lakoff, 2001; Brewster Smith, 2002; Jackson, 2005).

Back in the microgenetic moment, Terry then elaborates a particular aspect of the metaphorical contrast: war has *two opposing sides* whereas in terrorism the *enemy* is not to be seen across the metaphorical space of the conflict[7] but is *invisible* (89). He ends his turn with a reiteration of difference between terrorism and war, the unpredictability in time and place of terrorist events, and similarity: in the predictable outcomes of both – *people are going to get killed .. maimed* (93–97).

When Phil begins his turn in lines 100–4 by talking about the *bloodshed you'd get from it*, he is probably affected by Terry's immediately previous references to people getting *killed, maimed whatever* (95–7). One voiced thought may activate another, and local influences, as well as the more global, affect choices of words and phrases.

Metaphors in discourse can then be connected across the discourse event, from one metaphor to another and from metaphorical to literal language. They can be connected across discourse participants, and they can be connected from the moment of use into participants' lives and experiences. We can glimpse influences from the media and politicians, and suspect the influence of many other people and events that remain unknown to the researcher.

## The dynamics of metaphor emergence

Complex dynamic systems theory offers explanatory mechanisms of 'self-organization' and 'emergence' to theorize the relation between what happens in the moment of a discourse event with larger patterns of metaphor use.

In complex dynamic systems, the layering and nesting of systems supports the emergence of self-organized phenomena from one level or scale to another. In the natural world, examples of self-organization and emergence include: the termite nest that emerges from the activity of individual termites; the cloud that emerges from the interaction of wind, humidity and temperature; the forest that emerges from the interaction of many different species of flora and fauna. In each case, the emergent phenomenon is different in nature from the phenomena that produced it, and cannot be reduced to it; the processes have led to something new.

An analogy between the natural world and the discourse world would see a discourse event like a 'conversation' as emerging from the interaction of the individual participants. Within the discourse event, there may be other emergent phenomena, such as the words or phrases that emerge as a shared way of referring to a particular idea, described by Brennan and Clark as 'conceptual pacts' (1986), a label extended by Cameron (2007a) to 'lexico-conceptual pacts' in order to include both thinking and talking.[8] Cameron (2003) describes how the phrase *lollipop trees* emerged in the course of a classroom discourse event as a shorthand way to describe trees drawn as simple round shapes with stick-like trunks that the teacher disapproved of because they were not like their actual shapes. After the teacher used the phrase several times, a child was heard to produce it spontaneously as a comment on her drawing of trees. The phrase *lollipop trees* seemed to emerge over the course of several minutes of classroom discourse, not just as a lexical unit but as a phrase with particular pragmatic and evaluative meanings for the sociocultural group of that class. Any discourse community will have words and phrases, not only metaphorical but also technical, that emerge over various timescales as specific in form, use and meaning. These emergent ways of talking-and-thinking may be more or less permanent or temporary, used in single events or becoming conventionalised for years or decades.

Metaphorical language is subject to the dynamics of self-organization and emergence just as any language use but seems likely to play a particularly important role in supplying emergent ways of talking-and-thinking because, when first used, metaphor may be striking and memorable, and thus act as an attractor for future talking-and-thinking. Cooper (1986) suggests that metaphor is central to the language conventions that often emerge as characteristic or defining of groups. Within-group metaphors have a key purpose in sustaining intimacy among group members, marking the identity of groups through language that is obscure or inaccessible to outsiders. Conversely, being allowed access to within group language becomes an important marker of access to the group itself.

Another kind of emergence that happens in a focus group would be convergence in attitudes to topics of talk, the development of a framing around the topic which is internal to the group (Markova *et al.*, 2007). For example, following its initial voicing by Terry in Extract 5.1, the framing of terrorism as cowardly was further developed by other participants over the course of the discussion and could be considered to have emerged as a group framing or attitude.

Empirical study of metaphor dynamics has revealed various changes and adaptations that are made to metaphors as discourse proceeds, a process described as 'metaphor shifting' (Cameron, 2008b: 45). In the flow of talking-and-thinking on the microgenetic scale of a discourse event, linguistic metaphors shift as people negotiate meanings, extend their ideas, or enjoy exploiting an unexpected possibility opened up by metaphor. In Extract 5.1, we saw several types of micro-dynamic metaphor shifting:

- Terry's reformulation, or 'relexicalization', from *sneaky* to *bullying*;
- the non-metaphorical explication of the metaphorical link between *bullying* and terrorism;
- the introduction of a new metaphor through contrast, *not like war*;
- the further development of the metaphor through metaphorical and non-metaphorical language.

Metaphor shifting is seen as a key mechanism that drives the system dynamics and leads to the emergence of patterns in metaphor use. It is therefore part of the discourse dynamics theory of metaphor connecting the microgenetic level with the discourse event level and beyond.

### Types of metaphor shifting

Central to metaphor shifting is change in the vehicle of metaphor following its first use. Table 5.1 lists the ways in which the vehicle term of a metaphor can be developed, most of which we saw in Extract 5.1.

Table 5.1. Types of vehicle development (from Cameron 2008b: 57)

| Vehicle development | Description |
| --- | --- |
| Vehicle repetition | The term is repeated in identical or transformed form |
| Vehicle relexicalization | A near synonym or equivalent is used |
| Vehicle explication | Expansion, elaboration or exemplification of the term |
| Vehicle contrast | An antonymic or contrasting term is used |

In vehicle development, there is continuity in both the vehicle and topic of the metaphor. Metaphor shifting may also occur when continuity is maintained in only one of the vehicle or topic. Table 5.2 adds these possibilities to vehicle development, and in the right-hand column shows some of the discourse outcomes of the various types of metaphor shifting.

Vehicle 'redeployment' describes the shift in which a vehicle is used again with a changed topic. Vehicle redeployment occurred in the reconciliation context that we met in Chapter 1, when Jo Berry wrote in a poem, *my heart heals, as Ireland heals*, redeploying the vehicle *heals* from the topic *my heart* to the topic *Ireland*. When redeployment occurs across speakers, one of the discourse outcomes can be metaphor appropriation, in which a speaker adopts a metaphor vehicle previously used by another speaker and uses it for a new topic. We saw this phenomenon in Chapter 1, as the vehicle *healing* was appropriated by Patrick Magee, when he redeployed it to use with the topic of accepting responsibility for the damage done by the bombing.

Table 5.2. Types of metaphor shifting (adapted from Cameron 2008b: 61)

| Metaphor shifting | Vehicle | Topic | Discourse outcomes |
|---|---|---|---|
| Vehicle redeployment | The same or semantically connected lexical item is re-used with a different topic. | Changes | Include: metaphor appropriation; puns; text cohesion. |
| Vehicle development | Vehicle term is<br>• repeated<br>• relexicalized<br>• explicated<br>• contrasted | Remains the same<br><br>Moves to con-nected topics | Extended metaphors<br><br>Systematic metaphor |
| Vehicle literalization | Vehicle term is used non-metaphorically in reference to topic | Merges with vehicle; can become metonymic | Symbolization of topic. |

Vehicle literalization is the shift between metaphorical and literal uses of the same word or phrase (see also Chapter 4, this volume). Literalization occurs in the reconciliation conversation with the phrase *sitting down*, which Jo uses when she describes her process of understanding the bomber's motivation as a metaphorical journey: *the end of that journey/would be/sitting down and/talking to the people who did it*. The phrase *sitting down* is metaphorical when considered in relation to the *journey* metaphor but may also be interpreted as non-metaphorical since they did physically sit down together in order to talk; in later exchanges, it is used non-metaphorically but with some symbolic meaning, as when Pat uses *sitting* to emphasize the unexpected nature of the reconciliation conversations: *I was sitting in this wee kitchen/talking to this woman for the first time/whose father's dead*. Shifting between metaphorical and literal uses leads to words and phrases carrying symbolic meaning even when used in quite non-metaphorical ways. I have argued elsewhere (Cameron, in press a) that this symbolization happens at a speech community level as well as between individuals, and perhaps as an emergent outcome of individual language use. The process can be seen in conventionalized phrases like the above that link physical actions with speech action, e.g. *sitting down and talking* or *turn round and say*, in which retain symbolic potential seems to be passed from the physical action, which is often metaphorical, to the speech action, which may be literal, metonymic or metaphorical.

Returning to vehicle development, we can see that the outcome of intensive elaboration or explication of a particular vehicle over a short period of time will appear in the trace of the discourse as an 'extended metaphor'. Over longer periods of time, such as an entire discourse event, successive episodes and instances of vehicle development around closely connected topics produce what we call 'systematic metaphor' (Cameron, 2003, 2007a; Cameron *et al.*, 2009). Because of their importance to metaphor analysis, systematic metaphors are dealt with separately in the following sub-section.

### Systematic metaphors

A systematic metaphor is an emergent discourse phenomenon that is produced when discourse participants, over a discourse event or longer period of time, use a particular set of linguistic metaphor vehicles in talking about a particular topic, or closely connected topics. A systematic metaphor is not a single metaphor but an emergent grouping of closely connected metaphors. Within the discourse dynamics framework, a systematic metaphor is a collecting together of related linguistic metaphors that evolve and are adapted as the discourse proceeds. The collecting together is carried out by the researcher, on the basis of the semantics in context. However, it is hypothesized that a systematic metaphor may be more than just an aggregation of linguistic metaphors pulled together by an analyst. A systematic metaphor is seen as a kind of temporary stabilization in the dynamics of thinking-and-talking, which has the possibility of further evolution as discourse continues. As an emergent formulation, systematic metaphor may come to constrain and influence how discourse participants think and talk about topics.

The distinction between conceptual metaphors and systematic metaphors may not be clear in practice – since both claim to reflect metaphorical patterns of thinking – but theoretically they are very different. As we saw in Chapter 3, conceptual metaphor theory hypothesizes the pre-existence of conceptual metaphors underlying how people, at the social group level, think. Metaphorical expressions in language are then seen as manifestations of conceptual metaphors. In this theory, conceptual metaphors are held to be prior in three key ways: in thought as prior to language, across speech communities as prior to individuals, and in more general forms as prior to specific instantiations. In the discourse dynamics framework, people's language and cognitive resources are seen as prior to their participation in discourse events, and these resources may include conventionalized ways of thinking-and-talking, but no priority is given to thought over language or to the general over the specific. Discourse participants will use a range of types of thinking, most of which interact with language, and what happens in the moment of discourse can be influenced by factors on all scales and levels, not just from the macro or general 'downwards' (Gibbs and Cameron, 2008). What is shared by conceptual metaphors and systematic metaphors is the idea of connected patterns of metaphors as important tools in understanding and talking or writing.

In practice, and as we will see in Chapter 7, systematic metaphors are sets of semantically connected linguistic metaphors, collected together from transcriptions or texts across one or more discourse events, and labelled. For the researcher, a systematic metaphor emerges upwards through processes of analysis and interpretation, and serves as a way of condensing discourse data.

When, as researchers, we collect together connected linguistic metaphors and label them as a systematic metaphor, we are following, and constructing, a semantic trace of the coupled system through the data. The significance of that trace **for the discourse participants** will need to be interpreted very carefully, and will require other types of evidence if we are to claim cognitive reality. Theoretically, it is claimed only that emergent systematic metaphors **may** reflect patterns of metaphorical thinking-and-talking for discourse participants, not that these have a prior independent existence and necessarily do so.

## Stabilization and conventionalization of metaphors

In this section, we briefly summarize further theoretical explanations about the relationship between linguistic metaphors, occurring on the microgenetic timescale, and metaphors on the level of the speech community and on a longer timescale. These theoretical explanations adequately account for available empirical evidence, and complement the features of the discourse dynamics framework described above.

In a series of corpus studies, Deignan has shown how linguistic metaphors have stabilized connections across grammar, meanings and pragmatics (Deignan, 2005). Phrases like *down at heel* or *shouldering the burden*, in particular grammatical forms, come to be more likely to be used metaphorically than literally, come to have particular evaluative force, and come to be seen as appropriate or inappropriate for particular contexts. Cameron and Deignan (2006) developed a theoretical account of this phenomenon in terms of complexity/dynamic systems theory, developing the notion of 'metaphoreme' to describe a bundle of stabilized features around a word or phrase. It seems likely that the phrase that Phil uses in line 108 of Extract 5.1, *a flaw in the system*, has stabilized in this kind of way.

In a different type of empirical study, and investigating conventionalized ways of talking rather than just metaphor, Barr (2004) used multi-agent computer simulations of group dynamics to model convergence to conventionalized forms. Somewhat counterintuitively, the simulations showed that agents in a population do not need shared representations of common knowledge in order to converge to conventionalized systems of communication, but that such systems can self-organize across a population through activity at the level of individuals in communication. If the computer simulations can be extrapolated to human systems, then convergence through interaction can account for the conventionalization of metaphorical expressions. Contrary to conceptual metaphor theory, there is no need for conceptual metaphors to be hard wired into individual brains or to be represented at group level in order to account for what we observe in discourse; conventional metaphorical ways of talking-and-thinking can evolve through the dialogic dynamics of social interaction.

## From theoretical framework to methodology

This chapter has set out the discourse dynamics theoretical framework that underpins the methodological chapters that follow. In the next chapter, we begin working with the focus group data, demonstrating how linguistic metaphors can be identified. Chapter 7 then shows how identified linguistic metaphors can be grouped together and labelled as systematic metaphors as part of the research process that aims at in inferring people's ideas, attitudes and values from their discourse. Chapter 8 illustrates how analysing the structure of discourse events or products can help understand the function and effects of metaphor in the discourse.

### Notes

1. In some disciplines, theory is also required to be capable of making predictions about future behaviour; testing these predictions helps establish the usefulness of the theory. The requirement to predict does not apply to theory based on complex dynamic systems since these are by nature unpredictable.

2. A discourse event is a bounded and coherent human activity involving the use of language. Each reconciliation conversation used in Chapter 1 was a discourse event, lasting between one and two hours. Examples of other discourse events include: a school lesson or university lecture; an interview; a radio programme; a meeting; a doctor-patient consultation; a talk between friends or colleagues over coffee.

3. We leave open the discussion of whether discourse is the only location of metaphor, as discursive psychologists would argue/assume (e.g. Edwards, 1997), or whether metaphor may take on some mental existence outside of discourse, as cognitive theorists would argue/assume (see Chapter 3). In the end, researchers make a theoretical decision as to where they place themselves on this spectrum.

4. Technically, a complex dynamic system is composed of elements or agents and the relations between them. Both the elements/agents, and the ways in which they are connected, change with time. In the discourse system, the talk produced by each speaker can be considered as 'element', and 'relations' would be the interaction, i.e. how what one person says affects another person's talk. A person's talk is in turn an outcome of the interacting elements of the complex dynamic system that is the person, physical and mental.

5. The phrase '(something like)' is used as a reminder that we can only infer, not *know*, what speakers mean.

6. A methodological comment is needed at this point on the identification issues raised by the utterance *it's almost like bullying* and the later utterance *it's not like war* (86). These positive

and negative comparisons between terrorism and bullying/war are not metaphorical statements but are literally true: terrorism is not like war. However, the bringing together in each case of two distinct ideas – terrorism – bullying; terrorism – war – could be said to be a metaphorical act, and it is this that justifies its inclusion as metaphor.

7. Historically, *opposing sides* is metonymic, since battles in times gone by did in fact involve two groups of people facing each other. Contemporaneously, however, opposing sides are characteristic less of war than of various sports and games, including football and chess (Ritchie, 2003a; Howe, 2008; Chapter 4).

8. In fact, there is usually only evidence of lexical convergence; what is happening conceptually is not accessible to researchers and we only can know that participants share sufficient under-standing to make their talk work, not that they share a concept.

# Section 3

# Metaphor analysis

This section brings us to the heart of the matter, to the detail of methodological procedures and safeguards. After the initial identification of metaphor in Chapter 6, Chapter 7 takes readers through the grouping and labelling of metaphors that leads to finding patterns of metaphor use. Chapter 8 demonstrates how analysis of discourse activity complements metaphor analysis to reveal the functions of metaphor in the production and interpretation of talk and text.

In Chapter 9, Deignan and Semino illustrate how techniques of corpus linguistics and specially designed software can assist metaphor analysis, enabling larger quantities of data to be processed. A corpus is simply a collection of discourse data, usually large or very large in scale, often with millions of words. Corpus software can carry out automatic and very swift searches for patterns of word use across the corpus. Corpus techniques have much to offer metaphor analysis: from straightforward calculations of word frequency to comparisons of metaphor use in specific discourse events with metaphor use in the speech community; from supporting the extraction of implied meanings and cultural connotations of metaphors to automatically identifying semantic groupings.

Maslen, in Chapter 10, discusses techniques for dealing with the specific demands of studies that produce large amounts of metaphor data. The advantages of large amounts of data in providing stronger evidence or allowing comparisons across social groups must not be compromised by reducing research quality.

Having insisted in Chapter 1 on the multidimensionality of metaphor, we move in Chapter 11 beyond language and thinking to the physicality of gestural metaphor. Cienki illustrates how researchers are including gesture in metaphor analysis, and what this added dimension can reveal to researchers.

# 6  Identifying metaphors in discourse data

## Lynne Cameron and Robert Maslen

Chapters 1 and 2 presented the case for using metaphor as a research tool, while Chapters 3–5 explored some of the theoretical background which informs practice. Chapter 5 made the case for a discourse dynamics approach to metaphor, and our focus in subsequent chapters will be on analysing metaphor in language use. The methodology that we develop here and in the next three chapters is for application to discourse data, using linguistic metaphors as a tool to answer research questions about people's ideas, attitudes and values.

This chapter explains how researchers can identify linguistic metaphors in discourse data, and what makes for good practice in metaphor identification. Put another way, how does a researcher turn a source transcript like Extract 6.1a into a transcript with linguistic metaphors identified and ready for coding and analysis, like Extract 6.1b?

Extract 6.1a

| Terry | it's not like war, |
| Terry | ... where you've got two .. opposing sides. |
| Terry | ... terrorism .. is just a -- |
| Terry | an invisible enemy. |

Extract 6.1b

| Terry | it's not <u>like war,</u> |
| Terry | ... where you've got two .. <u>opposing sides</u>. |
| Terry | ... terrorism .. is just a -- |
| Terry | an <u>invisible</u> <u>enemy</u>. |

The answer to this question comes in several stages. First, we properly introduce the data that we met briefly in Chapters 4 and 5, and discuss how discourse data transcriptions are prepared for analysis. Next, we work through procedures for metaphor identification which have been used successfully in a number of research projects, and which have proved accessible to researchers who have not previously used metaphor as a tool of enquiry. Like any system of categorizing or coding language use, metaphor identification cannot always be entirely straightforward, and so we also explore the types of problems and ambiguities which tend to arise, suggesting techniques to ensure reliable and trustworthy metaphor identification.

Some researchers may only want to search for particular types of metaphors in their data; for example, one might look only for metaphors that relate to a particular topic, such as 'risk', or only for metaphors that draw on a particular domain, such as WAR. In qualitative or interpretive studies, however, there are several justifications for working to identify all linguistic metaphors across the whole dataset. First, in terms of reliability, checking every word minimizes the risk of missing metaphors. Second, in terms of validity, it is usually not possible to know before carrying out the analysis which metaphors might contribute to emergent themes across discourse events. For example, preposition metaphors in the focus group discussion (Extract 6.1), which may seem insignificant when considered in isolation, were found to contribute to a conceptualization of society as a set of contained spaces (*in the city; people in gangs*) and surfaces *(coming from over there)* in a starkly differentiated 'social landscape metaphor'.

## The data

The data used in chapters across this book come from two very different discourse events: a focus group discussion and a political speech. Details about both datasets are included in the Appendix. The focus group discussion took place as part of a research project investigating people's perceptions about the risk of terrorism, and the consequences for official risk communications. Of the 12 focus groups that were organized, we have selected the group of working-class, non-Muslim men in Leeds to use in Chapters 5, 6 and 7.

The second source of data is a speech made by then British Prime Minister Tony Blair to his (Labour) Party's spring conference on Sunday 13 February 2005 at the Sage Centre in Gateshead, UK. Chapter 4 gave us a glimpse of metaphors used in this speech, Chapter 8 analyses the discourse activity of the speech, and in Chapter 9, Deignan and Semino explore further some of the metaphors in the speech for their linguistic and cultural properties. The full speech is included in the Appendix. In political terms, this speech marked the unofficial start of campaigning for the election that would follow in May of that year, and was designed to address generally low approval ratings for the government and increasing calls for the Prime Minister to stand down. As with any major political speech, this text had more than one intended audience: among them, the Prime Minister's fellow party members in the hall, who gave him a warm reception, and the electorate as a whole, whose response was mixed. One newspaper journalist reported it as follows:

Blair's speech in Gateshead was a toe-curling embarrassment. (John
Rentoul, *The Independent*, 17 February 2005)

Clearly these discourse events produced very different discourse data with
contrasting characteristics and dynamics (see Chapter 5). The focus group transcription is a record of a spontaneous speech event where unscripted strangers
interacted for the first time. Although the moderator used a topic guide to direct
the discussion, the talk developed unpredictably, with participants addressing
their themes in ways which arose contingently out of the on-going conversation.
The Blair speech began as a text, written and delivered according to the conventions of public rhetoric. It is likely to have been composed with considerable
care, with both the immediate audience and subsequent reporting in mind.

The focus group talk shows many features common to spontaneous dialogue:
utterances tend to be short and marked by hesitations, restarts, non sequiturs
and interruptions. Participants develop lines of talk by agreeing or disagreeing with each other, and by elaborating the points they make. The moderator
used a prepared set of questions and topics designed to answer the research
questions. The political speech, in contrast, was carefully crafted and flows
from point to point according to a deliberately designed structure. The differing discourse dynamics reflect different discourse activity and structures, and
include strikingly different use of metaphor. We cannot examine metaphor use
without looking at the function that the metaphors play in discourse activity
and discourse design, and in Chapter 8 we return to the question of how to take
account of this in interpreting metaphors.

## Preparing data for metaphor analysis and identification

### Transcribing audio recordings for analysis

Depending on the kind of spoken discourse involved, and on the level of analysis appropriate to the research questions, transcripts need to be prepared by
listening to recordings and transcribing what participants said. Meaningful
analysis requires accurate data (see also Chapter 10) and preparing accurate
transcriptions takes several hours for each hour of recorded talk. However, this
effort allows the researcher to be confident that subsequent research findings
represent as closely as possible the event being analysed. Conclusions can be
based on clear evidence from the discourse, with audit trails traceable backwards
from findings through all stages of the analysis to the original recording.

It is inevitable that some contextual information from the original event is lost,
however carefully a written transcription is prepared. Transcripts do not tend to
include (and it would be very cumbersome to try) details such as what the room was
like, what people were wearing, or how much they had to drink. The importance

of participants' gestures is increasingly recognized – see Chapter 11 for evidence of how richly informative multimodal information can be – but again increases the time required for transcription. Having an observer present during data collection allows for some contextual information to be captured in field notes.

## Using intonation units in transcription of talk

One element of the original event which can be transferred relatively easily from recording to transcription is time. The passage of time plays a central role in the dynamics of discourse and in its interpretation. Transcribing talk in intonation units offers one approach to representing the temporal and dimension of dialogue (Du Bois *et al.*, 1993; Chafe, 1994). An intonation unit is a stretch of speech produced under a single intonation contour, often coinciding with a single breath. Each intonation unit occupies a new, numbered line in the transcript. This form of transcription has the advantage of representing language in a way that 'looks like it sounds' and is thus more readable for the researcher and for research users (see for example the extracts in Chapter 1, which use intonation units). Intonation units correlate highly with clause boundaries, while repetitions and restarts also tend to come under a single intonation or contour. Pauses inside and between intonation units are usually important to transcribe, particularly since stronger or more novel metaphors may be preceded by a pause.

Intonation units represent speech in a way that meshes with theories of metaphor in discourse and that are claimed to be cognitively realistic. Chafe's notion of the 'idea unit', from which the concept of intonation units developed, holds that an intonation unit tends to express only one idea (Chafe, 1994). The intonation unit is seen as arising out of the interaction between the dual constraints of cognitive processing and the physical task of producing language. Across units, ideas move in and out of focus as they are expressed. This has a clear resonance with the discourse dynamics approach to metaphor analysis presented in this volume, as does the intonation unit's status as a mind-body entity, since metaphor is viewed as essentially embodied in dialogic dynamics.

A further advantage emerges from the fact that intonation units are quite short (in our data, the time speakers take to produce an intonation unit averages out at less than two seconds), and so in transcription each unit contains a limited amount of text, which makes intonation units easily transferred to columns in spreadsheet software, such as Excel, for coding and analysis.

Using intonation units in the transcription of talk requires a commitment to training and extra time (see Stelma and Cameron, 2007). However, there is some room for discretion about how much detail is included, depending on the research questions to be answered. For example, complete analysis of stress may not be necessary, and orthographic transcription, rather than phonetic or phonemic, will usually be adequate for projects outside of linguistics. In Extract 6.2, which follows later in the chapter, four types of intonation contour are marked (the use of what look like familiar punctuation marks may be confusing at first; it is important to remember that these marks refer to intonation and not punctuation):

- A full stop/period indicates a final closing intonation.
- A comma indicates a slightly falling or level pitch and continuing intonation.
- A question mark indicates rising intonation.
- Dashes indicate an incomplete intonation unit.

The transcription also uses the following conventions for representing speech:

- Overlaps across speakers are marked with square brackets.
- Pauses are marked with double dots .. for a minimal micro-pause; three dots ... for a slightly longer micro-pause, and the approximate number of seconds in brackets for pauses longer than one second, e.g. (2.0) indicates a two second pause.
- The data include many instances of quasi-reported speech, in which a speaker adopts the voice of some other person or organization; these utterances are enclosed in <Q ... Q> brackets.
- <X ... X> brackets are used to represent a stretch of indecipherable talk.

The most frequently found alternative mode of transcription presents participants' talk turn by turn, and is formatted like the script of a play. Intonation and non-fluency features tend to be lost in this kind of transcription, and the large 'paragraphs' of talk can be more difficult to make sense of because of this. In the range of research projects we have carried out, we find intonation units to be useful, easy to work with, and theoretically valid.

### Preparing written texts

The written version of the political speech that we are using as data is separated into short numbered paragraphs, as in its original published form. It is included in the Appendix. Written texts can also be prepared for metaphor identification by being segmented by sentence or clause, if that seems appropriate or if software constraints demand it.

## An operational definition of metaphor

### Incongruity and transfer of meaning

In Chapter 1, we described metaphor as 'a device for seeing something in terms of something else' (Burke, 1945: 503). Once we start to work with data and want to identify metaphors in use, we need an operational definition (or operationalization), i.e. a description that can be used in analysing data. An operational definition ideally identifies all metaphors in the data while not identifying as metaphor anything that is not. However, the discourse world is not an ideal world and a watertight definition is not possible, for the simple reason that we are dealing with human language use, with its tendency to push boundaries, extend, and play around with ways of speaking. An operationalization will have to be as good as we can make it, given these problems, and will have to be accompanied by ways of dealing with the problems. Deciding on how good is good enough when constructing an operationalization is a key research skill, a judgement that requires both theoretical knowledge and empirical awareness.

Linguistic metaphor can be operationalized for our purposes through identifying words or phrases that can be justified as somehow anomalous, incongruent or 'alien' in the on-going discourse, but that can be made sense of through a transfer of meaning in the context. In Extract 6.1, the word *enemy* is incongruent when used in relation to *terrorism*, because *terrorism* is an abstract concept whereas *enemy* is a specific and concrete person or group. Another way of describing the incongruity condition is to say that these words or phrases have one meaning in the context and another, different, meaning which is more basic in some way, usually more physical or more concrete than the contextual meaning (Pragglejaz group, 2007). Thus, *enemy* has a basic meaning of a specific individual or group who has declared war on the speaker or speaker's group, and that is different from its contextual meaning, which is something like 'the frightening nature of terrorism'. Metaphorically used words or phrases must not only be semantically incongruent with the topic of the discourse at that point but must also support a transfer of meaning so that sense can be made of the word or phrase in context. In the example of *terrorism* as *invisible enemy*, *enemy* can be understood as personifying *terrorism*.

It is important to note that the operational definition identifies words and phrases that are **potentially** metaphorical. There is no claim made that readers or listeners will interpret the words or phrases as metaphor, nor that writers and speakers intended the words or phrases to be taken as metaphor. The operationalization captures, alongside obvious and novel metaphors, very conventionalized metaphors that are unlikely to be interpreted metaphorically, but still have the potential to be understood as metaphor. Researchers can separate conventionalized metaphors from novel metaphors later, if wished, although often we are interested in the cultural models indicated by conventional metaphors used by discourse participants.

Metaphor vehicles and metaphor topics

The incongruous words or phrases identified as above are called metaphor vehicle terms. They indicate the presence of a metaphor but are only one part of it. In conventional formulations, a linguistic metaphor consists of a vehicle term combined with a topic term, such as *Juliet is the sun* (where *Juliet* is the metaphor topic and *the sun* is the metaphor vehicle) or *a black hole of debt* (where *debt* is the metaphor topic and *black hole* is the metaphor vehicle). Explicit metaphor topics (*Juliet, debt*) may sometimes be present in discourse, but this happens only rarely in spontaneous talk. More often, the anomalous or contrasting metaphor vehicle words or phrases have to be picked out against the flow of discourse, in which topics remain implicit across considerable stretches of talk although usually easily inferred by discourse participants (Kittay, 1987).

In cognitive metaphor theory, vehicles would be called 'source domain' terms because they would be seen as instantiations of the conceptual domain that is the 'source' of the metaphor mapping (see Chapter 3). In the discourse dynamics approach (Chapter 5), it is more logical to use 'vehicle' as the label, than 'source domain term', because we are concerned with the language actually used in discourse, and want to avoid making assumptions about speakers' conceptualizations (see Cameron, 1999b).

## The process of metaphor identification

In this section, we set out a procedure for metaphor identification with two variations, the key difference between the variations being that one identifies metaphorically used words or phrases as metaphor vehicle terms, whereas the other identifies metaphorically used words. This difference in procedure arises from theoretical differences about the nature of language, and, although this distinction is theoretically profound, the actual outcomes of the identification procedure are in fact very similar. After an overview of the procedure, it is described in more detail, with problematic types of metaphors, special cases, and differences in outcomes between the two variations discussed. Extracts from both the spoken and written data are used to illustrate the procedure.

Overview of the metaphor identification procedure

The essential elements of the operational definition of linguistic metaphor are two meanings of a word or phrase that are incongruous in some way and a transfer of meaning within the discourse context that enables the incongruous word or phrase to be made sense of. Turning this into a procedure to apply to data gives four steps or stages (adapted from Pragglejaz group, 2007):

1. The researcher familiarizes her/himself with the discourse data.
2. The researcher works through the data looking for possible metaphors.
3. Each possible metaphor is checked for:
    (a) its meaning in the discourse context;
    (b) the existence of another, more basic meaning;
    (c) an incongruity or contrast between these meanings, and a transfer from the basic to the contextual meaning.
4. If the possible metaphor satisfies each of the above, it is coded as metaphor, usually by underlining or listing.

Each of these steps is now discussed in more detail.

### The researcher familiarizes her/himself with the discourse data

Metaphorical uses of words and phrases are most effectively identified against background knowledge of the whole discourse event, since this gives the best chance of recognizing anomalies or incongruities between the local discourse topic and the words or phrases being used metaphorically. For this reason, coders read through the transcription or text in order to get a feel for the structure and activity of the discourse, and to understand as far as possible the context in which metaphors were produced.

The focus group data used here was familiar to the coders because they had been involved in designing the question schedule and had moderated or observed each group. They also did much of the transcription, and, where the transcription was done by others, the coders listened to the audio recording and checked the transcription before proceeding to metaphor identification.

Reading the political speech in its entirety before coding for metaphors reveals its relation to the context of British electoral politics at the time and the recurring themes of Blair's physical, political and spiritual return.

### The researcher works through the data looking for possible metaphors

Having read and familiarized themselves with the transcript or text, coders next work carefully through the data looking at every word or phrase to see if it is a candidate for coding as a metaphor.

It is at this stage that the two variations of the procedure come into play. The method for identifying metaphors developed by the Pragglejaz group (2007) works at *word* level to identify metaphorically used words. The underlying view of language here is of language as a system in the minds of speakers, with words as the basic building blocks (for more on this view of language readers are referred to Steen (2007, 2008)). Some allowance is made in this version of the procedure for words that seem inseparable. The term 'lexical unit' is used to describe words and these phrases, and is defined in terms of dictionary head-words (see Pragglejaz group, 2007: 15).

This system/use view of the nature of language differs from the discourse dynamics view set out in Chapter 5, which takes the position that when people use language to express their thoughts and ideas, they 'soft assemble' words and phrases, adjusting them as they go for effective communication of meaning. What we see in talk or textual data is the outcome of this process of 'soft assembly', a trace of the mental activity that produced it (Larsen-Freeman and Cameron, 2008). What we look for when identifying metaphor are there-fore chunks or **stretches of language** that might be metaphorical, i.e. what we have called metaphor vehicle terms. The further reduction to word level built into the Pragglejaz group procedure is not theoretically valid in the discourse dynamics framework because neither language nor metaphor is seen to work only at word level. Sometimes individual words may be used metaphorically but often a group of words are used together metaphorically. By allowing meta-phor vehicle terms to be words or phrases, the identification procedure and the theoretical framework fit validly together.

There are some important implications that follow the decision whether to work with metaphor vehicle terms or metaphorically used words. If using vehicle terms, the coder has to decide where a vehicle term begins and ends; this is discussed below. Second, quantitative data analysis is affected because the units that are counted are different. The Pragglejaz group procedure allows a measure of metaphor density as a percentage of the total words that are used metaphorically, whereas the discourse dynamics procedure measures metaphor density as the number of metaphors (which is the same as the number of meta-phor vehicles) per thousand words (Cameron, 2003). Furthermore, researchers need to be aware of exactly what is being counted when reading studies that use metaphor analysis (Cameron, 2003; Low and Todd, Chapter 12, this volume).

## Checking each possible metaphor

Each word or phrase in the data is checked to see if it satisfies the two condi-tions for metaphor:

1.  there is a contrast or incongruity between meaning of the word or phrase in its discourse context and another meaning; together with
2.  a transfer of meaning that enables that contextual meaning to be under-stood in terms of basic meaning.

The Pragglejaz group procedure sets this out as follows (Pragglejaz group, 2007: 3):

3. (a)  For each lexical unit in the text, establish its meaning in context, that is, how it applies to an entity, relation or attribute in the situation evoked by the text (contextual meaning). Take into account what comes before and after the lexical unit.

   (b)  For each lexical unit, determine if it has a more basic contemporary meaning in other contexts than the one in the given context. For our purposes, basic meanings tend to be:

     (i)  More concrete [what they evoke is easier to imagine, see, hear, feel, smell, and taste];

     (ii)  Related to bodily action;

     (iii)  More precise (as opposed to vague);

     (iv)  Historically older.

     Basic meanings are not necessarily the most frequent meanings of the lexical unit.

   (c)  If the lexical unit has a more basic current – contemporary meaning in other contexts than the given context, decide whether the contextual meaning contrasts with the basic meaning but can be understood in comparison with it.

So, for example, we would look at the word ***strength*** as used in the Blair speech (line 36):

> *the people – have given me strength and support*

and decide that its contextual meaning refers to the positive mental energy which allows Blair to carry out the job of Prime Minister and which he feels is received through interaction with *the people*. *Strength* also has a more basic meaning of physical, muscular capacity to exert force on objects. This would be incongruous in the context of the political speech – or, in other words, the contextual meaning contrasts with the basic meaning. The contextual meaning can also be understood by comparison with the basic meaning: we can understand, for example, the ability to resist the arguments of others, or to continue with a course of action which is unpopular, in terms of the ability to exert physical force. *Strength* is thus identified as a metaphorically used word.

Figures 6.1 and 6.2 show extracts from the focus group discussion (Extract 5.1) and the Blair speech with metaphors identified, and a call-out showing the justification in each case. Following the discourse dynamics approach, metaphor vehicle terms are identified, rather than individual metaphorically used words.

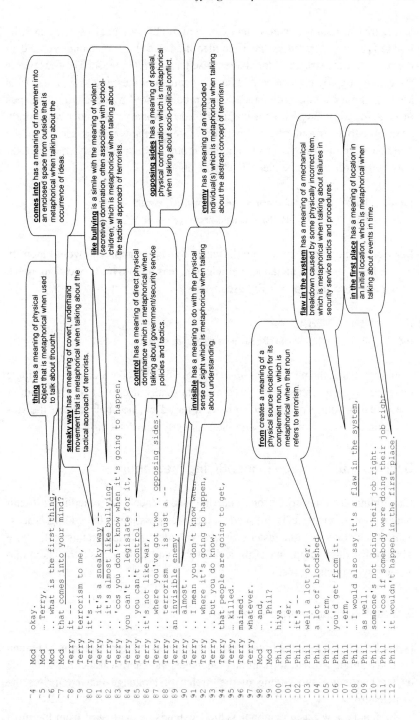

Figure 6.1. Metaphor vehicles underlined in an extract from the focus group discussion

Figure 6.1 includes several metaphor vehicles that are phrases. For example, in line 112, *in the first place* has been identified as a single metaphor vehicle on the basis that the stretch of language is used as a single phrase. The four words are conventionally collocated and have a contextual meaning as a phrase (this kind of idiomatic conventionalization can be checked by consulting a corpus of contemporary English or a corpus based dictionary); *in* and *place* jointly contribute to a particular basic, spatial meaning of the whole phrase. If, on the other hand, the word by word Pragglejaz group procedure had been followed,[1] only two words would be identified as metaphor:

| 111 | Phil | .. 'cos if somebody were doing their job right, |
| 112 | Phil | it wouldn't happen in the first place. |

Later on in the same extract, the discourse dynamics approach would identify *flaw in the system* as a metaphor vehicle, whereas an individual word approach would find three metaphorically used words:

| 107 | Phil | ..erm, |
| 108 | Phil | … I would also say it's a flaw in the system, |

In Figure 6.2, the phrase *face up to* in lines 78–79 is considered to be a single metaphor vehicle, rather than three metaphorically used words. The topic or contextual meaning of *face up to* here, inferred by the analyst from the surrounding text or talk, is something like: 'directly address a difficulty'.

## Decisions to be made in identifying metaphor

Identifying metaphor brings the researcher face to face with sometimes difficult issues. A set of clear decisions made as early as possible in the coding process helps researchers to make faster progress with identification. In this section, we describe the most important of these decisions and what needs to be taken into account when making them.

### Deciding where a vehicle term begins and ends

If the discourse dynamics framework is adopted, then a metaphor may extend beyond a single word to surrounding language, and the researcher has to decide on the beginning and ending of the stretch of language that comprises the vehicle term.

To decide how far a metaphor vehicle extends, we can start from the most clearly incongruous or contrasting word and work outwards. In line 87 of Figure

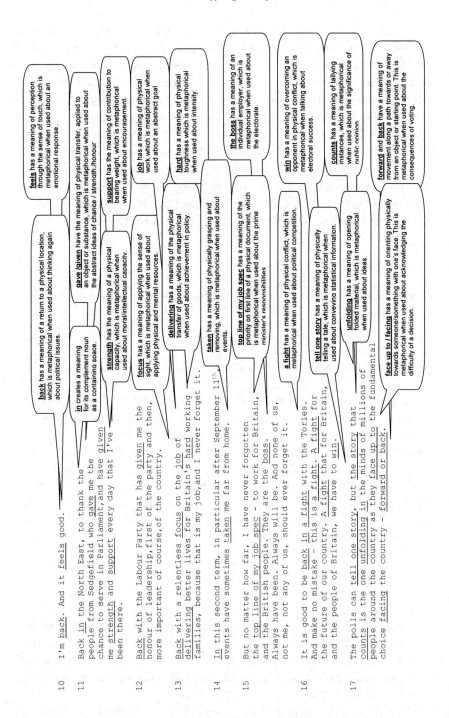

Figure 6.2. Metaphor vehicles underlined in an extract from the Blair speech

6.1: *where you've got two opposing sides*, the word *sides* stands out from the on-going talk because its basic concrete and physical meaning related to space and position contrasts with its contextual meaning, which is something like 'membership of different groups who are in armed conflict with each other'. Working outwards from *sides*, the adjective *opposing* is another word with a more basic meaning related to space and position. Furthermore, the phrase *opposing sides* is a semi-fixed expression in which the two words have come to be used together, or collocate. So the vehicle encompasses, at least, *opposing sides*. We might then ask whether the quantifier *two* should be included. However, *two* performs the task of enumerating the topic referents, just as it does the vehicle referents, and so no contrast or transfer of meaning is present. On these grounds *two* is not included as part of this metaphor vehicle.

## Metaphors and similes

The focus group extracts (Extract 6.1 and Figure 6.1) included two underlined metaphorical similes:

> *terrorism ... it's not like war*
> *it's a sneaky way ... it's almost like bullying*

Metaphor as described throughout this book requires the basic and contextual meanings of vehicle terms to contrast or to be incongruous. Simile does not require that incongruity, although it may be present. Instead simile, as traditionally defined, is a matter only of words used and not of underlying meanings, and requires an explicit term, such as *like* or *as* to connect its two parts. Both examples below are similes, but only the first is metaphorical. Here, there is incongruity or contrast between *he* as a male person and *a whirlwind*. The second simile is not metaphorical but is a literal comparison, with no 'alien' metaphorical term.

> *he was like a whirlwind*
> *she is like her sister*

Contemporary metaphor studies makes a distinction between metaphorical and non-metaphorical similes, and would describe the first of these examples as a metaphor that is signalled (Goatly, 1997) or 'tuned' (Cameron and Deignan, 2003) by the presence of the word *like*. The second example is a non-metaphorical simile.

As in the examples from the focus group discussion, the discourse dynamics procedure currently underlines the whole phrase including *like* as vehicle term, following Kittay (1987). The Pragglejaz group procedure, as being developed by Steen and colleagues, uses a special label (Mflag) for signalling words such as *like*, which indicate that it is a marker or signal of metaphoricity. Only *bullying* would then be underlined as a metaphorically used word.

While the actual labelling of the signalling words in similes remains an issue, metaphor scholars are agreed on the first point, that a distinction can be made between metaphorical similes and non-metaphorical similes.

## Very common verbs and nouns

> *make, do, give, have, get, put*
> *thing, part, way*

It is possible to state a basic meaning for most of these highly frequent words (e.g. *thing* is a concrete discrete object; *put* is to physically place something) so that metaphorical uses that contrast with the basic meanings can be identified:

> *I've <u>made</u> a new life here* (= developed)

the basic meaning of physical construction contrasts with, and contributes meaning to, the contextual meaning of 'developing social relations in a new place'.

> *you can <u>put</u> it <u>that way</u>* (= you can say that using those words).

the basic meaning of physically placing something contrasts with, and contributes to the meaning of, the contextual meaning of 'deliberately choosing words to express an idea'.

> *that's a large part of the decision...* (= a main reason for ...)

The basic meaning of a physically big section contrasts with, and contributes to the meaning of, the contextual meaning of 'a major factor'.

The frequency of these words, particularly in spontaneous talk, however, presents the researcher with a technical problem. Because there are so many of them, checking each one as a possible metaphor adds greatly to the project time spent on metaphor identification, and results in very lengthy lists of metaphors, most of which may not be of much relevance in answering the research questions. When research projects have limited time available, it may be more realistic to decide from the beginning not to look at particular highly frequent verbs or nouns. However, the risk in doing this, rather than initially including them, is that something interesting in metaphor use will be lost. In our work, we have omitted *have, do, get* but included the others in the identification stage, although not always making use of them in further analysis.

## Prepositions

As we have seen, some prepositions have a basic spatial meaning that is very clear, so that it is quite straightforward to find their metaphorical uses:

> *I got into a few scrapes*

*into* expresses an idea of physical containment which contrasts with the non-physical contextual meaning;

> *over the last five years*

*over* has the basic physical meaning of 'above' and 'from one side to another', which contrasts with the contextual meaning of the passage of time;

> *behind the times*

time is again expressed in terms of space and movement, with *behind* having the basic physical meaning of 'at the back of'.

The set of prepositions with basic concrete, physical meanings would also include *in, on, up, down, within, between, out of, from, through*. Other prepositions such as *by, for, of* do not have such clear basic meanings and are probably best ignored in metaphor identification. Particular research goals might render less obviously metaphorical prepositions interesting, in which case, the basic meaning would need to be clarified and used to test other instances for metaphoricity.

Because prepositions are also highly frequent in discourse data, the decision as to which are being included is best made early in the research process. It is easy to miss small words like prepositions when working through a large amount of text, so automatic word searches can help find all instances.

## The shared language of subgroups

People who share a discourse world – such as prisoners, football fans, engineers, parents – are likely to have a shared language in which expressions that seem metaphorical to outsiders have become conventionalized. An example from the reconciliation conversations (Chapter 1) is the description of the conflict in Ireland as *the struggle,* which became a shared way of talking for Republican sympathizers. The operationalization of metaphor described above would include this as metaphor since there is potential contrast and meaning transfer between a more basic meaning (physical struggle) and the meaning of the word or phrase in context. Clearly, from the perspective of a member of the sociocultural group who share a particular way of talking, that metaphoric potential is reduced in comparison to someone who is outside the group but a member of the larger speech community or general public. However, the potential remains and such phrases are not discarded as technical or jargon but included as metaphors. Depending on research priorities, a further round of analysis could identify metaphors specific to a particular sociocultural group.

## Personification

In personification something non-human is made animate:

> the river is <u>moving sluggishly</u>
> terrorism is an invisible <u>enemy</u>

The operational definition of metaphor that we have described in this chapter would include such personifications as metaphor, and metaphor identification would underline the animate words or phrases since these are the ones that are incongruent in the ongoing discourse.

## Etymology

The researcher must decide whether potential metaphoricity is to be relative to current usage or to usage at some other point in history. Some words and phrases are metaphorical in the way their meanings have developed over time, although their historical sense has been lost for most current speakers. For example, in *a reformed terrorist* the word *reformed* may originally have meant *re-formed* in the sense of 'physically made again'. However, for a user of modern English, it does not have any of that sense and just means something like 'having had a change of character'.

Etymology is likely to be a side issue in social science projects that do not have an explicit historical element. In the arts and humanities, the researcher may want to carry out a contemporary metaphor identification on an historical text, and would in this case need a great deal of information about language usage at that point in time in order to make a case for historical metaphoricity of words and phrases.

## Trustworthiness in metaphor identification

As explained earlier, good qualitative research concerns itself with trustworthiness at all stages of the process. At the identification stage, there are issues of validity – that what we operationalize as metaphor fits as closely as possible with our theory of metaphor – and of reliability – that what gets identified as metaphor is as consistent as possible over time and across different analysts.

A key validity issue arises from the need in identification to place boundaries on the category of 'metaphor' as we decide whether a particular word or phrase is to be included. As the previous section illustrated, these decisions are not always straightforward. A number of sources deal in some detail with the kind of problems which coders might face (e.g. Pragglejaz group, 2007; Cameron, 2003, Chapter 3).

It is impossible to define metaphor by necessary and sufficient conditions (Cameron, 1999a). This in turn means that the clear category boundaries that would smooth the wheels of coding cannot reliably be established. Because of this, coding involves making multiple decisions. Decision making is made more efficient by establishing certain criteria a priori, such as the inclusion or exclusion of highly conventionalized words and phrases, the inclusion or exclusion of articles (*a, an, the*) in noun phrases. These decisions place constructed boundaries on the category of metaphor. If thought through at the early stages of a research project, these decisions can also facilitate later stages of analysis. For example, excluding definite articles at the beginning of vehicle terms facilitates alphabetical ordering in sorting vehicles into groups (see Chapter 7).

As decisions are made, they should be carefully recorded in project notes. Project notes that are carefully kept and referred to will help all analysts work to the same set of guidelines and thus increase the trustworthiness of the research.

A large corpus of contemporary language use or a corpus based dictionary can be referred to check basic meanings (see Chapter 9), and to help resolve disagreements about meanings across a group of researchers.

Most important at the identification stage of research is that reliability is maximized, so that the procedure is applied in the same way at different points in time and by the different people engaged in the process. Reliability in metaphor identification is perhaps more accurately conceived as a continuous, iterative, cross-referential process of ensuring trustworthiness than as measurable by a single, discrete test with the result expressed in numerical terms. Reliability begins with a strong foundation of initial training. Reliability can then be increased by regular checks across data when coding is under way. A sample of each transcription should ideally be coded by more than one person, with a follow up discussion to reach agreement on items that are to be included or excluded as metaphor. A final step in which all items coded in a transcription are rechecked, after agreement on problematic cases has been reached, ensures consistency. In larger projects, this can be repeated for all transcriptions pooled together (see Chapter 10).

## Conclusion

This chapter has shown how researchers can use a trustworthy method to extract a set of metaphors from discourse data. Put succinctly, this involves:

- rigorous transcription to an appropriate level of detail;
- selection of method of metaphor identification and theoretical underpinning;
- training coders in metaphor identification and ensuring that they are familiar with the transcripts or texts;
- making clear and informed decisions about which words and phrases to consider for analysis;
- keeping notes on those decisions and applying them systematically across the data and across researchers;
- blind double checking of a sample of each transcription.

The outcome of this procedure is a list of metaphors identified in the discourse. Once this list has been prepared, the researcher can proceed to categorizing the metaphors and then looking for systematic relationships between metaphors and their referents, as it is particularly through these connections that metaphor has the power to unveil people's ideas, attitudes and values. These stages of analysis are addressed in the following chapter.

### Note
1. The authors are grateful to Anna Kaal of the VU University, Amsterdam, for applying the Pragglejaz group procedure and providing these examples.

# 7 Finding systematicity in metaphor use

## Lynne Cameron, Graham Low and Robert Maslen

## Overview: What can systematicity tell us?

A transcribed metaphor is like an excavated citizen of ancient Pompeii. Just as the shape in the ash distils a complex existence into one instant, so the record of language pinpoints a momentary state in a dynamic system of thought and expression. And just as the archaeologist might study the victims at the forum, the baths, and the Villa of the Mysteries to learn something of Roman society at the time Vesuvius erupted, so, from their use of words, the metaphor researcher can develop a picture of speakers' or writers' interacting ideas, feelings and language.

This chapter sets out a method for tapping into the potential of metaphors to reveal aspects of discourse. Based within the discourse dynamics approach described in Chapter 5, the method works from identified linguistic metaphors (Chapter 6) to establish systematic topic~vehicle connections. These systematic metaphors serve both as evidence for ideas, attitudes and values which may not be directly expressed in the discourse, and as a starting point for the further exploration of aspects of data which would not otherwise have come to light.

Previous chapters have explored in some detail the theories which underpin using metaphor as a research tool, but it is perhaps worth reiterating the significance of systematicity in metaphor use. Discourse is an outcome of the cognitive and linguistic processes that people engage in when they speak and write. What is expressed or understood in the flow of discourse is the best outcome available at that time, under those constraints and in those circumstances. These outcomes are not arbitrary; they reflect the multiple influences of past experience, sociocultural convention and the constraints of processing. Metaphor, like other aspects of language, is subject to these influences, but choice of metaphor has a particular revelatory capacity. A linguistic metaphor is connected into a dense network of ideas, associations, conceptual and affective patterns which are interwoven with correlates from embodied experience (Chapter 1). These connections and patterns are not expressed directly – indeed, we are not for the most part consciously aware of them – but they are fundamental to how we perceive, conceptualize and interact with the world. Systematic connections between semantically similar metaphor vehicles on the one hand and the topics they express on the other, open a window on the ideas, attitudes and values which may be active in speakers' or writers' minds at the time they engage in the discourse. The more robust the relationship, the stronger the claim that can be made about the underlying factors it reveals.

## Examples of systematic metaphors

The focus group data on the risk of terrorism introduced in Chapter 5 provided many examples of systematic metaphors (see Cameron *et al.*, 2009 for a more thorough exploration of these findings). For instance, a number of participants in the focus groups spoke about the risk of terrorism in terms relating to games. The risk was characterized as *a poker game* and *a game of bluff*, involving *lottery odds* for a public who were *pawns in a game*. One participant observed that if the worst happened, *my number's up*. Thinking of it from the perspective of the authorities as players in such games, another said, *they're actually dicing with your life*. What all these metaphors have in common is not just that they relate to games, but that the games have outcomes which affect the public in arbitrary ways; in other words, they are games of chance. These individual metaphors therefore contribute to a systematic metaphor we can formulate as:

*BEING AFFECTED BY TERRORISM IS PARTICIPATING IN A GAME OF CHANCE.*

The metaphors combine to show that the participants systematically represented that particular topic in those particular terms. The label was chosen carefully to reflect a collective or aggregate meaning of the linguistic metaphors, staying close to the actual words used while at the same time capturing the overall idea. Systematic metaphors are written in SMALL *ITALIC CAPITALS* to distinguish them from conceptual metaphors (Chapter 3), which are written in SMALL CAPITALS.

Another revealing set of metaphors emerged as participants discussed the actions of the authorities in response to terrorism, particularly in the UK. The opinions expressed tended to be very negative and suspicious, with participants talking about the authorities *acting shady* and doing things *behind the scenes*. The government going to war in Iraq with the Americans was characterized as *Billy the Kid*. One participant described official action as a *farce*. Together, these and other metaphors contributed to a systematic metaphor that was formulated as AUTHORITIES' RESPONSE TO TERRORISM IS THEATRE. (This metaphor is discussed further in Chapter 14.)

These examples give some idea of the potential outcomes of metaphor analysis in terms of systematic metaphors which can capture cognitive and affective information about the participants in discourse. This information is important to researchers in its own right, but might also have value for practitioners in other fields, such as therapy, communications or conflict resolution.

There are, however, certain obstacles to be dealt with in producing a trust-worthy set of systematic metaphors. Ninety minutes of focus group talk may contain 20,000 words and 1000 metaphor vehicles. Related metaphor vehicles are not necessarily produced in close proximity, and, among all the additional linguistic 'noise', important connections between vehicle terms are easy to miss, as are those between vehicles and topics. This chapter demonstrates in some detail how these stages of metaphor analysis within a discourse dynamics approach are carried out.

## Grouping metaphor vehicles

After identifying metaphor vehicles, the next step is to build larger groupings of related vehicles. Aside from making the coding process efficient, there are other good reasons for working exclusively on vehicles before considering topics. First, as we saw in the previous chapter, topics are often not explicitly referred to in the discourse and, when this is the case, retrieving them is in itself a stage in the analysis. Second, working just with the vehicles allows us to focus tem-porarily on the metaphorical 'world' rather than the discourse 'world', which provides an atmosphere of greater objectivity in establishing the semantic char-acteristics of vehicle groupings; in other words, we avoid trying to second guess what the speakers meant and concentrate on the words they actually said.

The vehicle grouping procedure in part resembles coding data within 'grounded theory' approaches (e.g. Charmaz, 2001), since it works inductively from the data, rather than starting from assumptions about what will be found. This contrasts with conceptual metaphor theory which starts from the assumption that particu-lar conceptual metaphors are active when a speaker produces a related linguistic metaphor. Nonetheless, some vehicle groupings, such as *SEEING* or *MOVEMENT* will look like the 'conceptual domains' of conceptual metaphor theory.

The researcher does not come entirely cold to vehicle grouping since, through working with the data to identify metaphors, they will have some knowledge of the data's structure and themes, its rhetorical highlights, and some of the metaphors used. For example, working with the Blair speech (Figure 6.2 and Appendix), the researcher is likely to have noticed the systematic use of the *MOVEMENT* metaphor (*backwards – forwards*), shortcutting the need to work upwards from the data to find it. A decision will still need to be made as to whether this label is the most appropriate for all the metaphors that connect within this grouping (see below).

Deciding on vehicle groupings for the hundreds of metaphors in an hour's talk requires various viable possibilities to be considered, and premature interpretive claims to be resisted. An important principle to bear in mind from the start is that the labels of groupings should remain as specific as possible. That is, researchers should try to avoid giving names to vehicle groupings which abstract or general-ize beyond the evidence in the data, and so run the risk of being over-inclusive or over-interpretive. As far as possible, labels for groupings are taken from the actual words that appear in a transcript. If, for example, a participant uses the word *feel* in the emotional sense, we assign this initially to a group labelled some-thing like FEELING rather than a more abstract category, such as PERCEPTION. Again this contrasts with conceptual metaphor theory which aims to generalize labels as much as possible in order to posit universals in human conceptualizing.

Grouping vehicles together is a flexible process. Initial decisions remain open to revision until the later stages of analysis, since each addition may change the nature of a grouping, and result in splitting or re-labelling.

### Working with the data, the evolution of groupings through splitting, combining, and renaming

The process begins with a list of linguistic metaphors.[1] We have found it useful to work in Excel software, which is readily available and straightforward to use. Examples in this chapter will include visuals from that particular software, although other software may do the job as well (see Chapters 9 and 10 for pos-sible alternatives). Figure 7.1 shows the Excel display of metaphors identified in the focus group data in Figure 6.1 before vehicle grouping. Each metaphor occupies a row of the table, with adjacent cells showing the following informa-tion: immediate discourse context in column F (the full intonation unit in which the metaphor appears); transcription line number in column C; data reference code in column D, if there are several sources (e.g. Blair speech or focus group, identified as 'Leeds CD Men'); and speaker's name, in column E.

| | Vehicle Group | Metaphor | Line | Transcript | Speaker | Intonation Unit |
|---|---|---|---|---|---|---|
| 2 | | thing | 76 | LeCDM | Mod | .. what is the first thing. |
| 3 | | comes into | 77 | LeCDM | Mod | that comes into your mind? |
| 4 | | sneaky | 81 | LeCDM | Terry | .. it's a sneaky way -- |
| 5 | | way | 81 | LeCDM | Terry | .. it's a sneaky way -- |
| 6 | | like bullying | 82 | LeCDM | Terry | .. it's almost like bullying. |
| 7 | | control | 85 | LeCDM | Terry | .. you can't control -- |
| 8 | | not like war | 86 | LeCDM | Terry | it's not like war. |
| 9 | | opposing sides | 87 | LeCDM | Terry | .. where you've got two..opposing sides. |
| 10 | | invisible | 89 | LeCDM | Terry | an invisible enemy. |
| 11 | | enemy | 89 | LeCDM | Terry | an invisible enemy. |
| 12 | | from | 106 | LeCDM | Phil | you'd get from it. |
| 13 | | flaw in the system | 108 | LeCDM | Phil | ...I would also say it's a flaw in the system. |
| 14 | | in the first place | 112 | LeCDM | Phil | it wouldn't happen in the first place. |

Figure 7.1. Metaphors in a stretch of talk ready for vehicle grouping in Excel

The next step is to work through the metaphor vehicles (in the case of this focus group discussion, the full list contained around a thousand) grouping them together on the basis of the semantics of the basic meaning of the metaphor vehicle, and choosing a label which generalizes as little as possible from the word or phrase used in the discourse.

Grouping metaphor vehicles is interpretive, in that there is no single 'right answer' and in that the researcher must make judgements about how best to group the vehicles on the basis of available evidence. The set of groupings evolves as the researcher works through the metaphor vehicles; each new addition may lead to adapting and adjusting the existing groups. Deciding on the range of each grouping and on how to select a label that best describes a grouping involves consideration of connections between metaphor vehicles and of the discourse evidence to support decisions. In turn, decisions about groupings contribute to what the analyst notices about patterns and themes in the data (Cameron *et al.*, 2009). In this way, metaphor vehicle grouping is a recursive procedure that must not be prematurely finalized. We need to work with what Cameron (2007a) calls 'principled flexibility'.

For trustworthiness in the grouping procedure, each decision carefully follows a central principle of this kind of interpretive analysis – rigorous assessment of the quality, and limits, of the discourse evidence for that decision. As with metaphor identification, reliability is maximized by discussion with, and cross checks by, colleagues, and project notes that aid consistency. However, although we strive for as much rigour as possible, the process is unavoidably hermeneutic, and its success depends upon imagination and creativity combined with as much trustworthiness as is possible. The vehicle groupings that we construct will inevitably at times have blurred boundaries and a degree of overlap.

Collaborative discussion among analysts allows the grouping decisions to be thoroughly tested, but researchers using this approach should not expect to come up with a set of categories which reliably accommodate every linguistic metaphor they find, since the dynamic nature of talking-and-thinking varies language in multiple and often subtle ways (Barsalou, 1989).

## Grouping the metaphor vehicles from Figure 7.1

In what follows, to give a flavour of the grouping process, we code the metaphor vehicles of Figure 7.1 as if we were researchers beginning this stage of metaphor analysis (see Figure 7.2):

> *thing* was initially selected on the grounds that it concretizes an abstract notion such as a thought. At a later stage there may be sufficient evidence to assign this metaphor to an abstract group such as CONCRETIZE, but for the first pass at grouping, the term provided its own label, THING. Also included in this category were: *something, everything, anything,*

although we excluded *nothing*, since, of all these terms, this one seemed to retain least connection with its *thing* morpheme.

The phrasal verb *comes into* expresses the idea of movement, but also of movement directed towards a contained space. Both of these might be important, so at an early stage, it is grouped as both MOVEMENT and CONTAINER.[2]

*sneaky* may evoke an image of a certain manner of movement, but the direct meaning of the word is more concerned with the act of hiding something, so we assign it to a grouping called CONCEALMENT.

*way,* though highly conventionalized, has a basic meaning of some kind of thoroughfare. Initially it is placed in a grouping, WAY.

*like bullying* is assigned to the grouping PHYSICAL ACTION.

*control*, like *way* and *thing*, is allocated to a grouping designated by the term itself, CONTROL. However, since the meaning of the metaphor vehicle includes an idea of physical restraint, a second possible vehicle group, PHYSICAL ACTION, is recorded for this metaphor.

*not like war* is a negated metaphorical comparison between conventional warfare and the unconventional conflict associated with terrorism. It is thus assigned to the vehicle group MILITARY.[3]

*opposing sides* in its basic meaning concerns adjacent points in physical space, so it goes initially in the group LOCATION.

*invisible* straightforwardly fits into a grouping designated SEEING, although we keep open the possibility of a separate group related to NOT SEEING.

*enemy* again evokes conventional conflict and so is assigned to the group MILITARY.

*from* is another MOVEMENT metaphor vehicle.

*flaw in the system* may suggest natural or artificial organization, but without further evidence, we make a vehicle grouping labelled with the term itself, SYSTEM.

*in the first place* again refers to a LOCATION.

The coded Excel list is updated as in Figure 7.2, with the vehicle groupings now added in columns A and B.

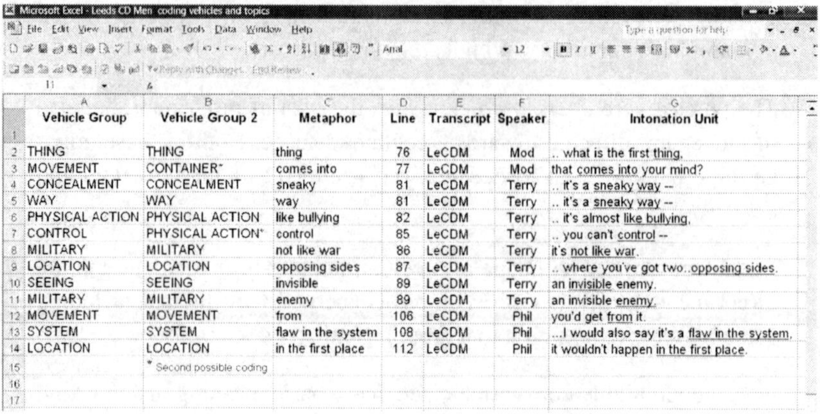

| | Vehicle Group | Vehicle Group 2 | Metaphor | Line | Transcript | Speaker | Intonation Unit |
|---|---|---|---|---|---|---|---|
| 2 | THING | THING | thing | 76 | LeCDM | Mod | .. what is the first thing, |
| 3 | MOVEMENT | CONTAINER* | comes into | 77 | LeCDM | Mod | that comes into your mind? |
| 4 | CONCEALMENT | CONCEALMENT | sneaky | 81 | LeCDM | Terry | .. it's a sneaky way -- |
| 5 | WAY | WAY | way | 81 | LeCDM | Terry | .. it's a sneaky way -- |
| 6 | PHYSICAL ACTION | PHYSICAL ACTION | like bullying | 82 | LeCDM | Terry | .. it's almost like bullying, |
| 7 | CONTROL | PHYSICAL ACTION* | control | 85 | LeCDM | Terry | .. you can't control -- |
| 8 | MILITARY | MILITARY | not like war | 86 | LeCDM | Terry | it's not like war. |
| 9 | LOCATION | LOCATION | opposing sides | 87 | LeCDM | Terry | .. where you've got two..opposing sides. |
| 10 | SEEING | SEEING | invisible | 89 | LeCDM | Terry | an invisible enemy. |
| 11 | MILITARY | MILITARY | enemy | 89 | LeCDM | Terry | an invisible enemy. |
| 12 | MOVEMENT | MOVEMENT | from | 106 | LeCDM | Phil | you'd get from it. |
| 13 | SYSTEM | SYSTEM | flaw in the system | 108 | LeCDM | Phil | ...I would also say it's a flaw in the system, |
| 14 | LOCATION | LOCATION | in the first place | 112 | LeCDM | Phil | it wouldn't happen in the first place. |
| 15 | | * Second possible coding | | | | | |

Figure 7.2. Metaphor vehicles assigned to groupings in Excel

As the grouping proceeds, the groups may be adjusted to better categorize the data. To illustrate the evolution of groupings, Table 7.1 lists the groupings from Figure 7.2 together with further examples from across the dataset. We then discuss the kinds of changes that would be made.

Table 7.1. Metaphor vehicles and their initial groupings

| Vehicle grouping | Metaphor vehicles collected into the grouping |
|---|---|
| *THING* | *thing, things, anything, everything, something, nothing, nowt (Yorkshire dialect – nothing), stuff* |
| *MOVEMENT* | *comes into, from, the end, comes, from behind, go, go away, go by, go for, go off, go up, goes off, going off, gone off, gone on, gone too far, lost the way, running, to a halt, to a standstill, went off, went on, went up, carry on, keep going, make a move, down the line, progressed, sliding, starts from, towards, went through* |
| *CONCEALMENT* | *sneaky, cover-up* |
| *CONTAINER* | *comes into, in, out, out of* |
| *WAY* | *way* |
| *PHYSICAL ACTION* | *like bullying, formed, hold on to, turned, work, flattened, hit, kicking back, hammered, knocking about, breaking, wrecks, a smacked hand, hit back, slapped down, stamping on* |

As we can see from Table 7.1, some groupings build quite quickly while others have just one or very few entries. Once several vehicles are grouped together, we can begin to explore the potential for revising the initial coding to produce a set of groupings that better reflect the data. Metaphors can be reassigned from one vehicle grouping to another, new groupings may need to be created, and existing groupings can be sub-divided or done away with altogether. Again, decisions should be made collaboratively by the research team, and recorded.

Table 7.1 suggests a number of changes that might be made to the initial groupings. First, the vehicle group *MOVEMENT* seems inadequate to accommodate the variety of metaphors it contains. In conceptual metaphor theory, this category is subdivided into the image schematic components SOURCE, PATH and GOAL, based on evidence of these distinctions in commonly used metaphors (Johnson, 1987). This subdivision is useful also for our purposes. *MOVEMENT* metaphor vehicles can be assigned to these new groups as in Table 7.2.

Table 7.2. *MOVEMENT* groupings of metaphor vehicles

| | |
|---|---|
| *MOVEMENT (SOURCE)* | *from, from behind, starts from* |
| *MOVEMENT (PATH)* | *carry on, down the line, go away, go by, go off, go up, goes off, going off, gone off, gone on, gone too far, keep going, lost the way, progressed, went off, went on, went through, went up* |
| *MOVEMENT (GOAL)* | *at the end, comes into, go for, to a halt, to a standstill, towards* |

The following vehicle terms do not contain an element of meaning corresponding to the new groups and so they remain in the more general grouping *MOVEMENT*: *comes, go, make a move, running, sliding*. Although it is a question for later in the analysis, we might already speculate at this stage whether the greater number of *MOVEMENT (PATH)* metaphors is revealing of something significant about participants' ideas, attitudes and values, is merely an artefact of the discourse context, or reflects conventionalizations in broader language usage. Splitting the *MOVEMENT* grouping in this way also allows us to merge the contents of the *WAY* group with *MOVEMENT (PATH)*, as the semantics of the latter match those which motivated *WAY*. One original vehicle grouping thus disappears.

The *PHYSICAL ACTION* group also appears under-refined. It contains metaphors which vary strikingly in the manner of action they depict. We can make a clear distinction between those actions which are neutral, and those which express an element of violence (Table 7.3).

Table 7.3. PHYSICAL ACTION metaphor vehicles subdivided

| PHYSICAL ACTION | *formed, hold on to, turned, work* |
|---|---|
| VIOLENT ACTION | *a smacked hand, breaking, flattened, hammered, hit, hit back, kicking back, knocking about, like bullying, slapped down, stamping on, wrecks* |

Again, the discrepancy in numbers between the two new groups is intriguing and may be noted for investigation at a later stage.

The metaphor *opposing sides* was originally grouped as LOCATION. However, from the rest of the data, an alternative grouping emerges – CONNECT/SEPARATE. This suggests not just location, but the positioning of one entity relative to another and the potential for access between the two. These criteria fit more closely with the semantics of *opposing sides* than those of the more general LOCATION group. The metaphor is thus moved to the new grouping with other vehicles such as: *apart from, connected, connection, hook up, mixed, stuck.*

## Principles applied in grouping vehicles

### Combining rigour and creativity

Throughout the process, researchers have to work with a combination of analytical rigour and creativity, which is not always the easiest balance to maintain. They must ensure the trustworthiness of vehicle group coding by applying the same principles as for metaphor identification, working with an awareness of categories which have emerged in previous work that are tailored by the particular needs of the research in hand. Precedents are borne in mind, but researchers respond to the data as they present themselves, attempting as far as possible to monitor for their subjective reactions to the text. Decisions are collaborative where possible, and these are discussed and recorded, ensuring that there is a 'paper trail' of thought processes from the beginning to the end of the analysis.

### Labelling groupings

In the discourse dynamics framework, systematic metaphors emerge 'upwards' from discourse data and remain connected to the specific discourse events from which data were collected. Therefore, we do not want to generalize the labels that we assign to vehicle groupings to too high a level. A label at too high a level may suggest entailments and implications that are not warranted from the data. What then counts as the 'right' level of generalization for labelling groupings? A guiding principle is that the label should cover all the vehicles included in the set and, as far as possible, only those. If the MILITARY metaphor vehicles, for example, had only included instances of *target*, we would not have been warranted to use a label of *MILITARY* or *WAR*, but only *TARGET*. The importance of restricting the level of generality of labels is illustrated by the vehicle grouping found to be important in the reconciliation data described in Chapter 1. Here, the large grouping *SEEING* included a smaller grouping *CHANGING A DISTORTED IMAGE OF THE OTHER* which became an important way in which participants talked about the outcomes of reconciliation.

A cognitive linguistic approach, while describing the process differently, has a parallel problem. If conceptual metaphors are assumed to pre-exist their use in discourse, then analysts describe their task, not as 'vehicle grouping', but as 'assigning linguistic metaphors to conceptual metaphors' (Deignan, Chapter 3, this volume). Their problem lies in choosing a conceptual metaphor label of appropriate level of generality without unwarranted entailments (Ritchie, Chapter 4, this volume; Semino *et al.*, 2004; Vervaeke and Kennedy, 1996).

Vehicle grouping designations – and changes to them – are applied throughout the data once they are made, so that similar items are not coded differently at different points. This is a particular challenge with large volumes of data (see Chapter 10).

## Using vehicle groupings from other studies

An alternative to starting from scratch in grouping metaphor vehicles in discourse data is to use groupings from other studies, such as those described in Chapters 1 and 2. The risk with doing this is that the 'shape' of the discourse data will be flattened or lost by using categories designed for other discourse events and contexts. If this risk is guarded against, then the time-saving benefits may well make it worthwhile. The advice would be that if a grouping doesn't feel like a good fit to the data, it shouldn't be used.

Even when groupings from other studies are used as a starting point, some new metaphor vehicles are likely to be found that may require groupings to be adjusted. For example, within the Perception and Communication of Terrorist Risk project, the fifth focus group analysis produced *BUILDING* metaphor vehicles that had not been found in the first four.

## Building vehicle groupings: the Blair speech

Figure 7.3 shows the groupings of metaphor vehicles from the Blair speech extract that was used in Figure 6.2.

Again, vehicle grouping labels reflect as far as possible the semantics of the basic meanings of the metaphor vehicle terms. It is somewhat easier to label the vehicle groupings in the Blair data since the text has been deliberately crafted around a small number of figurative themes and most of the selected metaphors contribute to these.

| | A | B | C | D |
|---|---|---|---|---|
| 1 | Text | Line | Metaphor | Vehicle group |
| 2 | I'm back | 30 | back | DIRECTION |
| 3 | it feels good | 31 | feels | FEEL |
| 4 | back in the north east | 32 | in | CONTAINER |
| 5 | who gave me the chance | 34 | gave | GIVE/TAKE |
| 6 | have given me strength and support | 36 | given | GIVE/TAKE |
| 7 | have given me strength and support | 36 | strength | STRENGTH |
| 8 | have given me strength and support | 36 | support | STRENGTH |
| 9 | that has given me | 39 | given | GIVE/TAKE |
| 10 | the honour of leadership | 40 | leadership | DIRECTION |
| 11 | Back with a relentless focus | 44 | focus | SEEING |
| 12 | on the job of delivering better lives | 45 | job | JOB |
| 13 | on the job of delivering better lives | 45 | delivering | GIVE/TAKE |
| 14 | for Britain's hard working families, | 46 | hard | HARD |
| 15 | In this second term | 49 | In | CONTAINER |
| 16 | taken me far from home | 52 | taken | GIVE/TAKE |
| 17 | the top line of my job spec | 55 | top line of my job spec | JOB |
| 18 | they are the boss | 58 | boss | JOB |
| 19 | it is good to be back | 65 | back | DIRECTION |
| 20 | in a fight with the Tories | 66 | in | CONTAINER |
| 21 | in a fight with the Tories | 66 | a fight | FIGHT |
| 22 | this is a fight | 68 | fight | FIGHT |
| 23 | a fight for the future of the country | 69 | fight | FIGHT |
| 24 | a fight that for Britain | 70 | fight | FIGHT |
| 25 | we have to win | 72 | win | FIGHT |
| 26 | The polls can tell one story | 73 | tell one story | STORY |
| 27 | the story that counts | 74 | the story | STORY |
| 28 | the story that counts | 74 | counts | NUMBER |
| 29 | is the one unfolding | 75 | unfolding | STORY |
| 30 | in the minds of millions of people | 76 | in | CONTAINER |
| 31 | as they face up to | 78 | face up to | BODY |
| 32 | facing the country | 80 | facing | BODY |
| 33 | forward or back | 81 | forward | DIRECTION |
| 34 | forward or back | 81 | back | DIRECTION |

Figure 7.3. Metaphor vehicle groupings for extract from the Blair speech

## From vehicle groupings to systematic metaphors

Once all the linguistic metaphor vehicles have been coded, a final check is made of the groupings. In keeping with the 'principled flexibility' that has informed the process throughout, it is quite possible for a category introduced at a late stage in the process to influence a change in coding for items that have been there since the start. This flexibility ensures that the vehicle groups are as trustworthy a resource as possible for the next stage of the analysis, finding systematicity in metaphor use.

A 'systematic metaphor' is a set of linguistic metaphors in which connected vehicle words or phrases are used metaphorically about a particular topic. Up to this point, we have been working with the vehicle terms of metaphors because these are what appear in the discourse as incongruous or anomalous in some way. A metaphor, though, is usually seen as having two parts to it, the vehicle and the topic, which are syntactically combined in the traditional formulations of metaphor: a conceptual metaphor is presented as a combination of target and source domain, as in UNDERSTANDING IS SEEING, and a prototypical metaphor in language is usually given a copular form, with the vehicle connected to the topic by the verb *to be,* as in *no man is an island* (John Donne). The topic or target of the metaphor is what it is about, the contextual meaning: in the above examples, the conceptual topic domain described as SEEING would be UNDER-STANDING, and the linguistic topic described as *an island* would be *person/man.* The next step is to identify topics to go with the metaphor vehicles.

## Identifying the topics of metaphors

Sometimes the topic of a metaphor is clear; it is explicitly expressed in the discourse, as in the examples above, either in close proximity to the metaphor vehicle or elsewhere, and is thus easily recoverable by the analyst. However, this tends not to be the case for most metaphor topics, particularly in spoken discourse (Cameron, 2007a), where the metaphor may enter the flow of discourse without being explicitly assigned to a topic (Kittay, 1987). A topic may also not be made explicit if the metaphorical way of talking about it has become so conventionalized that it is almost the *only* way to talk about it, and in some cases there may be no other way of talking about a topic than metaphorically. As a result, finding metaphor topics in discourse may be quite a problematic task.

The elusive nature of many metaphor topics is often a consequence of the dynamic nature of discourse interaction. A group discussion does not operate like a cognitive tennis match, with neat packages of information passing back and forth to be decoded deterministically. Themes develop throughout the inter-action; contributing to or making sense of what is said requires participants to refine constantly the conceptualizations and multiple layers of meaning which constitute their understandings. Added to this is the problem of presumed shared knowledge, which means that some metaphor topics are considered 'given' without the need for definite reference. These characteristics are part of the nature of communication, and contribute to our ability not just to exchange information, but to engage in richly nuanced, empathetic interaction. They often also make it difficult to decide on an unequivocal topic label to go with each metaphor vehicle.

Researchers have to decide on a reasonable level of granularity for topic labels. This decision may well be driven by the volume of data. Since establishing fine grained topics often involves detailed reading of the data, a large degree of inference and a considerable investment of time, this may sometimes not be a viable approach with large datasets.

One possible technique for rationalizing the process is the use of a refined set of topics related to a project's particular research questions. This approach was taken in the Perception and Communication of Terrorist Risk study. The aims of the project were to establish people's perceptions of the risk of terrorism and explore issues relating to the communication of the risk. With this in mind, the following broad topic categories, called 'key discourse topics', were established:

1.  terrorism, including acts, risk, causes, perpetrators;
2.  communication, by the authorities (2A) and by the media (2N);
3.  responses to terrorism, including responses by the authorities (3A) and responses by, or particularly likely to affect, Muslims (3M);
4.  society and social groups, including Muslims (4M); and
5.  topics outside the project's main areas of interest, including the focus group discourse itself.

Rationalizing the topics in this way allowed researchers to decide from the surrounding discourse what was being talked about, rather than define a specific topic for each individual metaphor. It is necessary to do this with close reference to the source transcript, as apparent topical relationships between entries in a list of selected metaphors can mask changes that take place in the flow of intervening dialogue (see Chapter 10). Given that caveat, and keeping an eye out for subtler distinctions which can subdivide systematic mappings in interesting and important ways, this type of topic coding can speed up the process considerably.

## The emergence of systematic metaphors

Once topic codes are assigned to the metaphor vehicles, all the necessary information is in place to begin a search for systematic metaphors. Preliminary insights and hunches which may have come to the researcher while working with the data up to this point can now be investigated more rigorously. The process involves a further sorting of the coded data. Within each vehicle grouping, all the linguistic metaphors that relate to a particular topic are collected together into a set. This set of related linguistic metaphors is what we call a 'systematic metaphor'. A systematic metaphor is a construct of the researcher, not necessarily of the participants, created to help condense the discourse data, and to summarize metaphorical ways of expressing ideas, attitudes and values.

Since the set of related metaphors were used at different times in the discourse event, or at different points in a written text, a systematic metaphor can also be seen as a 'metaphor trajectory', using the discourse dynamics terminology introduced in Chapter 5. Systematic metaphors or metaphor trajectories are to be distinguished in significant ways from conceptual metaphor. Whereas conceptual metaphor theory (Chapter 3) claims cognitive reality for conceptual metaphors, i.e. that people make active use of conceptual metaphors and turn them into linguistic metaphors as they speak or write, the discourse dynamics approach does not claim that systematic metaphors necessarily exist for individual discourse participants, only that they may do so. Whereas conceptual metaphor theory is concerned to generalize conceptual metaphors to the highest level possible in order to make statements about universals in human cognitive processing, finding systematic metaphors in discourse data aims to contribute to understanding what specific people do when engaging in specific discourse events.[4]

Constructing systematic metaphors by collecting together all the linguistic metaphors related to a particular topic within each vehicle grouping can be assisted by computer software, such as Excel, with a capacity for multivariate data sorting. However, the importance of a particular systematic metaphor must be judged by the analyst. Sometimes there may only be a couple of related linguistic metaphors in a set, and at other times there may be quite a number. The size of the set does not automatically relate to its importance, since a small set may include really powerful metaphors and a large set may collect together conventionalized and not very relevant metaphors. What matters is the discourse function of the metaphors connected together in a systematic metaphor. In the next chapter, we show how discourse function can be analysed. Alongside the contribution of the metaphor to the unfolding discourse event, we may also want to ask further questions about systematic metaphors in order to decide on their importance and relevance, and how to label them:

- Which participants used these metaphors? All of them? Or only particular individuals?
- Do all participants use the metaphors in the same way? Or do some disagree or resist the metaphors?
- Do the metaphors singly or in combination carry evaluation or attitude? e.g. Are they positive or negative? Are they highly emphatic?
- What is the nature of the metaphor trajectory? Did the metaphors all occur at a particular point in the discourse or are they scattered about?
- How do the connected linguistic metaphors change with different uses?

The answers to questions like these, together with consideration of the systematic metaphors in relation to the research questions of a particular project, will contribute to the analyst's decision about the significance of the systematic metaphors.

The process of finding systematic metaphors from the coded data involves imagination and creativity alongside carefulness and rigour. It is at this point that the metaphor analyst bears the greatest responsibility to the research process. It is all too easy to over-interpret the data, to give too much importance to metaphorical patterns or to select descriptive labels that are more vivid than the data warrants. Chapter 12 returns to this point in emphasizing good practice.

## Systematic metaphors in the focus group data

In this section, we present some of the systematic metaphors which emerged from analysis of this one focus group discussion. These were later compared with systematic metaphors produced by other focus groups.

### Systematic GAME metaphors

A set of metaphors relating to games and playing were used with direct reference to the topic of terrorism, as in Figure 7.4.

In contrast to the finding from the overall data which was cited at the start of the chapter and characterized terrorism in terms of *A GAME OF CHANCE*, the Leeds CD Men focus group spoke of games with rules, but rules which were unclear or being broken by the terrorists. This is perhaps best expressed through two

| | A | B | C | D | E |
|---|---|---|---|---|---|
| | Topic | Metaphor | Line | Speaker | Intonation Unit |
| 1 | | | | | |
| 2 | 1 | kicking off | 1329 | Phil | they're all kicking off now, |
| 3 | 1 | level playing field | 1087 | xx | [] it's not a level playing field |
| 4 | 1 | pawns in a game | 3276 | Terry | .. pawns in a game, |
| 5 | 1 | team | 1201 | Terry | .. this is our team, |
| 6 | 1 | team | 1202 | Terry | .. that's your team, |
| 7 | 1 | teams | 1211 | Finn | who's to draw up the teams? |
| 8 | 1 | who's on which | 1215 | Finn | who's on which team? |
| 9 | | | | | |
| 10 | | | | | |
| 11 | | | | | |
| 12 | | | | | |

Figure 7.4. Examples of metaphors contributing to the GAME systematic metaphor

connected systematic metaphors: *VIOLENT CONFLICT IS A GAME WITH RULES* and *TERRORISTS BREAK THE RULES.*

The multiple coding of each linguistic metaphor, and the sorting carried out by the software, shows the researcher at a glance both how many linguistic metaphors were used and who by. Claims of patterns in the data can be made very precisely – we are able to say whether a systematic metaphor was used across the group or just by certain members of the group. The inclusion of a metaphor's full intonation unit, as immediate discourse context, usually reminds us whether the use of a metaphor was in response to someone else's prior use or initiated by the speaker. The line numbers indicate whereabouts in the dynamics of the discourse the metaphors were used, with several numbers close together indicating a cluster of similar metaphors. (Chapter 10 gives more detail about metaphor clusters.) Further information about the metaphor dynamics comes from noticing repetitions or very similar formulations of linguistic metaphors at different points in the discourse event. So Figure 7.4 shows that the *TEAM* metaphor was used by Terry in a two-part formulation contrasting the two parties in military action as *our team* and *your team*, and then picked up by Finn and elaborated as he disagrees with Terry by questioning who would choose the *teams*. All this information about the discourse dynamics of the metaphors is packed up into the systematic metaphor, and can be readily unpacked to interpret findings.

## Systematic metaphors of *VIOLENT PHYSICAL ACTION*

The systematic metaphor *TERRORISM IS VIOLENT PHYSICAL ACTION* is built up from a number of more specific topic-vehicle mappings, as in Figure 7.5.

| | A | B | C | D | E | F | G |
|---|---|---|---|---|---|---|---|
| | Topic | Metaphor | Line | Speaker | Intonation Unit | | |
| 2 | 1 | bullying | 152 | Ray | it's a form of bullying, | | |
| 3 | 1 | hit and run | 124 | Eddie | .. hit and run, | | |
| 4 | 1 | hit and run | 1193 | Terry | .. it's hit and run, | | |
| 5 | 1 | kicking back | 1336 | Phil | and that's why they're kicking back. | | |
| 6 | 1 | kicks | 166 | Reece | .. and they get kicks out of it. | | |
| 7 | 1 | killing | 4962 | Terry | it is killing me. | | |
| 8 | 1 | like bullying | 82 | Terry | .. it's almost like bullying. | | |
| 9 | 1 | shook up | 763 | Josh | well it shook the whole world up. | | |

Figure 7.5. Linguistic metaphors contributing to the systematic metaphor *TERRORISM IS VIOLENT PHYSICAL ACTION*

While an act of terrorism is by definition a violent act, committed by the terrorist(s), the words and phrases in the table in Figure 7.5 metaphorize terrorist violence in terms of violent interpersonal contact. These metaphors all have an element of interpersonal intimacy which is absent in terrorist acts such as bombings or shootings.

*VIOLENT PHYSICAL ACTION* metaphors are not just used to talk about terrorism, however. Metaphors from this group are also produced when people talk about their own and society's responses to the threat of terrorism, foregrounding another facet of the topic. The systematic metaphors form a larger network of metaphors using *VIOLENT PHYSICAL ACTION* vehicle terms. The response of the UK public to the terror threat is talked about as *VIOLENT PHYSICAL ACTION* in a small set of metaphors, including *hits* as in Extract 7.1:

Extract 7.1

| Josh | ... if it's a distance away, |
| | I don't think it is -- |
| | <u>hits</u> you as much, |
| | as what it would be, |
| | if it's on your doorstep. |

There are ten instances when government responses to terrorism are spoken of in terms of *VIOLENT PHYSICAL ACTION*, Table 7.6:

| | A | B | C | D | E | F |
|---|---|---|---|---|---|---|
| | **Topic** | **Metaphor** | **Line** | **Speaker** | **Intonation Unit** | |
| 2 | 3A | a smacked | 3850 | Eddie | is <u>a smacked</u> hand. | |
| 3 | 3A | banged up | 3873 | Phil | ... to get <u>banged up</u>. | |
| 4 | 3A | hit back | 136 | Eddie | .. so there's no <u>way</u> you can <u>hit back</u>. | |
| 5 | 3A | kick | 2618 | Finn | <u>kick</u> 'em all <u>out</u>. | |
| 6 | 3A | kick | 2625 | Finn | why <u>kick</u> 'em all <u>out</u>, | |
| 7 | 3A | kick | 2636 | Terry | <u>kick</u> 'em all <u>out</u>. | |
| 8 | 3A | kicking | 2605 | Eddie | or <u>kicking</u> people <u>out</u>. | |
| 9 | 3A | kicking | 2610 | Finn | or <u>kicking</u> people, | |
| 10 | 3A | slapping down | 5396 | Eddie | they need <u>slapping down</u>. | |
| 11 | 3A | stamping on | 1514 | Josh | .. and .. they're <u>stamping on</u> it, | |

Figure 7.6. Government responses to terrorism as violent physical action

## Systematic metaphors of the SOCIAL LANDSCAPE

The *VIOLENT PHYSICAL ACTION* metaphors examined above employ interpersonal and visceral metaphor vehicles as central to the way they work, and tap into memories of contact and pain. In contrast, the spatial metaphors in the data, while also relying on physical experience, evoke a sense of location or movement through space and over surfaces.

Metaphors in the focus group discussion represent social differences as physical separation in space, through a set of what we call *SOCIAL LANDSCAPE* metaphors. Social group differences may be religious, socio-economic or cultural; whatever the differences, they metaphorically create spaces and distance between groups, as in Figure 7.7. *SOCIAL LANDSCAPE* metaphors include *GROUPS WHO THINK DIFFERENTLY ARE PHYSICALLY SEPARATED* and *POLITICAL / PHILOSOPHICAL / RELIGIOUS BELIEFS ARE PHYSICALLY LOCATED.*

## Systematic metaphors about TERRORISM AS MOVEMENT

Spatial metaphors are not only static. *MOVEMENT* metaphors are widely used to talk about a number of topics and when they apply to terrorism, they produce a systematic metaphor and personification in which *TERRORISM MOVES SNEAKILY THROUGH THE SOCIAL LANDSCAPE TO A GOAL OF MAXIMUM DESTRUCTION.*

*TERRORISM* is seen as having *started from somewhere* (*behind*, where it cannot be seen) (i.e. its *SOURCE*); it progresses in *a sneaky way*, *through* the churches which help it and *through* the *system* which is supposed to prevent it (i.e. its *PATH*), in order to create the greatest possible destruction (its *GOAL*). Examples are shown in Figure 7.8.

| | A | B | C | D | E | F |
|---|---|---|---|---|---|---|
| 1 | Topic | Metaphor | Line | Speaker | Intonation Unit | |
| 2 | 1 | opposing side: | 87 | Terry | .. where you've got two .. opposing sides. | |
| 3 | 3A | against | 4232 | Eddie | .. it's against human rights, | |
| 4 | 1 | around | 179 | Josh | .. it's all around you. | |
| 5 | 1 | behind | 218 | Finn | there's something behind it, | |
| 6 | 1 | behind | 241 | Finn | .. some sort of justification behind it. | |
| 7 | 1 | somewhere | 1834 | Phil | .. it starts from somewhere, | |
| 8 | | | | | | |
| 9 | | | | | | |

Figure 7.7. Examples of *SOCIAL LANDSCAPE* metaphors

| Topic | Metaphor | Line | Speaker | Intonation Unit |
|---|---|---|---|---|
| 1 | came from | 1024 | Josh | came from Leeds. |
| 1 | come from | 369 | Finn | where they come from? |
| 1 | directed at | 406 | Finn | it wasn't directed at us. |
| 1 | from behind | 130 | Eddie | .. attack you from behind. |
| 1 | get across | 215 | Finn | it's just someone trying to get a point across. |
| 1 | get through | 2950 | Josh | .. but somebody's going to get through. |
| 1 | get through | 2954 | Josh | .. they're going to get through. |
| 1 | go for | 731 | Finn | .. they do go for. |
| 1 | go for | 715 | Josh | they go for the -- |
| 1 | go for | 716 | Josh | they go for the most destruction, |
| 1 | in a way | 53 | Owen | .. (2.5) lot of people hurt in a nasty way. |
| 1 | in another way | 1439 | Phil | .. in another way. |
| 1 | in ways | 3150 | Phil | in their ways. |
| 1 | start up | 3602 | Phil | .. and want to start hisself up? |
| 1 | started from | 232 | Finn | .. it all started from somewhere. |
| 1 | starts from | 1829 | Phil | [] this is where terrorism starts from. |
| 1 | starts from | 1834 | Phil | .. it starts from somewhere. |
| 1 | through | 1527 | Terry | [] X through the system. |
| 1 | through | 3297 | Owen | .. X done through' IRA, |
| 1 | through | 3191 | Phil | it's all done through' churches. |
| 1 | way | 121 | Eddie | .. sneaky way of doing it, |
| 1 | way | 191 | Josh | .. they want their own way. |
| 1 | way | 81 | Terry | .. it's a sneaky way -- |

Figure 7.8. *TERRORISM MOVES SNEAKILY THROUGH THE SOCIAL LANDSCAPE TO A GOAL OF MAXIMUM DESTRUCTION*

There is an interesting parallel with MOVEMENT metaphors in the Blair speech here, in which phrases such as *we go forward with Labour or back to the Tories* built the very clear (and deliberate) systematic metaphor: *VOTING LABOUR IS GOING FORWARDS AND VOTING TORY IS GOING BACKWARDS*. These MOVEMENT metaphors draw on the affective quality of the spatial terms, in which words like *forwards* and *up* tend to have positive associations, while *backwards* and *down* have negative ones (Lakoff and Johnson, 1980; Gibbs, 2006a; Ritchie, Chapter 4).

## Systematic metaphors of UNDERSTANDING AS SEEING

Highly conventionalized linguistic metaphors that fall into highly conventionalized patterns of use represent the point where systematic metaphors come closest to conceptual metaphors (although their theoretical underpinnings remain very different). For example, one of the most extensive metaphor vehicle groupings in the focus group data is SEEING. Metaphors of sight are highly frequent and conventionalized in English (as in other languages). Figure 7.9 gives some examples.

| | A | B | C | D | E |
|---|---|---|---|---|---|
| | Topic | Metaphor | Line | Speaker | Intonation Unit |
| 2 | 1 | invisible | 89 | Terry | an invisible enemy. |
| 3 | 1 | see | 1100 | Finn | .. they don't see it like that. |
| 4 | 1 | see | 1116 | Finn | .. that's what they see it as. |
| 5 | 1 | see | 1150 | Finn | .. like terrorists do see it as a war. |
| 6 | 1 | see | 1833 | Phil | you can see, |
| 7 | 1 | see | 5021 | Ray | I can see it now. |
| 8 | 1 | seeing | 1075 | Finn | they're seeing it as a war. |
| 9 | 2 | point of view | 4642 | Phil | … my point of view is, |
| 10 | 3 | see | 51 | Owen | that's the way I see it. |
| 11 | 3 | see | 5271 | Ray | I can see something, |
| 12 | 3 | seen | 958 | Finn | have seen it. |
| 13 | 4 | see | 4544 | Finn | .. no one's going to see, |
| 14 | 4 | see | 4439 | Phil | might see things different, |
| 15 | 4 | views | 2730 | Finn | [] at least they challenge the views, |
| 16 | 4 | views | 4536 | Finn | .. identically the same views, |

Figure 7.9. SEEING metaphors in the focus group data

When topics are put together within the *SEEING* vehicle group, patterns begin to emerge, and what is clear first of all is that all these examples refer to thinking or understanding in some way. The systematic connection between vehicle and topic can be expressed as UNDERSTANDING IS SEEING, in parallel with the conceptual metaphor. While the conceptual metaphor may or may not exist as a mental structure, when researching metaphor use in particular discourse events by specific people, what is of interest is the finer grained, more specific, systematic metaphorical patterns. Close examination of the discourse evidence requires, for example, taking account of the grammatical subject of the metaphorical *SEEING*, and suggests subtler patterns more specifically relevant to the aims of the terrorist risk research. For instance, linguistic metaphors such as those in Figure 7.9 suggest a systematic metaphor TERRORISTS' BELIEFS AS SEEING.

A total of eight metaphors in the focus group discussion use the verb *see* in the same way, with all but one are produced by one speaker, Finn. The evidence thus warrants the claim that this speaker uses the metaphor systematically, but not that the rest of the group necessarily does.

## Systematic metaphors as a starting point for further investigation

The examples given here are drawn from a single focus group and are far from being an exhaustive list of the systematic topic~vehicle connections in that sample of data. Intriguing patterns of relations emerge from this subset which might lead us to pursue particular connections or extrapolate to broader themes. The systematic use of *VIOLENT PHYSICAL ACTION* metaphors for the action of the UK authorities is one case in point. How do participants in other groups, with different demographic profiles, speak about the same topic?

In fact, comparing the sample transcript with the full dataset of 12 groups reveals some stark differences. Most striking of all is the use of *VIOLENT PHYSI-CAL ACTION* metaphors by Muslim focus groups. While Muslim groups, like the other groups, used these *VIOLENT PHYSICAL ACTION* metaphors to talk about the actions of terrorists and the responses of the authorities, they also used them to talk about the effects on British Muslims of societal and official responses to terrorism, creating a systematic metaphor *A RESPONSE TO TERRORISM IS VIOLENT PHYSICAL ACTION TOWARDS MUSLIM GROUPS* emerges from data such as those in Figure 7.10.

The impression that Muslims present different metaphors in their talk about terrorism is strengthened by analysis of *LABELLING* metaphors, which were almost exclusively produced by Muslim participants in the research and mostly negative (Figure 7.11).

These linguistic metaphors contributed to the systematic metaphor *A RESPONSE TO TERRORISM IS NEGATIVE LABELLING OF MUSLIMS.*

This is one example of how a systematic metaphor which emerges in analysis can start a thread of investigation and further analysis, in turn revealing further systematic metaphors with implications for research aims.

**Microsoft Excel - Leeds CD Men  coding vehicles and topics**

File  Edit  View  Insert  Format  Tools  Data  Window  Help

| | A | B | C | D | E | F | G |
|---|---|---|---|---|---|---|---|
| 1 | Topic | Group | Metaphor | Line | Speaker | Intonation Unit | |
| 2 | 4 | LeMM | breakdown | 1218 | Rashid | community breakdown, | |
| 3 | 3M | LeMW | thrown | 1542 | Dina | (official response is) thrown at us. | |
| 4 | 3A | LoMM | squashed | 3127 | Farid | the human rights have been squashed, | |
| 5 | 3M | LoMM | backlash | 677 | Farid | and .. the backlash .. is another-- | |
| 6 | 3M | LoMM | backlash | 678 | Farid | we feel more the backlash. | |
| 7 | 3M | LoMM | backlash | 943 | Sarfraz | but because of the backlash as well. | |
| 8 | 3M | LoMM | backlash | 3414 | Farid | the violence of the backlash of terrorism, | |
| 9 | 3M | LoMM | impact | 986 | Sarfraz | what sort of any impact, | |
| 10 | | | | | | | |
| 11 | | | | | | | |
| 12 | | | | | | | |

Figure 7.10. *A RESPONSE TO TERRORISM IS VIOLENT PHYSICAL ACTION TOWARDS MUSLIM GROUPS*

| | A | B | C | D | E | F |
|---|---|---|---|---|---|---|
| | Topic | Group | Metaphor | Line | Speaker | Intonation Unit |
| 2 | 2 | LeMM | label | 87 | Rashid | or at least the label of terrorism, |
| 3 | 2 | LeMM | label | 132 | Nuri | that's a .. label, |
| 4 | 2 | LeMM | labelled | 156 | Nuri | then you might be labelled a terrorist. |
| 5 | 2 | LeMM | labelling | 189 | Nuri | labelling question. |
| 6 | 1 | LeMW | bad name | 601 | Haifa | a very bad name. |
| 7 | 3 | LeMW | label | 1479 | Haifa | they'll just label all of us. |
| 8 | 3 | LeMW | labelling | 2795 | Haifa | everybody is labelling -- |
| 9 | 4M | LoCDM | brand | 1998 | Ben | .. so you can't .. brand .. one lot bad, |
| 10 | 3A | LoMM | on the list | 3291 | Farid | the asylum seeker is on the list. |
| 11 | 3M | LoMM | labelled | 471 | Farid | they are being labelled as terrorists. |
| 12 | 3M | LoMM | labelling | 116 | Farid | ..an awful lot of labelling, |
| 13 | 4M | LoMM | a good name | 2082 | Aasif | if you want a good name for yourself |
| 14 | 3M | LoMW | brand | 1218 | Yasmina | I do brand people SQ>, |
| 15 | 3M | LoMW | branded | 1445 | RMk | about how Muslims have got branded. |
| 16 | 3M | LoMW | labelled | 2743 | Farah | and 99% .. Muslims are labelled as terrorists, |
| 17 | 3M | LoMW | name | 181 | Daania | .. we get a bad name again <@>, |
| 18 | 4M | LoMW | branded | 577 | Yasmina | ...(6.0) just the fact that you're branded. |
| 19 | 4M | LoMW | trademark | 635 | Aalia | ..it's like a trademark, |
| 20 | 4M | LoMW | trademark | 650 | Aalia | just because you have got .. trademark, |

Figure 7.12. LABELLING metaphors in the focus group discussion

## Types of systematicity

Systematicity of metaphor use can operate in a number of ways. We conclude the chapter by considering two important kinds of systematicity: metaphor framing and metaphor narratives.

### Metaphor framing

Metaphors like A RESPONSE TO TERRORISM IS NEGATIVE LABELLING OF MUSLIMS emerge from the metaphor analysis as ways of 'framing' the ideas, attitudes and values of discourse participants. Because we know exactly who used the related linguistic metaphors and in what discourse context, we can make quite precise claims: for the Muslim participants, women and men, in the focus group discussions NEGATIVE LABELLING emerged as a way of framing responses to terrorism in the UK, by the authorities and by non-Muslims in society. Participants may bring their existing frames into a discourse event, and/or they may adapt and change their framings as the discourse proceeds (Markova et al., 2007). Large scale and corpus studies can make larger, but less precise, claims about framing metaphors across the speech community.

Within conceptual metaphor theory, conceptual metaphors are claimed to act as overarching frames which inform and influence discourse. Chilton (1996), for example, explored the significance of the CONTAINMENT metaphor in shaping American policy towards the Soviet Union during the Cold War through analysis of political discourse. In recent US elections, Lakoff (1996) has argued that national political discourse in the United States is framed by certain key metaphors, or metaphorical cognitive models, claiming, that changes in metaphors can drive changes in the sociopolitical landscape.

Claims about metaphor framing need to avoid the danger of over-generalization, beyond what is warranted by empirical data. In an empirical study of a corpus of political discourse, Cienki (2005a) tested Lakoff's hypothesis that two metaphorical cognitive models serve to frame morality in the US political system. He found only a small number of linguistic metaphors used in presidential debates that could be said to reflect the hypothesized conceptual metaphors. More evidence for the cognitive models was actually found in non-metaphorical language, reminding us that a metaphor analysis starts with metaphor but does not stop there. One of Cienki's conclusions is that large, overarching, cognitive metaphorical models are more likely to be found in collections or corpora of texts from multiple discourse events than in data from specific discourse events, i.e. to be evidenced across social groups rather than for individuals.

## Metaphor scenarios and metaphorical stories[6]

Another type of metaphor systematicity is narrative – metaphors work together to create a sequence of linked events. As with metaphor framing, narrative systematicity can be seen as operating either cognitively across sociocultural groups or more locally in the dynamics of specific discourse events. The cognitive version of metaphorical narrative systematicity, the 'metaphor scenario', like overarching conceptual metaphor frames, often works at the level of sociocultural groups rather than specific discourse events (Musolff, 2004).[6] However, when describing actual narratives in a particular stretch of discourse, we find we need to add a slightly different type of description, which we shall call a 'metaphorical story'. We begin by describing scenarios.

Musolff characterizes a scenario as follows:

> a set of assumptions made by competent members of the discourse community about 'typical' aspects of source-situation, for example, its participants and their roles, the 'dramatic' storylines and outcomes, and conventional evaluations of whether they count as successful or unsuccessful, normal or abnormal, permissible or illegitimate, etc. These source-based assumptions are mapped … onto the respective target concepts.

(Scenarios) not only present action-schematic accounts of (e.g.) *MARRIAGE, BIRTH* etc., derived from the source domain, but...they include narrative-normative assumptions about the possible success of (e.g.) *extramarital flirts* (in a political 'couple'). (Musolff, 2006: 28)

Scenarios enable the speaker to not only apply source to target concepts, but to draw on them to build narrative frames for the conceptualization and assessment of (e.g.) socio-political issues. (Musolff, 2006: 36)

A metaphor scenario can thus be thought of, for present purposes, as the combination of some sort of event with a set of conventional expectations, attitudes and evaluations. The event can, again according to Musolff (2006), be relatively large scale, with several component activities (LOVE–MARRIAGE), or small scale, comprising fewer activities (SEPARATION). Listeners or readers, it is claimed, draw on scenarios to help them rapidly connect and interpret sections of discourse; they speed up the work of inferring connections and overtones, and of applying these to the topic.

In his comprehensive longitudinal studies of how Europe and the EU are treated by the European press, Musolff has found that writers repeatedly develop, extend and refer intertextually to, metaphor scenarios (Musolff, 2000, 2004, 2006). These metaphorical narratives are worded in terms of a specific vehicle grouping and operate in the source domain. One of Musolff's scenarios involves the mapping of MARRIAGE and PARENTHOOD scenarios on to the development of the European Union: countries get engaged to, marry, flirt with, get into bed with, fall out of love with, and even divorce each other. One journalist even noted that if France and Germany were a couple, Tony Blair (standing for the UK) had to be the lover/mistress. Few further details were given, but the conventional MARRIAGE scenario, with the couple at its centre, allows the reader to rapidly draw the conclusion that being a mistress may flag desirability and panache, but more importantly it flags lower status and influence on the family unit – in this case the EU (Musolff, 2006: 28).

Scenarios do not, however, exhaust the narrative potential of metaphor in discourse. Speakers can create narratives explicitly within specific discourse events. At a general level, these have been treated by conversation analysts under labels such as 'stories in conversation'. Our interest here is purely in stories involving metaphors. The point about a 'metaphorical story' is that it recounts (rather than assumes), normally within a single text or discourse event, actions involving one or more participants in settings. The story teller may recount the whole story in one go, or it may emerge progressively as the discourse proceeds. Indeed a story could be negotiated by two or more speakers.

Stories and scenarios may interact, in that stories may allude to conventional metaphor scenarios; however, there is no necessity for them to do so. The Tony

Blair speech contains a good example of a single speaker metaphorical story (Extract 7.2).

Extract 7.2

> all of a sudden there you are, the British people ... And before you know it you raise your voice. I raise mine. Some of you throw a bit of crockery. And now you, the British people, have to sit down and decide. (paragraphs 37-38)

In this case, the metaphor involves public unhappiness with politics being seen as a domestic argument. The metaphorical story has two explicit participants, *the British people* and Blair as sparring partners, engaging in at least three sequential actions, shouting, shouting back, and *throwing crockery*, followed by a possible outcome, *sitting down* (implying calming down) and *deciding* whether to stay or go. The teller, Blair, adds formal storytelling devices throughout (like time markers and present tense), with start and end markers, to emphasize that this is indeed a short (metaphoric) story. *Throwing crockery* can also be seen, from its use in other texts, to involve reference to an inferrable metaphoric argument scenario involving a husband and wife (treated in detail in Chapter 9).

Further examples of metaphorical stories can be found in a university lecture on Corporate Strategy, analysed in Low *et al.* (2008).[5] The recurrence of *fighting* throughout the lecture suggests the systematic metaphor BUSINESS COMPETITION IS FIGHTING. This is elaborated to cover: (1) a battle between Greenpeace and Shell; (2) changing the business model within a company; and (3) price wars between companies, the latter being treated as: (a) bare knuckle fighting; (b) a swearing match; and (c) kamikaze pilots. The simplest stories involve an explicit metaphor being extended or elaborated in the same turn by the same speaker via a single clause or phrase, in a way that suggests the progression of an event. Extract 7.3 shows the shortest of metaphorical stories as the lecturer evaluates a short, exaggerated narrative of a price war.

Extract 7.3

3274     Lect: I mean it is completely shooting yourself in both
         feet
3275     and then trying to run a hundred yards (.)

The metaphorical idiom *shoot(ing) yourself in the foot* conventionally involves a person, a gun, a typical action of an incompetent person, and a result, namely the inability to walk afterwards. The story is created here by exaggerating the action (not just *one foot* but *both feet*), adding a virtually impossible follow up action, and using multiple story-telling markers (framing the start with *I mean*, using the present tense for immediacy and *then* for narrative sequence). The details involving *shooting yourself in the foot* may possibly involve the assumptions needed for an inferred scenario, but even if they do not, lines 3274–3275 still form a short metaphoric story.

A slightly more complex example of a story based on extending a metaphor to create a narrative comes inside a longer anecdote (Extract 7.4). This anecdote relates a conversation that took place in an Icelandic restaurant between the lecturer (who had been served raw whale meat), the head of Greenpeace and two Norwegians, one of whom appears to have commented on whale killing:

Extract 7.4

| | |
|---|---|
| 1347 | in this actual room |
| 1348 | two two Norwegians |
| 1349 | and said the wonderful classic phrase (.) |
| 1350 | what is so wrong |
| 1351 | about killing minke whales |
| 1352 | and and to see the sort of head of Greenpeace |
| 1353 | virtually go through the ceiling |
| 1354 | before coming down (.) |
| 1355 | and sort of killing all in his path (.) |

The metaphor *go through the ceiling* is extended to create a brief three-action narrative of going up – coming down – result. The last action (1355 *killing all in his path*) changes the image from a person going upwards to a rampaging wild beast, with the middle action (1354 *coming down*) functioning as a transition: connected semantically to going up, but positioning the angry man on the ground ready to run. The rising and the rampaging are connected, as both figuratively describe angry people. The *coming down* may also have an anger dimension if it is taken as implying a heavy bang (as with an explosion); one could, however, see this as *coming down* simply taking on an extra resonance by being sandwiched between two expressions of anger (or following a reference to whales (1351)) which are large and heavy.

The question lastly arises of how the listener fits all the bits of the story together and comes to a rapid, if rough, interpretation of the action of the head of Greenpeace as understandable, if socially inappropriate behaviour. An intersection with Musolff's scenarios can account rather neatly for this. The scenario here is one of the attacking and strong monster (or alien entity) which brings down (literally) unwanted chaos, destroying entities as it goes.

Staying at the level of story, there is a certain narrative similarity in terms of 'local possibility' between the *kill* and the *shoot in the foot* examples, even though different images are involved. In the shooting story, running was something that would be impossible if you had shot yourself; here, *coming down* is something that is possible if you had gone up, and rampaging is something that is possible if you had come down.

There is variation in the extent to which metaphoric stories require inferencing by the listener/reader before they can be identified as such and interpreted in a way that is relevant to the discourse as a whole. The *shoot in both feet* (Extract 7.3) and *go through the ceiling* (Extract 7.4) stories were fairly obvious plays on conventional metaphoric phrases which were mentioned (albeit in altered forms) at the start. The price war example below (Extract 7.5) is slightly different:

Extract 7.5

| 3255 | Lect: you know |
|------|----------------|
| 3256 | one of the worst examples of competing <u>on</u> price (.) |
| 3257 | was Sainsbury |
| 3258 | and Tesco's <u>getting into</u> a price <u>war</u> (.) |
| 3259 | you know |
| 3260 | so Sainsbury's <u>goes down</u> threepence (.) |
| 3261 | <u>on</u> |
| 3262 | # baked beans (.) |
| 3263 | you <u>bastard</u> |
| 3264 | fourpence <u>on</u> ravioli |
| 3265 | you <u>swine</u> |
| 3266 | frozen peas <u>down</u> |
| 3267 | and who the <u>hell wins</u> (.) |
| 3268 | Stud: we do |

The listener is told that the topic is a *price war* (3258), that it is an extreme example (3256) and that some sort of illustration is coming (*you know*, 3259). The story itself (3259–3268) involves two opponents (Sainsbury and Tesco as personified supermarket chains) engaging in a pantomime-like duel and three actions.

The first action comprises three tone groups (3260–3262), as the speaker seemingly thinks out the plot. The focus of the first action (*baked beans*) and the last two actions (price cuts on *ravioli* and *peas*) are given short tone groups. The beans and ravioli reductions are followed by the other party swearing, again involving short tone groups. The intonation thus reinforces the idea of short, violent blows and emotional reactions to them. There finally is a potential outcome (*wins*). There is also some minimal interactivity between speakers, in that a student answers the rhetorical question.

As with previous stories, the narrative is carefully tied into the larger account; here, the *you know* implies the listener can make a connection with price wars, and the final interactive couplet *who the hell wins? We do* shifts the focus away from the fighters and their swearing and back to the audience.

The difference between this and the previous two stories is that from line 3260 to line 3267, the listener has to infer what is happening, since no actual warfare words (or even words referring to fighting) occur. Indeed, none of the three actions (reducing beans, ravioli and peas), is war related, but literally something that a supermarket might do. Only the swearing could lead one to infer that the war metaphor was still in operation – or being alluded to, if one sees a shift from war to personal duel, or from real war to comic war. In short, the price war story blends fighting and supermarket trading, and requires a degree of inferencing that the war metaphor is still relevant.

Metaphoric storytellers can at times be seen to work hard to pull the threads of complex stories together. The Strategy lecture contains a good example of this, shown in Extract 7.6 below. In the middle of the lecture, the lecturer treats changes in company policy and management as being first like the Trojan War (about which a radio series had recently been broadcast) and then like a palace revolution (1656–1705, Extract 7.6). While both relate to the systematic metaphor of COMPETITION (OR BEING COMPETITIVE) IS FIGHTING, the Trojan War involves personal combat between champions, whereas palace revolutions do not. In lines 1674 to 1683 (bolded) the speaker seems to be trying to transition from one situation to the next, to smooth over the inconsistencies and integrate the two – not with great success it must be admitted, but he appears to see the need to try.

Extract 7.6

| | | |
|---|---|---|
| 1657 | Lect: | # anyone watched |
| 1658 | | The |
| 1659 | | the Troj- |
| 1660 | | or watched (.) |
| 1661 | | listened to |
| 1662 | | the Trojan wars |
| 1663 | | <u>on</u> Radio Three |
| 1664 | | <u>over</u> (.) |
| 1665 | | <u>over</u> (.) |
| 1666 | | Christmas time |
| 1667 | | g- |
| 1668 | | # if you want blood |
| 1669 | | lust (.) |
| 1670 | | I mean you know |
| 1671 | | it's it's all <u>there</u> |
| 1672 | | I mean you s- |
| 1673 | | you don't (.) need to read Charles Handy |

| | |
|---|---|
| 1674 | but (.) |
| 1675 | essentially there is <u>bloodletting</u> (.) |
| 1676 | because |
| 1677 | if you change the <u>model</u> (.) |
| 1678 | you actually need |
| 1679 | to change |
| 1680 | not just the <u>model</u> |
| 1681 | but |
| 1682 | but its <u>champions</u> (.) |
| 1683 | you know |
| 1684 | you (.) |
| 1685 | so what you e- |
| 1686 | normally get |
| 1687 | is there is a <u>clean sweep</u> |
| 1688 | and you're you're seeing some of that actually happen(.) |
| 1689 | even in the august chambers |
| 1690 | of Marks and Spencer's |
| 1691 | because (.) |
| 1692 | the <u>old guard</u> |
| 1693 | cannot then |
| 1694 | be the new <u>guard</u> |
| 1695 | they cannot say |
| 1696 | well |
| 1697 | actually (.) what we said |
| 1698 | for the <u>last</u> (.) |
| 1699 | three years |
| 1700 | was a complete |
| 1701 | utter <u>load of bollocks</u> |
| 1702 | you know |
| 1703 | so (.) |
| 1704 | but we've got a really good <u>model</u> now (.) |
| 1705 | so it tends to be <u>bloodletting</u> (.) |

To sum up, metaphorical stories occur within a single discourse event, and tend to be marked out by the speaker in various ways, so that the listener or reader will recognize that a story, however short, is being told. The events in the story are not always linked with explicit connections – or the story would be ruined. This is where metaphor scenarios help out. As culturally-entrenched schemas with conventional expectations and evaluations, listeners can draw on them to help them rapidly connect and interpret (or add overtones to) actions in an ongoing story. Scenarios and stories need to be seen as complementary, if sometimes overlapping, aspects of metaphor-related narrative in discourse.

## Conclusion

This chapter has set out a method for establishing metaphor patterns in discourse activity. The idea of the systematic metaphor, or metaphor trajectory, lies at the heart of metaphor analysis – systematic connections between metaphor vehicles and topics in discourse events which have the potential to reveal cognitive and affective aspects of participation. The method proceeds by collecting linguistic metaphors into vehicle groupings with similar semantic characteristics, then identifying topics which are repeatedly expressed by metaphors within a vehicle grouping. As with earlier stages of the discourse dynamics metaphor process, this approach works mainly inductively upwards from the linguistic metaphor data. It aspires to trustworthiness rather than numerically demonstrable reliability achieving this through collaborative decision-making, note-taking and the rigorous application of changes throughout the data so that coding remains systematic and traceable. Systematicity in metaphor use exists on many levels, from very specific topic~vehicle connections, through framing metaphors and metaphorical stories in discourse events, to more generalized cognitive models and metaphor scenarios with multiple entailments across large collections of discourse data.

### Notes

1. The Perception and Communication of Terrorist Risk project used software that produces an alphabetical list of metaphor vehicles from the identification procedure. This software is not commercially available, so other researchers may begin grouping from some other starting point, having carried out the identification of metaphors in discourse data.
2. It is important to note here that placing multiple codings in multiple adjacent cells can lead to difficulties when data are sorted in Excel because blank cells of metaphors in just one grouping will be listed meaninglessly together. One solution is to fill empty cells with a copy of the single metaphor vehicle grouping, as is done in Figure 7.2.
3. An alternative label would be *WAR*. However, a previous study (Cameron, 2007b, Chapter 1, this volume) had used *MILITARY* and so this label was used for consistency across studies.
4. It would be possible to subscribe to conceptual metaphor theory and to carry out the kind of analysis we have been concerned with here and in Chapter 6. The difference would be that assuming pre-existing conceptual metaphors allows the researcher to work top down and analyse linguistic metaphors as instantiations of conceptual metaphors. The inductive, bottom-up vehicle grouping would be replaced by an allocation of each linguistic metaphor to one of a set of conceptual metaphors assumed to be in action.
5. The recordings and transcriptions used in this study come from the British Academic Spoken English (BASE) corpus. The corpus was developed at the Universities of Warwick and Reading under the directorship of Hilary Nesi and Paul Thompson. Corpus development was assisted by funding from BALEAP, EURALEX, the British Academy and the Arts and Humanities Research Council. The transcripts follow the BASE convention of marking a filled pause by a hash sign #. Unfilled pauses are marked by brackets containing the time to the nearest whole second, e.g. (4). (.) represents a noticeable pause but one lasting less than a second. The extracts

used here have been reanalysed to underline linguistic metaphors, as is done by Cameron and colleagues in the rest of the chapter.

6. Our thanks to Andreas Musolff for his helpful comments on this section of the chapter, and particularly for his suggestion about scenarios in the whale killing example.

# 8   Metaphors and discourse activity

## Lynne Cameron

This chapter addresses an aspect of metaphor analysis that arises from adopting a discourse perspective. If, as we claim, metaphor is shaped by the discourse context in which it is used, then researchers need to take account of that shaping context as they interpret people's use of metaphor. For example, structured interviews and written biographies, to take just two types of discourse that might be used as research data, create very different discourse contexts and conditions for metaphor use. Metaphors will not necessarily directly reflect people's ideas, attitudes and values, but will be chosen and adapted to fit their environment of use, reflecting ideas, attitudes and values through the prism of the discourse event in which they are expressed. Metaphor analysis must therefore be integrated with analysis of discourse activity.

Figure 8.1 (first encountered in Chapter 1) illustrates these two dimensions of metaphor-led discourse analysis.

In Chapters 6 and 7, we worked down the left side of the diagram, finding metaphors, building metaphor groups, identifying systematicity in metaphor use through systematic metaphors, metaphor framing and metaphorical stories

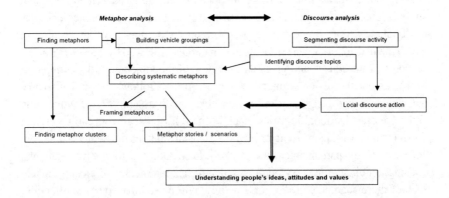

Figure 8.1. Metaphor-led discourse analysis

(metaphor clusters are dealt with in Chapter 10). This chapter starts from the right side of the diagram, and shows how analysis of discourse activity and local discourse action can be integrated with metaphor analysis.

## Analysing discourse activity

Chapter 5 introduced a way of thinking about discourse as dynamic, and we develop that perspective further in this chapter. Readers are also referred to Chapter 6 of Larsen-Freeman and Cameron (2008) which discusses in more detail a complex dynamic systems view of discourse as activity. A dynamic view fits more easily to spoken language than to written language; it is relatively unproblematic to think about a conversation or discussion as an event in which what participants say is influenced by various dynamic forces, such as wanting to justify an opinion, disagreeing with other participants or answering a question. As described in Chapter 5, spoken discourse data offers a trace of the activity that occurred in the discourse event. A written text, such as an official document or a work of fiction, can also be seen in this way, as a trace of activity in the discourse event that was the composition of the text by the writer. Although writing the text might have been a solitary activity, it was dialogic in the (Bakhtinian) sense that the writer had listeners or readers in mind while composing the text, and was influenced by previous encounters with texts and talk. The deliberate process of textual composition usually erases evidence of spontaneity, leaving a final text with a clear, and often conventionalized, structuring. The political speech we have been considering might be analysed as a spoken event, if a recording was available, but here we consider it as a written text prepared for oral delivery.

As researchers, our data are traces of discourse activity within discourse events; data come as transcriptions of spoken discourse or as written texts, and analysis proceeds by segmenting texts or transcriptions into smaller episodes of discourse action. For example, a classroom lesson may have an opening in which the teacher organizes students and materials, followed by a teacher fronted section that introduces and gives an overview of the topic and tasks coming up in the lesson; the major segment of the lesson then follows, as students carry out their assigned tasks, and the lesson closes with a summary of work done and more organizational logistics. Each of these lesson segments can be broken down further, perhaps by topic or by the actions of students or teacher (Cameron, 2003). A doctor-patient interview is likely to include the following segments: opening, an elicitation of symptoms, a diagnosis, treatment, and closing. Inside each of these segments of discourse activity will be smaller episodes of action: for example, the opening may start with a greeting and response; the elicitation of symptoms is likely to contain sequences of questions and answers.

Discourse analysis offers a range of methods and tools for segmenting the activity of talk and text – see Schiffrin *et al.* (2001). For example, conversation analysis may be appropriately employed for revealing local discourse action inside episodes of talk, rhetorical structure theory may be used to help break texts into chunks, and critical discourse analysis has been used with a particular focus on metaphor (e.g. Koller, 2004). The usual warning is appropriate: before adopting any particular method of discourse analysis, it is necessary to check the theoretical assumptions involved and be sure they are compatible with the rest of the research project. As an applied linguist carrying out research projects with different kinds of spoken discourse data, I have found that I needed to develop categories of discourse activity that fit specific research purposes, and that balance the requirements of theoretical validity with the demands of practicality. To illustrate the process of analysing discourse activity, the political speech data, as a written text, will be analysed in detail in the following sections. The full text of the speech can be found in the appendix, and it will be useful to have read it all the way through in order to make sense of the analysis that follows.

## Finding boundaries of segments

Generally segments of discourse activity are identified by **boundaries** that mark a change from one kind of activity to another. To describe discourse activity, the analyst can ask: 'What is the discourse producer (i.e. the author or speaker) doing here?' Of course, s/he is usually doing more than one thing, but the idea is to describe the primary activity, which is usually evidenced by the words used and/or by the reactions of other participants. For example, in the first two paragraphs of the speech, Blair is 'Opening the speech by thanking people'. Following the text to find the point at which this activity changes to some other activity, we see this opening segment continuing with what might be called 'locating', making mention of local landmarks. He doesn't finish thanking people until the end of paragraph 9, where there is a shift from the opening segment into a new kind of discourse activity, and thus a new segment. The boundary comes just before the short and punchy lines, *I'm back. And it feels good.* The segment which opens at this point introduces and previews both the topics of the rest of the speech and the rhetorical patterns. This previewing activity continues until the end of paragraph 29, when a change of topic, grammatical subject and goal marks the start of another section.

Detailed examination of the discourse dynamics of the first segment (paragraphs 1–9) shows how the discourse actions of 'opening by thanking and locating' flow from one to another. The segment is, as it were, bracketed by the first and last paragraphs which refer to Blair's visits in the area prior to the speech, and express his appreciation of that visit. Alongside mention of local attractions, the segment includes references to achievements supported by the Labour government, which is an example of fulfilling several discourse goals at the same time. A sub-segment boundary occurs in the middle of the second paragraph, as Blair moves from thanking people to locating the speech by talking about the local area. The shift in discourse activity is indicated by the phrase *a great place*; the adjective *great* relates back to appreciation, while *place* serves to introduce mentions of locations. There follows mention of particularly impressive places in the area, with the implication that the government has supported these new or newly refurbished buildings. Paragraph 5 continues the theme of change and achievement but moves from building to education and adds statistics. Paragraph 6 describes the changes and achievements with unemployment, and paragraphs 7 and 8 summarize achievements in the local area, connected to the national and party politics. Paragraph 9 moves back to Blair's visit, and contains a change in grammatical subject to 'I' that prepares listeners for the pivotal *I'm back* coming up in paragraph 10. The flow of the discourse is managed through choices of grammar, of lexis, and of topic, and somewhere inside this flow are the metaphors (see below).

The decision to label the segment up to paragraph 9, rather than just to paragraph 2, is motivated by wanting to construct an initial, broad segmentation of the whole speech. Smaller sub-segments will be identified as fits the research goals. Boundaries may not always be as sharp as here but there should, at least, be distinct evidence in the text or transcript of the two types of discourse action between which a boundary occurs (see Cameron, 2003 for more detail on segmenting transcripts of talk).

### Evidence for boundaries in discourse activity structure

Language features that offer evidence for discourse activity boundaries can include:

- Pauses in talk or change of paragraph in written text.
- Discourse markers that explicitly signal a move to new activity e.g. *Having looked at xxx, we now move to ....*
- Changes in topic, e.g. from buildings to education.
- Changes in lexis, which may be connected to topic change or may be a change in level of specificity, e.g. in a doctor/patient interview, the lexis in the opening may be quite general: *fine, OK*, while more specific lexis is used in the next section: *a stabbing pain in my leg.*
- Changes in use of grammar, e.g. of grammatical subject, from third person location-related topics to first person *I.*

A clear boundary will probably display several of these features.

Some types of discourse events are easier than others to segment. Cultural conventions or rituals lead to some discourse events being tightly structured and highly predictable, and thus easily segmented. A structured or semi-structured interview will segment easily by the questions that the interviewer asks. Problems can arise with deciding on the segments that make up a text or discourse event because one type of activity may be nested inside another. Furthermore, in talk, speakers can drift from one topic to another without clear boundaries, while written texts are often more intricately structured than conversation because the writer has had time to construct complicated shifts in discourse activity. Sometimes a change in discourse activity only becomes obvious some time after it is under way and it is not possible to pinpoint a precise boundary. The dynamic potentialities of language use will always produce problems for analysts, and we have to deal with them as best we can. Metaphor identification presents problems because people stretch and play with the possibilities of metaphorical language, and discourse activity analysis will face problems because of processing constraints, and because people stretch and play with the possibilities of discourse design

## Segments of discourse activity in the Blair speech

Figure 8.2 shows a possible segmentation of the Blair speech in terms of discourse activity. It divides the speech into five segments around pivotal points, each carrying out a particular kind of discourse activity.

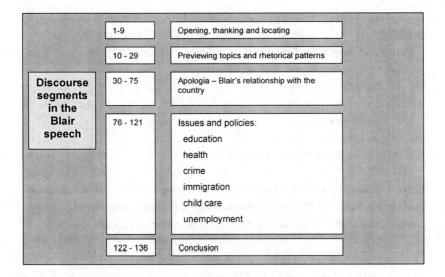

Figure 8.2. Discourse activity segments in the Blair speech

The segments are unequal in length, with the fourth being the longest, and most easily divisible further into sub-sections by topic. The boundaries of sections sometimes blur and overlap, probably in order to construct a more coherent speech for listeners and to create the desired impact on supporters and voters.

## Metaphors and discourse activity in segments of the Blair speech

The discourse activity analysis is mapped on to the analysis of linguistic metaphor in a detailed and recursive process that requires close attention to lexical choices, to grammatical form and to rhetorical patterning, in order to reveal how metaphors are incorporated in discourse activity.

It is difficult to offer a single template for the process of combining analyses of metaphors and discourse activity since it has to be sensitive to the research goals. Researchers will need to move between the metaphors and discourse activity in order to understand how metaphors are used to frame and elaborate ideas (see Chapter 7) and how metaphors contribute to expressing attitudes and values. In what follows, I try to indicate the kinds of things about metaphor and other language that might strike a researcher exploring the Blair speech.

Words and phrases in italics are from the text of the speech; underlined terms indicate useful dimensions of discourse activity analysis:

### Segment 1: 1–9: Opening, thanking and locating

The speech moves outwards from the local to the national – from the *Centre* (paragraph 1) to *Gateshead* (paragraph 2) to *Britain* (paragraph 8).

The major **agents** in this speech are all introduced in paragraph 8:

> *Tories/Tory Government*
>
> *l*
>
> *people* (which refers to all those mentioned so far, whose lives have been changed)
>
> *we / the New Labour Government*

There are many words and phrases with **affective** content – that express the speaker's perspective in terms of **emphasis**, **evaluation** or **alignment** (Cameron and Deignan, 2006; Graumann, 1990)) – in this same paragraph:

> *so passionate, historic, never again, neglected, achieve so much, neglected and left behind, uncaring*

The affective words and phrases are grouped around the agents so that the following **relations** are constructed:

*people – achieved, talented,* but at risk of being *neglected* and *left behind*
*Labour – passionate, winning, historic, worked with people*
*Tories – uncaring, neglected and left behind*

The strongest metaphors prefigure the attitudes and values of the rest of the speech. These are the metaphors about social injustice that describe deprived lives as *untouched by change* (paragraph 7) and people as *neglected and left behind by an uncaring Tory Government* (paragraph 8). Both *untouched* and *left behind* suggest isolation and deliberate lack of action. The sadness and isolation are also suggested by the Dickensian metaphorical allusion in paragraph 4 to empty factories as *ghosts of times past.* These early metaphors will connect into the rhetorical structuring of the main body of the speech, which metaphorizes political choices as *moving forward* or *going back*, with the Labour government positioned as both caring and progressive.

Paragraph 9 seems to be a brief bridging passage, closing down the subsegment about achievements in the area before returning to more practical and current content as exemplified by the lexis: *touring, texted, yesterday.*

### Segment 2: 10–29. Previewing topics and rhetorical patterns

The short sentence *I'm back* (paragraph 10) is very significant. Its short length contrasts with the longer sentences of previous talk. A contrast is also made by putting *I* in the subject position, in a striking declarative grammatical form. It is followed by an affective sentence containing a positive evaluation, also grammatically declarative: *And it feels good.* The import of this sentence is investigated by Deignan and Semino using corpus analysis (Chapter 9, this volume), and by Ritchie, taking a perceptual simulations approach (Chapter 4, this volume; 2008).

In this speech, Blair had the task of re-establishing his credibility with his party and with the British people after the debacle of the initial stages of the Iraq invasion and war and in advance of an upcoming election. The phrase may also carry resonances from Schwarzenegger films, where *I'll be back* is part threat, part promise.

Paragraph 10 is very interesting in terms of metaphor because it is not immediately clear whether *I'm back* is a linguistic metaphor or a non-metaphorical statement. It is in some ways non-metaphorical because Blair is geographically *back* in his constituency in the north-east of England. But such a punchy sentence at this point is likely to be figurative in some way. As the speech continues, he unpacks the different meanings of *I'm back* and the figurative meanings are strengthened (Table 8.1). It is as if this first utterance contains the potential for various later figurative and literal meanings.

Table 8.1. Literal and metaphorical meanings of *back* in the Blair speech

| | |
|---|---|
| *Back in the north east* (paragraph 11) | Literal, meaning returned to a geographical place |
| *Back with the Labour Party* (paragraph 12) | Both literal and metaphorical: literal in that Blair is speaking to Labour Party supporters so is literally returned to the place where they are them; metaphorical if *the Labour Party* means the values of the party as well as the physical location of supporters |
| *Back with a relentless focus* (paragraph 13) | Both literal and metaphorical as above. The prepositioning *with* is also now metaphorical since it refers to adopting an attitude rather than being physically co-located |
| *It's good to be back in a fight with the Tories* (paragraph 16) | Metaphorical: the more basic sense of the vehicle *be back*, returning to a place, is used to mean participating again in an action. Followed by strong metaphor *fight*. |

*Being back* would be placed in a vehicle grouping such as JOURNEY or MOVEMENT (Chapter 7) but it is more accurately and specifically about RETURNING TO A PLACE, and more specifically about RETURNING TO A PLACE WHERE ONE BELONGS. After the first two uses of these *back,* there is a contrast with *taken me far from home* (14). This phrase is also rather ambiguous as to metaphoricity – *home* can be both physical and emotional; it carries connotations of safety and belonging, while being *far from home* suggests loneliness and losing touch with important values. The full clause – *events have taken me far from home* – sounds poetic because of the combination of alliteration of *far* and *from*, assonance of *from* and *home*, the succession of four monosyllabic words, and the rich cultural connotations of words and phrase. The grammatical choice of passive verb *have taken* metaphorically makes *events* the agent and cause of Blair's absence or straying, thereby reducing his responsibility for these actions.

The idea of *far from home* is then connected, through metaphor, to responsibilities at home. In paragraph 15, the phrase *the top line of my job spec* is a linguistic metaphor in which employment in more everyday jobs of ordinary *people* that have *job specs* becomes a source domain for the topic of Prime

Ministerial responsibility. When the *British people* are described as *the boss*, the employment story or scenario is being developed, although it is rapidly replaced with the *fight with the Tories* scenario in paragraph 16.

When Blair ends paragraph 15 with *None of us, not me, not any of us, should ever forget it*, he gives a first hint of the apologia which is to be developed shortly. This sentence also uses a three part repetition *none ... not ... not*, a rhetorical pattern that is common in public speeches, and also found at the end of paragraph 21.

A lexical chain (a repeated use of a word or connected word across a piece of discourse), emphasizes the metaphorical conceptualization of political elections as physical fight:

*in a fight* → *this is a fight* → *a fight for the future* → *a fight that* → *we have to win*

Paragraph 17 changes the FIGHT metaphor abruptly to a STORY metaphor, which constructs the framework for the first use of the speech's central metaphor at the end of paragraph 17: *the fundamental choice facing the country – forward or back*. This is a different metaphor from the earlier instances of *back* which carry the idea of a positive and powerful return to a place where one belongs. In this instance, the result of moving *back* would not be a return to a warm and welcoming home, but a negative return to the previously mentioned *uncaring* (8) government and *ghosts of times past* (4). The thematic or framing metaphor is repeated in fuller form in paragraph 27: *do we go forward with Labour, or back to the Tories?*

In building metaphor groups, two separate groupings would be appropriate for the two uses of *back* as metaphor vehicle. One might be labelled RETURNING TO A PLACE WHERE ONE BELONGS, which is positively valenced, whereas the other, negatively valenced, might be labelled RETURNING TO AN OLD AND LESS FAVOURABLE PLACE. The topics of the metaphors are also different: in one case it is Blair's choices and in the other case choices made by the people of Britain.

Throughout the speech, the opposition *forward/back* is used to emphasize the negative outcomes of choosing the Tories, with the implication that *going back to* this situation would be a mistake. For example, paragraphs 19 and 20 contain a series of CHAOS metaphors used about the opposition: *mess – disaster – spread – wasted – in tatters*. The *forward/back* metaphor recurs as a refrain throughout the speech, and full analysis would need to examine all instances in their discourse activity to reveal its impact and interplay with other metaphors and ideas (readers are referred to Chapters 4 and 9, and to Ritchie, 2008).

## Segment 3: 30–75: Apologia

The first hint of Blair's regret came at the end of paragraph 15, and returns in paragraphs 22–24 in a sequence of five sentences that each begin with meta-phorical *where* (a word referring to a physical place is used to talk about event or process). The pivot and middle of the five sentences pre-announces the theme of the Apologia segment of the speech which starts at paragraph 30. The segment is labelled *apologia* (from the Greek, *'speaking away'*) since Blair is more concerned with explaining and defending himself than with actually apologizing.

The segment boundary is marked by a change of grammatical subject, from *we,* the party, to *I,* Blair, (in paragraphs 30) and explicit reference: *a lot of it is about me* (31). There is also a change of register, from what we might call public oration to more intimate talk about feelings: *I understand why people feel angry.*

The apologia is structured through two metaphors:

*BLAIR'S RELATIONSHIP WITH THE VOTERS IS LIKE A DOMESTIC RELATIONSHIP.*
*MAKING POLITICAL MISTAKES IS LEARNING LESSONS.*

First comes the development of the metaphor scenario of Blair's relationship with the people he governs as like an interpersonal domestic or sexual relation-ship (mentioned in Chapter 7). As was the case earlier with *I'm back*, the use of metaphors gradually builds up the scenario. When Blair first says in para-graph 32: *I think a lot about my relationship with the country*, it is not clear that the word *relationship* is being used metaphorically, as well as literally and non-specifically to mean simply a connection between people. The more meta-phorical potential is only activated in paragraph 33, when he explicitly sets up the analogical mapping: *it's not a bad idea to think of it in terms of being like any relationship*. There then follows a set of lexical choices, some of them metaphorical, that might apply in the metaphor scenario of a domestic or sexual relationship (again, see Chapter 9 for a corpus analysis of these data):

| | |
|---|---|
| *warmth growing; expectations rising;* | (paragraph 34) |
| *euphoria; euphoric moments;* | (paragraph 35) |
| *mood turning; the thousand little things that irritate and grate* | (paragraph 37) |

This climaxes at the end of paragraph 37 with the scenario in which the public act as an offended partner: *raise your voice; throw a bit of crockery.*

In terms of metaphor identification (Chapter 6), the gradual shift here into something like allegory presents problems in underlining metaphor vehicles, because by the end of paragraph 37, the discourse dynamics have moved us completely inside the scenario and it is not clear which words would not be underlined as metaphorically used, other than the pronouns *I, my, you, your.* The metaphor scenario is connected back into the real world at paragraph 38, with an explicit mention of the election: *now you, the British people, have to sit down and decide.* This last phrase is an example of a 'physical-speech-and-action' verb phrase (Cameron, in press b), in which a metaphorical verb (*sit down* as in the couple scenario, where sitting down to talk about relationship issues would fit) and a non-metaphorical verb (*decide,* as in vote for one party and not another). The metaphor RELATIONSHIP scenario is further elaborated a little later when the British people's choice between Labour and Tory or Liberal Democrat is spoken of in terms of choosing a sexual partner: *want Mr Howard; go off with Mr Kennedy.* The scenario is closed with a return to the political domain, and a reiteration of the *forward/back* metaphor at paragraph 39.

The RELATIONSHIP scenario is perhaps intended to serve as the background against which Blair's *mistakes* are to be understood. A partner may make mistakes, but if the partnership is strong, these can be accommodated if sufficient regret is shown and if promises about future behaviour are sufficiently convincing. Such an appeal seems to come in paragraph 66: *I'm still the same person. Older. A little wiser, I hope. But still with the same commitment and belief.* The choice of words here that can be used in both the RELATIONSHIP metaphor scenario and in the topic domain of politics, such as *commitment,* works to 'bridge' between the two.

The LEARNING LESSONS metaphors are used to describe how Blair became this wiser person, beginning in paragraph 41, and including the following vehicles:

> *learnt some lessons; a harsh teacher; wise one* (paragraph 41)
> *learnt, learned* (paragraphs 43, 48, 49, 50, 54, 55, 56)

This metaphor is not elaborated into a detailed scenario as the RELATIONSHIP metaphor was, but gains its significance from the repetition of *I learnt.* Interwoven with the LEARNING LESSONS metaphor are JOB metaphors that resonate with the RELATIONSHIP metaphor to suggest a scenario in which Blair is Britain's breadwinner, going out to work doing a tough job but also, as a 'new man', learning to listen.

There is a shift at paragraph 51 in grammatical subject from *I* to *we,* as the focus gradually moves from Blair's learning to government action. In paragraphs 51 to 61, the set of topics that will be dealt with in more detail are introduced, including the topic of Iraq where people were most likely to perceive *mistakes* to have been made:

| anti-social behaviour | (paragraph 51) |
| work and education | (paragraph 52) |
| immigration | (paragraph 53) |
| Iraq | (paragraph 54) |
| economy | (paragraph 58) |
| public services | (paragraph 61) |

In paragraphs 61 and 62, there is a return to the RELATIONSHIP metaphor as Blair urges the electorate to believe what he has *learned* from *this journey,* that *a partnership* is the best way, and asks the British people not to dump him but to go *forward together* (paragraph 64).

In paragraph 70, Blair describes himself as having *the same passion and hunger* as when he was elected (or, metonymically, *first walked through the door of 10 Downing Street*). As the corpus analysis in the next chapter shows, *passion and hunger* are an unlikely combination, resonating with the RELATION-SHIP metaphor scenario but is equally applicable to political ambition.

The Apologia segment comes to an end somewhere around paragraph 75. This paragraph repeats the metaphors *the hunger and passion* as being what takes Blair forwards to further change.

From paragraph 76 onwards, the speech deals sequentially with a range of social issues and policies, explaining the background of each and the government action in terms of 'pledges'.

### Segment 4: 76–121. Issues and policies

This section is not explored to the same level as detail as the previous ones, but we note the refrain of the *forward/back* metaphor to frame each policy issue, as progressive Labour is contrasted with *backward* Conservative policies. Blair's rhetorical strategy here is, in respect of each issue, to start from specific instances that he has the witnessed and learnt from, then to generalize to the issue and remind people of the government action taken.

### Segment 5: 122–end. Conclusion

The last subsection, on the economy, gradually merges into the concluding section, with a pivot point around paragraph 122:

> *We can't promise paradise. But we can make progress.*

The mention of *paradise* links back across the discourse to the *miracles* that the people might have expected but politicians couldn't deliver, in paragraph 35.

Both *RELIGION* metaphors reflect unrealistic expectations, of partners in relationships and of politicians.

Paragraphs 122–127 become very short, highlighting the importance of the coming election. The conclusion is a call to the party supporters, reminding them of *how we got here* (paragraph 132), of their traditional values (paragraph 133) and urging them, with the final use of the *JOURNEY TO A NEW AND FAVOURABLE/OLD AND LESS FAVOURABLE PLACE* metaphor, to continue *forward not back* at all levels from party to country.

## Metaphors and discourse activity in the Blair speech: Synthesis and summary

The discourse activity analysis carried out on the Blair speech in this chapter has involved a simple segmentation of discourse in terms of discourse participant activity, followed by identification of patterns of language use including phonological, lexical, grammatical and rhetorical strategies. Bringing these together with patterns of metaphor use allows the following insights into the speech writer's use of metaphor to be brought together as a synthesis and summary, similar to the metaphor synthesis of reconciliation data analysis in Chapter 1.

- The metaphors of *RELATIONSHIPS, JOB, LEARNING LESSONS,* and *JOURNEYS* are interwoven and connected throughout the text. They are used both to convey ideas and affect, and to construct and highlight the rhetorical structure of the speech.
- The discourse dynamics of the speech showed shifting between literal and metaphorical uses of the same words, sometimes in the gradual building up of metaphorical scenarios as with the *RELATIONSHIP* metaphor to describe Blair and the British voters. This metaphor contributed to a key function of the speech, to repair Blair's standing with the British voters. In the *RELATIONSHIP* metaphor scenario, Blair was constructed as the repentant partner who has *learned his lessons* by listening and who, despite falling out, wants to maintain his political partnership with the British people. The relationship between Blair and the voters was also expressed using *JOB* metaphors, with the British people as boss and Blair as employee.
- The *forward/back* metaphor was used to encapsulate the choice between Labour and Conservatives, and used to structure the discourse by acting as a recurring frame or refrain. This particular linguistic metaphor was the most significant in the speech, and was complemented with others that can be grouped in the same systematic metaphor: *CHOOSING LABOUR/CONSERVATIVE IS A JOURNEY TO A NEW AND FAVOURABLE/OLD AND LESS FAVOURABLE PLACE.*

- Additionally, *CHAOS* metaphors were used to construct negative evaluations of Conservative policies in contrast with Labour policies, and
  to heighten the undesirability of a Conservative government as a *PLACE
  TO GO BACK TO*.

## Conclusion

Using metaphor as a research tool involves understanding what people do with
metaphors, as well as which metaphors they use. Metaphor identification and
analysis needs to be combined with analysis of discourse activity. One aspect
of that analysis is the identification of discourse topics and themes (see Chapter
7), and their evolution in the text or talk. The other aspect, as illustrated in
this chapter, involves using some kind of discourse analysis methodology to
describe local discourse action and its interplay with metaphors. Having analysed and described local metaphor and discourse action, the researcher can
then zoom out to the discourse activity as a whole to research findings in the
form of a synthesis and summary of the use of metaphor to express ideas, attitudes and values.

In the next chapter, we move out from activity within a specific discourse
event to consider metaphor across the multiplicity of discourse events that make
up the language experience of a sociocultural group or speech community, as
represented in a corpus.

# 9 Corpus techniques for metaphor analysis

## Alice Deignan and Elena Semino

## Introduction

A *corpus* (plural *corpora*) is a collection of naturally-occurring texts, either written or transcripts of speech. Since the 1980s, it has been possible to store texts on computer and to search them using specialized software. The rapid developments in computational memory and processing speed since then have enabled enormous increases in the size of corpora and the speed at which they can be analysed. Scholars in both the humanities and the social sciences have come to recognize the importance of studying authentic language data (as opposed to examining invented examples and/or their own intuitions about language use), because the study of naturally-occurring language, especially through corpus research, has repeatedly revealed patterns that do not seem to be discoverable using the researcher's unaided intuitions (see Sinclair, 1991, 2004 for the development of this point). Hunston (2002), for example, discusses modern corpora and the ways in which they have been used to tackle language analysis. Baker *et al.* (2008) combine corpus linguistics with critical discourse analysis in order to investigate the representation of refugees and asylum seekers in the UK press.

Corpora are usually studied from a linguistic perspective, but findings can be relevant to researchers in other, related fields. There are a number of ready made general corpora available (see below). However, researchers often build their own corpora of texts relevant to their own discipline, which they sometimes search in conjunction with existing general corpora, using techniques described below. In this chapter we begin with a brief introduction to corpora, and then go on to show how a variety of corpus-based analytical techniques can be used in metaphor research. We refer specifically to the speech by Tony Blair that is also discussed in other chapters in this volume.

## Types of corpus

### Large corpora

Large modern corpora contain many millions, usually hundreds of millions, of words of running text. Two well-known British ones are the Bank of English and the British National Corpus (see websites section for URLs). These attempt to provide a representative sample of contemporary English, as experienced by a British speaker – though the issue of representativeness is a very thorny one. These corpora are so large that it is impossible to search them by hand. Tasks that specialized software can perform include:

- identifying the part of speech of each word in the corpus, a procedure known as **tagging** or **annotation**
- counting the **frequencies** of each word form in the corpus
- showing each instance of a word form, with its surrounding context (that is, producing a **concordance**)
- counting which words frequently co-occur with a particular word (its **collocates**) and giving statistical measures of the significance of this.

Some of these tasks are exemplified below; see Hunston (2002) for more detailed descriptions, and Deignan (2005) for applications to metaphor analysis.

Most large corpora are divided into **sub-corpora**, which can be studied separately. For example, the Bank of English has sub-corpora of informal speech, various newspapers, books and magazines, BBC World Service broadcasts, and spoken and written data from the USA and Australia.

## Specialized corpora

Specialized corpora can consist of several million words from a particular genre, or can be much smaller. They are usually compiled with the goal of investigating language use within a specific genre, sometimes with the additional aim of comparing this to related genres, or to the language as a whole. For instance, Skorczynska and Deignan (2006) compared metaphors used in academic economics publications with those used in popular economics texts, using two small corpora. Specialized corpora may be small enough to search by hand, or may be searched automatically using software such as WordSmith Tools (Scott, 2008). A compromise is to search a large sample by hand, then use the results as the basis for automatic searches over the whole corpus, a technique used by Charteris-Black (2004). The Blair speech, which is examined in this chapter, is an example of a specialized corpus, but one that is very small. In this chapter we use the speech to show how corpus techniques can enable the analyst to gain insights into the uses of frequent words and expressions within this speech. If the analyst wished to examine Blair's discourse more generally, a larger corpus would be needed, consisting of a number of speeches and samples of other speech types, depending on the analyst's exact goals. The collection of 12 focus group discussions that is analysed elsewhere in this book is also an example of a small corpus.

## A technique for examining metaphors in a text

To use corpus techniques to examine the metaphors in a text or collection of texts, the researcher first needs to turn the texts into a machine readable corpus. This is straightforward for small collections of texts; at its simplest, the process involves transcribing data, or converting it, into text files, which are then stored in an identifiable and discrete location on a computer hard drive. The next step is to design the analysis procedure, which will usually involve choosing software. There are several commercially available packages for analysing corpora; one of the best known is WordSmith Tools (Scott, 2008), which was used for the analysis described below.

Information about word use in a specialized corpus can be of interest in itself. It can also be compared with the results of the same searches performed over other corpora. Some researchers use a large general corpus as a source of information about typical language use, against which results from the specialized corpus are compared. A large corpus used in this way is referred to as a **reference corpus**. This technique can suggest whether metaphors from the specialized texts are used in ways that are typical of the language more widely, or not. Researchers look for points such as frequency, typical collocates, variations on idioms and fixed phrases, **connotation** (the positive or negative orientation that some words have; for example, *slim* has positive connotations) **register** (a subset of the language, used in a particular setting, such as medical language) and grammatical structure. There is a danger of such an analysis being over-simplistic if the reference corpus is too small to expect many examples of infrequent words and expressions, or if the analyst's own text is of a highly specialized register. In the following section, we exemplify these techniques using the speech by Tony Blair given in February 2005 at Gateshead (see Ritchie, 2008 for an analysis of this speech that builds on the same project which gave rise to this chapter; also Chapters 4 and 8, this volume). Note that the corpus consists of the entire speech (in the Appendix), although only extracts are quoted here.

## Word frequencies in the Blair speech

The relative frequency of words in a text can be a useful starting point for analysis. The words occurring most frequently in the Blair speech are as shown in Table 9.1. The numbers in column 1 give the rank order of frequency of each word in the text.

This information is unsurprising. Words such as *the*, *a* and *of* are highly frequent in almost all texts, and it would be unusual if they did not appear in the top ten most frequent words of almost any corpus. A distinction is sometimes made between words such as this, called 'grammar' or 'function' words, and words which seem to carry more meaning, sometimes called 'lexical' or 'content' words. The distinction can be difficult to maintain for some words, such as modal verbs, but is nonetheless useful as a general guide.

Table 9.1. Most frequent word forms in the Blair speech, in rank order

| Rank order | Word |
|---|---|
| 1 | *the* |
| 2 | *and* |
| 3 | *to* |
| 4 | *a* |
| 5 | *of* |
| 6 | *//* (used to denote pauses) |
| 7 | *in* |
| 8 | *we* |
| 9 | *I* |
| 10 | *for* |

The most frequent lexical words in a text are usually more informative. For the Blair speech, these are shown in Table 9.2, in descending order of frequency, with the number of occurrences in column 1.

Table 9.2. Most frequent lexical words in the Blair speech, with number of occurrences.

| Number of occurrences | |
|---|---|
| 43 | *people* |
| 20 | *back, new* |
| 19 | *country* |
| 15 | *school, Tory* |
| 12 | *time, work* |
| 11 | *know, Labour* |
| 8 | *best, go, learnt, life, party, same, things. think* |
| 7 | *choice, first, government, just, lives, lot, police, right, said, say, sometimes, spending, thing, told, want* |
| 6 | *British, care, centre, future, hard, long, million, together, Tories, worthless* |
| 5 | *change, community, cuts, fight, Gateshead, half, job, leader, lost, Mr, place, policy, real, response, seen, take, term, values, vote, waiting, working, world, year, years* |

A study of frequent lexical words can provide one way into a more detailed corpus search (though not the only possible starting point – the researcher might decide to focus on a particular semantic theme for instance, as we show below). For example, the above list suggests the questions: Why does Blair use the word *Tory* more frequently than *Labour*? Is this typical of addresses to party workers? Is it typical of Blair's speeches? Clearly, more texts need to be examined to answer questions of this sort. There may be a linguistic or contextual explanation, or the use may be a rhetorical tactic.

In a full analysis, all of the frequent words in Table 9.2 would be subject to an initial study to determine whether they showed metaphorical uses. A number of these words are potentially of interest, including the following:

*back; forward; cuts*
*job, work, working;*
The set of words associated with *fighting;*
The set of words associated with *time (future, months, years).*

Space limitations do not allow a discussion of all these words here; some are analysed in more detail in the following sections, in order to exemplify the process of analysis and the kinds of insights that can be gained.

## Concordance analysis of 'back'

WordSmith Tools was used to produce a concordance for the word form *back*, shown in Figure 9.1.

```
1.  should ever forget it, it is good to be back in a fight with the Tories. And make
2.           we try to persuade them to come back to the fold. Where we have made
3.   important of course, of the country. Back with a  relentless focus on the job
4.        to save money. But we should not go back to those days. Not now, not ever
5.  uyers. I do not want this country to go back to those failed Tory policies. Not
6.          not a Labour government. Going back not moving forward. But for me I
7.    from me. I'm back. And it feels good. Back in the North East, to thank the
8.  re a lot- will get a reply from me. I'm back. And it feels good. Back
9.  ost support we go out and try to win it back. Where we have lost old friends, we
10.           lives. And the same night, back in my constituency, a woman
11. help for first time buyers. Forward not back. The 1997 pledges met and more
12.  it is tempered by realism. Forward not back. The biggest choice in politics for
13. Renewed for each each time. Forward not back. For us. For Britain
14.   Choice facing the country- forward or back- and that story will not be told until
15.          Do we go forward with Labour or back to the Tories? Our task is to
16.   Backward? We must never let them put back the notion that high standards in
17.      Redwood speaking, the one they put back on the Tory front bench to show
18.  Not power by the front door but by the back door. Spread disillusion and cynicism
19. Support every day that I've been there. Back with the Labour party that has
20.      With the Big Conversation. I went back out, and rather than talking at
```

Figure 9.1. Concordance for *back* in the Blair speech

To produce Figure 9.1, the WordSmith Tools concordancer has identified all citations of *back*, and arranged them so that the search word, *back*, appears down the middle of the screen, with its immediate textual context on either side. The citations have been ordered alphabetically according to the word on the immediate left of the search word. The researcher can re-order citations, a facility which is very useful when examining longer concordances.

While concordance software can assist greatly in identifying prominent words and patterns, and can arrange these conveniently, it cannot, as yet, replace qualitative analysis conducted by a human researcher. Detailed manual analysis leads to a number of interesting observations.

First, when *back* is used to talk about Tories, it occurs in the following expressions:

- *forward not back*: (citations 11, 12, 13, 14, 15)
- *go back*: (citations 4, 5, 6)
- *put back*: (citations 16 and 17)
- *by the back door* (citation 18)

In all of these expressions, *back* is used with negative meaning. In *forward not back*, and *go back*, *back* suggests a negatively evaluated past, contrasted with a positively evaluated future. *Put back* is less clearly negative in itself, but an examination of the citations shows that the object of the phrasal verb is something from the past that is negatively evaluated. *by the back door* connotes deception.

When *back* is used to describe Blair or the Labour party, it occurs in the following expressions:

- *(I'm) back* (citations 1, 3, 7/ 8, 9, 19)
- *I went back out* (citation 20)
- *back in my constituency* (citation 10)
- *come back to the fold* (citation 2)

The first expression, *I'm back*, is interesting in that it is sometimes used literally, as in citation 7 *I'm back. And it feels good*. In citation 19, *back with the Labour party*, there is a possible literal interpretation, given the context, of a speech to Labour party workers. However, this could also be interpreted figuratively, if the Labour party is understood as an abstract entity rather than as the people physically present. Citation 8, which is taken from immediately before citation 7, is ambiguous, while citation 1, *back in a fight with the Tories* is figurative.

These latter uses seem to be positively oriented, while the use of *back* in referring to Tories is negative. It is not especially interesting to find that politicians speak positively of themselves and negatively of their opponents, though

metaphorical sense. Blair's absence from the North East seems bound up with another kind of being away, and his return to the area is associated with a metaphorical return. The non-literal absence and return are not stated on-record, and their nature is left to the hearer to infer. It is possible that hearers will infer that he admits having strayed from party principles, or from the central duties of his job, but the nature of any admission is not specified.

## Concordance and frequency analysis of work

WordSmith Tools was used to produce a concordance, shown in Figure 9.2, of the word form *work*, as well as inflected forms such as *worked*, and derived forms such as *worker*.

The Wordlist program in WordSmith Tools tells us that the various forms of *work* account for the following percentages of the whole text:

| | |
|---|---|
| *work* | 0.28% |
| *working* | 0.11% |
| *workers* | 0.02% |

Intuition suggests that this is more frequent than would be expected, so these frequencies were compared with a reference corpus. To study the use of a frequent word with a general meaning such as *back*, it is not vital to get a very close match with the genre of the reference corpus. However, to compare frequencies of a word that has a more specific meaning, such as *work*, and could be expected to be more genre-bound, it is useful to get as close a match as possible with the reference corpus. The closest match within the Bank of English is the component containing BBC World Service broadcasts; like the Blair speech, it consists

```
1.        a million people through as education work. Just along from this magnificent
2.           the New Labour government who have worked with them, are so passionate
3.  delivering better lives for Britain's hard working families, because that is my job
4.           the top line of my job spec- to work for Britain, and the British people
5.      the country's hopeless, the NHS can't work, the education system is in tatters
6.      and earn every vote, every seat as we work towards earning a majority. I said
7.      and I learnt. I learnt than when I'm working hard, trying my damnedest and
8.       third pledge because that is what hard-working families told us they needed
9.  ld not have been possible without the hard work of people who work for and run
10.      without the hard work of people who work for and run our businesses. I don't
11.      give them ours and ask them to keep working with us to keep our economy
12.      a lot going for us because of the work, the strength, the creativity and the
13.      and year to value and respect the work of the real deliverers, the people
14.  officers, local council staff and people working together, using the new ASB
15.       ID cards and strict controls that work to combat asylum abuse and illegal
16.      their ability to juggle family and work. I saw the new computers and the
17.  Cutting the housing programme for key workers and first time buyers. I do not
18.       More people off benefit and into work using minimum wage and more
19. survive. More people off benefit and into work. Worthless? Yes, to the Tory
```

Figure 9.2. Concordance for *work*, including inflections and derived forms, in the Blair speech

of scripted speech, and a good deal of its content concerns current affairs. The Bank of English software gives frequency figures as per-millionages, so the percentages generated by WordSmith Tools need to be multiplied by 10,000 to get a comparison, which is shown in Table 9.3.

Table 9.3. Frequencies of *work, working, workers* in BBC World Service corpus and Blair speech

|  | *BBC World Service corpus*<br>Occurrences per million words | *Blair speech*<br>Occurrences per million words |
|---|---|---|
| *work* | 511.5 | 2800 |
| *working* | 233.3 | 1100 |
| *workers* | 239.1 | 200 |

This analysis supports the intuition that *work* and *working* are a good deal more frequent in the Blair corpus than in a comparable reference corpus. However, *workers* is less frequent in the Blair corpus. A more detailed semantic analysis would then need to be carried out to see whether there are specific uses by Blair which account for these differences, and, if some of these are metaphorical, what the metaphor connotes.

## Identifying metaphors manually to examine in a reference corpus

Where a text is short enough to be searched by hand, as is the case for the Blair speech, metaphors can be identified and then compared with their use in a reference corpus. There are some differences between the use of metaphor in the Blair speech, and its use in the reference corpus. Three examples are given here.

### An analysis of *crockery*

Blair uses the image of an angry domestic scene in which one partner throws crockery at another, as follows:

> 8.  And before you know it you raise your voice. I raise mine. Some of you *throw a bit of crockery*.

There are only four citations referring to *crockery* being broken in anger in the Bank of English, as follows:

> 9.  She would scream, *break crockery*, threaten to kill us all.

10.    ...other capable officers, notably Cal Waller, could be sent to Riyadh to help sweep up the CINC's *broken crockery*.

11.    [He] has been booted out of his luxury home by his outraged wife – under a hail of kitchen-ware. Mac Okamoto last night told how partner Olivia, 49, *threw* a toaster and 'many items of *crockery*' at him.

12.    'Perhaps he doesn't enjoy *dodging the crockery*,' Rose said.

The British National Corpus, yielded three citations of crockery being broken in anger, in a sample 50 citations of *crockery*, as follows:

13.    When he came back she said she'd go out herself tomorrow, and if he tried to stop her she'd *smash up all his crockery*.

14.    I'm having a row with a girl, *the crockery is flying against the wall*, and I'm thinking: 'That's a fucking great line, I must use that.'

15.    My mother *threw* insults and then the *crockery*, while my father ignored the insults, caught the crockery, and produced endless cups of tea when they eventually decided to make up.

In the reference corpus citations, it seems that, where gender is specified, all throwers are females and victims male. They seem to refer to a culturally-shared scenario (see Chapter 7), in which the female thrower is irrational, and the male victim long-suffering and more detached. This is interesting when considered in relation to Blair's use, in which the thrower represents the Labour party, also his audience, and the victim is Blair himself; it could be argued that by drawing on this scenario and its stereotypical evaluations, Blair suggests that their dispute was overly emotional, but ultimately not very significant.

### An analysis of *face/face up to*

Blair describes the voters' decisions at the forthcoming general election, using the sentence:

16.    ...the story that counts is the one unfolding in the minds of millions of people around the country as they *face up to* the fundamental choice facing the country – forward or back.

The use of the metaphorical phrasal verb *face up to* was checked against a reference corpus. In the Bank of English, *face up to* usually collocates with words and expressions describing problems. The most frequent lexical right collocates in the Bank of English are:

*fact(s), reality, responsibility(ies), problem(s), concern, future, challenges*

Examples are:

17. It took a lot of strength for me to *face up to* the fact that I had a problem.
18. We now have to *face up to* the fact that Debbie has gone.

When *face* is used without *up*, it is less strongly negative and collocates with *choice*, in citations such as:

19. Last time the people were given this opportunity they were *faced* with the choice of a group which told lies and one which told the truth.

Blair's choice of *face up to* rather than *face* is, on the surface, atypical, unless its object, 'the fundamental choice facing the country' is constructed as a highly negative entity.

## An analysis of *passion* and *hunger*

Blair speaks of his aims in the following sentences:

20. I have the same *passion and hunger* as when I first walked through the door of 10 Downing Street. Because I have seen what our progressive values applied to the modern world can do. [...] And the *hunger and passion* is there for me because though I can see change happening, I know it's not nearly enough.

The metaphorical use of *hunger* was analysed in the Bank of English. The collocation of *hunger* with *passion*, which occurs twice in Blair's speech, does not occur in the sample of the Bank of English consulted.

The most frequent objects of metaphorical *hunger* are as follows, in order of frequency:

*success, power, glory, winning*

As these collocates would suggest, in terms of meaning, *hunger* is used metaphorically to talk about the desire to win, especially in sporting contexts. Metaphorical *hunger* is also used, though less frequently, to talk about the desire for entities such as freedom and knowledge, but when this is the case, the object of *hunger* is specified. When it is not specified, as in Blair's speech, context suggests that *hunger* refers to personal ambition.

For the three examples discussed in this section, there is the interesting question of the motivations for these language choices: is Blair following the norms of lexical use? If not, why has he broken them? Corpus analysis cannot answer this, because it concerns the speaker's intentions and inner meanings, which may not be consciously accessible even to him. If we decide that the choice of *throw a bit of crockery, face up to the fundamental choice* and *passion and hunger* break normal lexical use, we may conclude that this is due to the speaker's (or speech writer's) need to express difficult and sensitive concepts, which have led him or her to distort slightly the normal meaning and use of these words. On the other hand, it could be argued that these language choices are leaking meanings which exist in the speaker's mind but which are not overtly present in the speech. These would be that the Labour party is over-emotional but ultimately powerless faced with its leader (throwing crockery), that when they come to vote they must confront difficult truths that they have been avoiding (face up to), and that one of Blair's strongest drivers is not the desire for change but personal ambition (hunger). The potential implications of the 'crockery-throwing' scenario in particular were not lost on political commentators, who, in the days following the speech, repeatedly remarked on the way in which Blair had constructed a personal relationship between himself and the electorate, characterized at different times as a blossoming romantic relationship or as a marriage. For instance, the BBC News website reported the speech under the headline 'Rekindling the Labour love affair' (Wheeler, 2005), while the *Independent* newspaper began its report on the speech 'Tony Blair tried to rekindle his jaded relationship with the British people yesterday' (Russell, 2005).

In each of the cases that we have studied in this section, a corpus approach has enabled us to identify atypical uses of words and grammar, often in comparison with other language users.

## Studying 'keyness' with Wmatrix

In the preceding sections we have used concordances to carry out comparisons between the uses of particular expressions in Blair's speech and in a large reference corpus. We have shown how this can reveal the likely associations of individual expressions (e.g. *crockery*), and more generally contribute to the investigation of the peculiar characteristics of a particular set of data as opposed to a much larger and more representative sample of the language. In the rest of this chapter, we introduce a software tool (Wmatrix) that is especially designed to compare different corpora, and we discuss its potential for metaphor analysis.[1]

Wmatrix is a web-based software tool that automatically compares the frequencies of different linguistic categories in different corpora, such as a specially built corpus on the one hand (be it a single text or a collection of texts) and a larger reference corpus on the other. The two-million word BNC sampler is provided for comparison, but it is also possible for the researcher to upload their own reference corpus. Comparisons can be carried out at three levels:

1. The word level
2. The part of speech level
3. The semantic field level.

At the word level, the software generates word lists for each of the two corpora and compares them with one another.[2] Statistically significant differences between the two corpora are calculated via log likelihood, which has a threshold value of 6.63 for 99 per cent significance ($p = 0.01$). The output of this tool enables the analyst to see which words are used significantly more frequently in the specialized corpus than in the reference corpus. Such unusually frequent, or overused, words are known as *key words*[3] (NB: WordSmith Tools also includes a key word facility). The page displaying the results of the key word analysis includes links to concordances of each word, which can be used, among other things, to identify metaphorical instances of each expression.

The analysis of key words is a useful complement to the examination of raw frequencies of words in texts and corpora. In Section 4 we provided a list of the most frequent lexical words in Blair's speech, i.e. lexical words that occur more than five times. Amongst other things, we noted that this list includes the word *back* (20 occurrences), which is used metaphorically on several occasions and in different ways in the speech. More specifically, one of Blair's uses of *back* is part of a metaphorical opposition with *forward*, whose ten occurrences in the speech are all metaphorical. The expression *forward not back* occurs three times in the speech, and was also used as the slogan for the Labour party's 2005 election campaign (*Britain forward not back*). These observations are valuable, but they cannot be used to claim that Blair makes an unusually frequent use of these words in the speech in comparison with English generally or with comparable genres.

We therefore used the key word facility in Wmatrix to compare Blair's speech with the 'context-governed' spoken section of the BNC sampler, which includes approximately half a million words of transcribed speech from a range of institutional contexts, such as classroom interaction, business meetings, news commentaries, lectures, political speeches, and so on. The comparison revealed that 428 words are overused in the speech with a log likelihood value of 6.63 or above. The ten most overused items are: *1997, Tory, pledge, country, Britain, worthless, learnt, people, new* and *spending*. Several of these expressions are also included in our earlier list of words with five or more occurrences (e.g. *Tory, people*) while others are not (e.g. *learnt, spending*). More specifically, *forward* is the fifteenth most overused word (log likelihood = 34.46) and *back* is the sixty-fifth most overused word (log likelihood = 18.21). These results indicate that Blair does use these words unusually frequently, but also enable us to make more precise claims. In terms of frequency, Blair's use of *forward* (which is exclusively metaphorical in the speech) is more idiosyncratic than his use of *back* (which oscillates between literal and metaphorical uses). The top 100 most overused words include several other expressions that are only used metaphorically in the speech, such as: *backward*, *delivered* and *fight*. In other words, this kind of analysis reveals the words which are most characteristic of the specialized corpus, and enables the metaphor analyst to investigate the presence of metaphorical uses via links to concordances for each word.

The other two tools in Wmatrix work in a similar way, but operate on versions of the two corpora that have been automatically annotated (or tagged), i.e. enriched with additional information. The part of speech component allocates each word in the two corpora to a grammatical word class (e.g. noun, verb, etc.), and then compares the frequencies of each word class in the two corpora.[4] The output enables the analyst to see which word classes are overused in one's own data as compared with the reference corpus. Similarly, the semantic field component allocates each word in the two corpora to a semantic field (e.g. people, objects), and then compares the frequencies of each semantic field in the two corpora. The output enables the analyst to see which semantic fields are overused in one's own data as opposed to the reference corpus. In the next section we will show how the semantic annotation tool can be exploited in order to search for metaphorical expressions. This, we will argue, is particularly relevant when dealing with data that, unlike Blair's speech, is too large to be analysed manually.

### Semantic annotation, key semantic fields and metaphor analysis

The semantic annotation component in Wmatrix relies on the USAS tool, which was developed at Lancaster University and is continuously being refined (http://ucrel.lancs.ac.uk/usas/). This tool exploits a multi-level semantic tagset which includes 21 main semantic fields (e.g. 'Government and Public', 'Life and Living Things', 'Time'). Each of these broad fields of meaning is subdivided into more specific semantic fields, often involving several sub-levels. For example, the broad field of 'Life and Living Things', is further subdivided into several more fine-grained semantic fields, including 'Alive', 'Dead', 'Plants' and 'Living creatures: animals, birds, etc.'. In the process of annotation, the software uses a purpose-built lexicon to allocate all words in the corpora under analysis to a semantic field. This process has been found to have an accuracy of 91–92% (Rayson *et al.*, 2004). In addition, it is possible to obtain a list of further semantic fields that each word can potentially belong to, in addition to the one which it has actually been allocated to by the tool.

The USAS tool was not developed for metaphor analysis, but has considerable potential as an aid to metaphor researchers (see Hardie *et al.*, 2007; Koller *et al.*, 2008; Archer *et al.*, 2009; Koller, 2009). As we suggest below, the semantic fields included in the tagset can be broadly related to the domains of conceptual metaphor theory (Lakoff and Johnson, 1980, 1999). Hence it is possible to examine the output of the annotation process to identify any semantic fields that may correspond to metaphorical source domains (e.g. the semantic field 'Health and disease' in a corpus of press articles on the economy). The analyst can then view concordances of all expressions included under those semantic fields, and identify any metaphorical uses. In this way, it is possible to extract from the data open-ended sets of metaphorical expressions, without being limited to specific word forms as is the case with concordances, frequency lists and key words.

We used the USAS tool to compare Blair's speech with the context-governed section of the spoken part of the BNC sampler. We obtained a list of semantic fields that were found to be overused in the speech as compared with the reference corpus. Of these, 44 were found to be overused with a log likelihood value of 6.63 or above, and can therefore be described as 'key' semantic fields in the speech. The five most overused semantic fields were: 'Politics', 'Alive', 'Education in general', 'People', 'Government'. These provide an overview of the general topics that dominate the speech, but are unlikely to correspond to metaphorical source domains (NB: the 'Alive' semantic field is overused as a consequence of the frequency of two word forms only: *life* and *lives*). An examination of the list of 44 overused fields does, however, include several more likely candidates, such as (in order of decreasing statistical significance): 'Tough/strong', 'Location and direction', 'Hindering', 'Stationary' and 'Religion and the supernatural'. In the light of our earlier comments on metaphorical expressions relating to motion, we will consider particularly the semantic fields that relate to movement. In terms of conceptual metaphor theory, this means that we will focus primarily on metaphorical expressions that realise the PATH image schema (Chapter 3) and/or the JOURNEY source domain.

One of the 21 main semantic fields included in the USAS tagset is: 'M: Movement, location, travel and transport'. This broad field subsumes nine more specific semantic fields, which are as follows:

M1   Moving, coming and going
M2   Putting, pulling, pushing, transporting
M3   Vehicles and transport on land
M4   Sailing, swimming, etc.
M4–  Non-swimming

M5   Flying and aircraft
M6   Location and direction
M7   Places
M8   Stationary

Four of these semantic fields (M1, M2, M6 and M8) are included as overused items in the output of the semantic analysis of the Blair speech as compared with our reference corpus. In two cases (M6 and M8) the overuse is statistically significant (log likelihood = 6.63 or above). All four semantic fields are included in Table 9.4, in decreasing order of statistical significance. The table also provides the following information: the number of word types[5] from the speech that were subsumed under each semantic field; the number of word types from each semantic field that have at least one metaphorical use in the speech, and the percentage out of all types ('Met word types'); the number of word tokens in the speech that were subsumed under each semantic field; the number of metaphorical word tokens in the speech from each semantic field, and the percentage out of all tokens ('Met word tokens'); the log likelihood value for each field.

Table 9.4. Overused semantic fields included under 'M: Movement, location, travel and transport' in the Blair speech

| Semantic fields subsumed under M: movement, location, travel and transport | Word types | Met word types | Word tokens | Met word tokens | Log likelihood value |
|---|---|---|---|---|---|
| M6 Location and direction | 28 | 21 (75%) | 70 | 44 (63%) | 17.69 |
| M8 Stationary | 5 | 3 (60%) | 9 | 4 (44%) | 10.37 |
| M2 Putting, pulling, pushing, transporting | 21 | 21 (100%) | 28 | 28 (100%) | 2.77 |
| M1 Moving, coming and going | 32 | 17 (53%) | 43 | 24 (56%) | 0.59 |
| **Total** | 86 | 62 (72%) | 150 | 100 (66%) | – |

The high log likelihood associated with the M6 semantic field in particular indicates that Blair uses expressions to do with location and direction unusually frequently in the speech. More specifically, the fact that 63% of the word tokens included under the M6 semantic field are used metaphorically provides some indication that Blair makes a particularly frequent use of metaphorical expressions that are to do with motion and location. For the purposes of metaphor analysis, however, it is worth examining all semantic fields that are likely to correspond to metaphorical source domains, whether or not they are overused to a statistically significant extent.

As Table 9.4 shows, an examination of the words that were subsumed under all four semantic fields enabled us to identify, in total, 62 different types of metaphorical expressions, and 100 actual occurrences. These are not limited to the expressions we had noted by considering word lists and key words (e.g. *back*), but include a much larger number and variety of further expressions, such as *route, journey* and *gone* in the extracts below (NB: below we underline the metaphorical expressions that were allocated by the software to one of the overused semantic fields included in Table 9.4):

19. a modernised Labour Party is the <u>route</u> to a Britain modernised in a way that benefits the many and not the few.
20. So this <u>journey</u> has <u>gone</u> from 'all things to all people' to 'I know best' to 'we can only do it together'.

None of the three underlined words occurs sufficiently frequently in the speech to be noticed via an examination of key words or of lists of the most frequent lexical words. However, they are all part of a complex network of motion metaphors that contribute to the internal structure and rhetorical force of Blair's speech. Similar considerations apply to other metaphorically used words included under the four semantic domains in Table 9.4, such as *settled, rising, position, comes from*, etc. When analysing small amounts of data such as Blair's speech, it would of course have been possible to identify all these expressions via a traditional manual analysis. With larger amounts of data, however, a thorough manual analysis is not possible, and the contribution of the semantic annotation tool is therefore much more valuable.

As we mentioned earlier, the list of semantic fields that are overused in Blair's speech includes a number of further examples of likely metaphorical source domains, such as Tough/strong, Hindering, Religion and the supernatural, Lack of food, and so on. A detailed investigation of each of these semantic fields would have yielded several instances of metaphorical expressions. The 'Lack of food' semantic field, for example, includes the two metaphorical uses of the word *hunger* we discussed above.

The manual search of the output of the USAS tool for potential metaphorical source domains does have a major limitation, however. The metaphorical senses of some highly conventional metaphorical expressions are, not surprisingly, included in the lexicon. In such cases, the software may therefore (correctly) allocate the word to a semantic field that, for our purposes, corresponds to the target domain of the metaphor. This is the case, for example, for the three instances of the word *backward*, which are used by Blair to describe the Tories and their policies as antiquated and inadequate (e.g. *the stupidest most backward policy you could think of*). All three instances of this word were allocated to the semantic field 'Inability/unintelligence'. In contrast, novel uses of metaphor will always be placed under a semantic field corresponding to the source domain. The word *crockery*, for example, was placed under 'Food'.

There are two ways to overcome this relative unpredictability of the classification of metaphorical expressions. One is to look closely at those semantic fields that are likely to correspond to target domains, i.e. those that relate to relatively abstract, complex and subjective areas of experience. This applies to 'Inability/unintelligence', for example, as well as to semantic fields such as 'Failure' and 'Helping'. The other method involves a development of the USAS environment in Wmatrix which has been made specifically in order to facilitate metaphor analysis (Hardie *et al.*, 2007; see Koller *et al.*, 2008). The semantic annotation tool includes a 'Broad Sweep' search facility, which enables the researcher to find all expressions that include a particular semantic tag in their profile, whether or not it has been chosen by the software as the one it should be associated with in a particular case. For example, we have mentioned that the word *backward* in the Blair speech was allocated to the semantic field 'Inability/unintelligence'. In this case, this particular semantic tag was (rightly) chosen by the software among a range of possibilities for the word, which also included M6 ('Location and direction'). A broad sweep search of M6, or of the whole larger field of 'Movement, location, travel and transport' includes *backward* among many other further expressions, some of which are used metaphorically in the speech.

Another potential limitation of the software is that it is unlikely to recognize *ad hoc* metaphorical scenarios such as the one where Blair and the country are involved in a rather tempestuous relationship. In the USAS output, the different expressions that evoke this scenario are not all placed under the same semantic fields. However, some small subsets of these expressions *are* placed together, so that an analyst may have been able to follow them up and discover the whole scenario. For example, the concordance for the M2 semantic field ('Putting, pulling, pushing, transporting') includes the following three consecutive lines:

| | | |
|---|---|---|
| And before you know it you | raise | your voice. I raise mine. |
| it you raise your voice. I | raise | mine. Some of you throw a bit |
| I raise mine. Some of you | throw | a bit of crockery. And now |

These lines contain part of the scenario, which could then be explored in full by clicking the links that provide more context for each citation. Nonetheless, one cannot be certain that all cases of similar metaphorical scenarios can be identified in this way.

Clearly, the use of the USAS semantic annotation tool for the study of metaphor involves careful manual analysis (and some ingenuity) on the part of the researcher. Familiarity with one's data is also crucial in deciding what semantic fields are likely to reward detailed investigation. Overall, however, the crucial advantage of this analytical method is that the researcher is able to explore metaphorical patterns relating to a range of potential source domains without being restricted to individual word forms or pre-determined lists of potential metaphorical expressions.

## Conclusions

In this chapter we have provided a brief overview of corpus based techniques which can be of use to metaphor researchers in a variety of disciplines. In spite of the inevitable use of technical terminology, we hope we have managed to suggest that relatively little technical expertise is needed to use corpora for one's own research goals. What we have not been able to do, for reasons of space, is to discuss in detail the potential significance and implications of the metaphorical phenomena that can be uncovered via corpus based methods. These will of course vary depending on the researcher's goals. Koller (2004), for example, adopts a corpus based approach to the exploration of the relationship between metaphor and gender in business magazine articles. A number of recent studies have similarly demonstrated the relevance of corpus-based approaches to the study of metaphor in, amongst others, politics and the media (e.g. Charteris-Black, 2004; Koller, 2004; Musolff, 2004; Semino, 2008).

### Notes

1.  Wmatrix was developed by Paul Rayson at Lancaster University, and can be accessed here: http://ucrel.lancs.ac.uk/wmatrix/. Free trials are available on request.
2.  The software recognizes multi-word expressions such as phrasal verbs and proper names, but here we are using the general term 'word' for the sake of simplicity.
3.  The tool also identifies underused words, i.e. words that are used significantly less frequently in one's own data as compared with a reference corpus.
4.  The part-of-speech annotation is carried out by means of the CLAWS tool, which has been shown to have an accuracy of 96–97% (see websites section for URL).
5.  Here 'word type' refers to word forms, rather than lemmas. For example, the different forms of the verb lemma *go* (i.e. *go, goes, gone*, etc.) are treated as separate types.

### Websites

The Bank of English: http://www.collins.co.uk/books.aspx?group=153
British National Corpus: http://www.natcorp.ox.ac.uk/
CLAWS tool: http://ucrel.lancs.ac.uk/claws/
USAS tool: http://ucrel.lancs.ac.uk/usas/
Wmatrix: http://ucrel.lancs.ac.uk/wmatrix/
WordSmith Tools 5: www.lexically.net/wordsmith/

# 10 Working with large amounts of metaphor data

## Robert Maslen

> *Thus all things are presented by shadows.*
> Erasmus, *The Praise of Folly* (1511/1941, 14)

When technology makes one of its periodic advances, we should always accompany the leap forward with a backward glance. This was known in the fifteenth century, when the printing press revolutionized the way words and texts could spread, but also raised questions about the accuracy of the Vulgate bible, sending scholars back to the oldest Greek and Hebrew source documents. And the same is true today: information technology has opened up a great array of prospects in language research. It is now possible to gather data in volumes unimaginable a generation or two ago. But it is also easier than ever to construct analytical abstractions which lose contact with the texts they are drawn from. The study of figurative language use is particularly demanding in this regard, and so the rallying cry of the Renaissance humanists is always worth keeping in mind: *ad fontes*, they said: 'Back to the sources'.

Following this principle was a key aspect of the metaphor analysis carried out as part of the Perception and Communication of Terrorist Risk (PCTR) project which provided the data we used in Chapters 6 and 7. To recap, the project was a multi-method exploration of conceptualizations of terrorist risk. It applied the approach to metaphor identification explored in this book to twelve 90-minute focus group discussions of approximately 190,000 words in total, and identified 12,363 linguistic metaphors for analysis (Cameron *et al.*, 2009). The researchers were unaware of work of a similar scope on the same sort of data and so they developed techniques *in situ* for managing the project material through coding and analysis, and for maintaining links to the source texts. This chapter presents some of the key lessons learned during that process. It is not intended to be prescriptive and is not an exploration of corpus techniques *per se* (dealt with in detail in Chapter 9); rather, it examines one experience of research practice which others with limited experience of metaphor analysis might adapt to their own circumstances.

## A word about software

In Chapters 6 and 7, which covered metaphor coding and analysis techniques, several examples are given from Excel tables which were used in the PCTR project for managing data. However, Excel is by no means the only software package available for large-scale metaphor studies, and a number of worthy (and, in some regards, superior) alternatives are suggested below. Deciding between them is a matter of matching software characteristics to the aims of research, and in the case of PCTR, Excel proved most appropriate, due to a number of useful features:

- Excel is based on an (for most purposes) endless spreadsheet and so can handle a very large volume of listed data simultaneously.
- The tabbed worksheet format makes it possible for the source text to be 'next to' the worksheet where extracted metaphors are listed and coded. This is very valuable during the coding process, when one has to make constant reference to the context of extracted items.
- All the information relevant to a particular metaphor (such as line number, speaker, etc.) can be presented for ease of reference in adjacent cells. However, some of this advantage is lost if data are transcribed into long turns, rather than intonation units (see Chapter 6).
- Layers of coding can be added to a worksheet adjacently, simply by entering new information in the next column along, or inserting a new column where necessary. The order of columns can be rearranged as required, depending on the focus of interest.
- Data can be sorted by multiple criteria, using the 'Sort Data' function. This is useful, for example, when gathering topics within vehicle groups.
- Once individual texts have been selected and coded, data can be consolidated into a single spreadsheet. This facilitates systematic coding and makes late-in-the-day coding revisions far easier to apply to a full dataset.
- 'Pivot tables', which automatically map the contents of Excel columns against each other quantitatively, make it possible to measure the co-occurrence of different coded elements. For example, a pivot table can quickly produce a matrix which gives the number of times given topics are referred to by metaphors in given vehicle groups.
- Charts, drawn automatically from spreadsheets and pivot tables, show up patterns which can be difficult to discern from numerical or textual data alone.
- If more advanced statistical work or numerical data manipulation is part of a project, Excel data are reasonably easily transferred to the SPSS statistics package. In the PCTR project this was very helpful in combining the metaphor analysis with other strands of the research.

Figure 10.1 shows an extract from the PCTR 'master' spreadsheet, which compiled data for analysis from the project's 12 focus groups following the process described in Chapter 6. The metaphors, codes and contextual information, though they ran to more than 12,000 lines, were, given the characteristics listed above, relatively straightforward to manipulate and search for coherent patterns.

Other software packages have their own advantages. With ATLAS.ti qualitative analysis software, for example, the coding interface keeps the source document in view, which is less easily achieved with Excel and does away with the possibility of reading wrongly between the lines of a list of extracted metaphors. Figure 10.2 shows the portion of the Leeds focus group used in Chapter 6 coded for vehicles and topics in ATLAS.ti. Although this software lacks some of the sorting capabilities of Excel, several of its features are superior. Initial 'in vivo' coding, in which a selected item is coded by its own name, soon builds up a list which can be applied to subsequent items and then refined. 'Coding by list' then serves as a very efficient method of processing the rest of a transcript (and subsequent transcripts). 'Quick coding', which codes an item with the code used previously, can speed up topic coding considerably, since

| | KTs | V Group | Group | Metaphor | Line | Speaker | Text |
|---|---|---|---|---|---|---|---|
| 10725 | 3 | VIOLENT ACTION | LeABM | backlash | 1770 | Peter | I don't think there's been much backlash at-- |
| 10726 | 3M | VIOLENT ACTION | LoMM | backlash | 943 | Sarfraz | but because of the backlash as well. |
| 10727 | 3 | VIOLENT ACTION | LeABM | backlash | 961 | Sean | . a bigger backlash. |
| 10728 | 3A | VIOLENT ACTION | LeCDM | banged up | 3873 | Phil | ... to get banged up. |
| 10729 | 2N | VIOLENT ACTION | LeCDM | break | 3973 | Josh | they break into programmes. |
| 10730 | 3 | VIOLENT ACTION | LoCDW | break down | 2558 | Eve | you'd have a nervous break down. |
| 10731 | 1 | VIOLENT ACTION | LeMM | break down | 1216 | Rashid | to break down the civil order. |
| 10732 | 2N | VIOLENT ACTION | LeCDM | break in | 3971 | Josh | I mean they break in -- |
| 10733 | 2N | VIOLENT ACTION | Lo ABM | break it down | 3556 | Jeff | break it down for you. |
| 10734 | 4 | VIOLENT ACTION | LeMM | breakdown | 1218 | Rashid | community breakdown. |
| 10735 | 2N | VIOLENT ACTION | LeABW | breaking | 905 | Diane | when it was breaking. |
| 10736 | 2N | VIOLENT ACTION | LeABW | breaking | 908 | Diane | and it was all breaking news |
| 10737 | 4 | VIOLENT ACTION | LeCDM | breaking | 3862 | Eddie | who are breaking the laws, |
| 10738 | 2N | VIOLENT ACTION | LeCDM | breaking | 3972 | Josh | they're breaking that newsflashes. |
| 10739 | 2N | VIOLENT ACTION | LeABW | breaking | 2999 | Lynne | when there's different news items breaking |
| 10740 | 2N | VIOLENT ACTION | LeCDM | breaking | 3922 | Terry | ..<X breaking X>.. news. |
| 10741 | 4 | VIOLENT ACTION | LoMM | breaking apart | 1376 | Sarfraz | .Russia's breaking apart? |
| 10742 | 3A | VIOLENT ACTION | LeABM | broken down | 4081 | Peter | . a place that should be broken down so easily |
| 10743 | 2N | VIOLENT ACTION | LeABM | broken loose | 345 | Mike | . hell that's broken loose. |
| 10744 | 3A | VIOLENT ACTION | LoMM | broken up | 3196 | Farid | ... (1.0) today Iraq is completely broken up |
| 10745 | 1 | VIOLENT ACTION | LeCDM | bullying | 152 | Ray | it's a form of bullying. |
| 10746 | 1 | VIOLENT ACTION | LeABM | burst in | 3234 | Adam | but if a guy's burst in with guns. |
| 10747 | 4M | VIOLENT ACTION | LoABM | conflict | 2336 | Roy | in conflict with our, |
| 10748 | 3 | VIOLENT ACTION | LeABW | crushed up | 154 | Celia | when you're crushed up. |
| 10749 | 3 | VIOLENT ACTION | LoCDM | cut | 3302 | Leo | we'd . cut that down. |
| 10750 | 4M | VIOLENT ACTION | LeABW | cut off | 1593 | Diane | so cut off from society. |
| 10751 | 4M | VIOLENT ACTION | LeABW | cut off | 1612 | Diane | cut off the dialogue, |
| 10752 | 1 | VIOLENT ACTION | LoABM | cut off | 255 | Roy | all the mobiles were cut off. |

Figure 10.1. PCTR master focus coding spreadsheet containing data from 12 focus groups

it is interesting that different meanings of the same word can have opposite orientations.

The uses of *(I'm) back* were then studied in detail, using a 59 million-word sample of the Bank of English as a reference corpus (see above). There are 62,542 citations of *back* in the reference corpus. Of these, there are 1,692 citations of *Back* (that is, with upper-case *B*); the vast majority of these are accounted for back in expressions such as *Back to Basics*, or song titles such as *Baby Come Back*, or begin sentences with an adverbial group, in citations such as:

1. *Back* in the seventies you could start a job one week and start another one the following week.

Within the concordance for *back*, with lower case *b*, a search for '*m back*', to find instances of '*I am back*' and '*I'm back*' produces 1655 citations. Citations such as '*[bring] him back*' need to be taken out. This has to be done by hand, but sorting alphabetically reduces the time needed. Citations containing strings such as '*him back*' and '*them back*' appear together if the concordance is sorted alphabetically to the left of the search word, *back*, making it fairly straightforward to identify and delete them. After reducing the concordance to '*I'm back*' and '*am back*', 107 citations remain. These can be divided into two roughly equal sized groups: clearly literal (50 citations), and those with varying degrees of metaphoricity (57 citations). Examples are as follows:

*Literal*

2. I let myself out and drive home. I am *back* in my own bed by 6 a.m.

*Metaphorical*

3. I'm *back* to the level where I can compete.
4. I'm *back* in business.
5. I'm *back* with a bang.
6. I'm *back* on course for a British title shot.
7. The world should know that I'm *back* – and ready to rock.

In each of the metaphorical citations, the subject has been performing below par, ill, out of favour or in some other way metaphorically 'away'. The use of *back* therefore indicates the positive process whereby the person has newly acquired their full mental and/or physical abilities, and is once again ready for action.

Blair's use of *I'm back* seems to combine the two uses found in the reference corpus. Most uses are apparently literal, but they also seem to evoke the consecutive metaphors often refer to the same discourse topic, if not the same referent. Although it must be used with caution, ATLAS.ti also has an automatic coding function, whereby all instances of a designated string can be assigned a particular code. High frequency terms often used metaphorically (such as prepositions) could be coded in this way, assuming that a post hoc check was made to exclude errors.

However, it is at the analysis stage that ATLAS.ti may be particularly useful as a tool in metaphor research. Its 'network view' feature allows the on-screen manipulation of coding tags – which in metaphor research may be vehicles, topics or other features of the data – in a high-tech version of the traditional table sort. This provides a useful starting point for seeing significant systematic relationships which can then be explored in the verbatim transcripts. The 'query tool' is a powerful function which allows the user to explore mappings between different codes. Codes can be grouped hierarchically and frequency information about individual items and co-occurrence between items can be generated easily. Rees *et al.* (2007) (see also Chapter 2) provides an example of research conducted with the aid of ATLAS.ti.

Like ATLAS.ti, NVivo qualitative analysis software automatically maintains the link between coded items and source data, including the potential to link

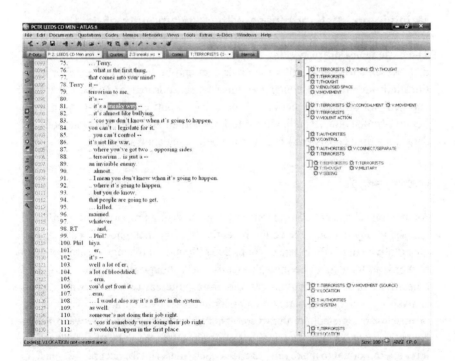

Figure 10.2. Example of metaphor coding in ATLAS.ti (PCTR Leeds CD men transcript)

to the original sound file. Its capacity to facilitate the building of hierarchical structures and networks from node categories (which might represent vehicles and topics) is clearly applicable to the emergent approach to systematic relationships advocated in this book.

Researchers whose metaphor work has a technical linguistic focus, and particularly if it includes grammatical analysis, may consider preparing and searching their data using the conventions and software developed by the CHILDES project (http://childes.psy.cmu.edu/, see MacWhinney, 1991 for an overview). The software is available for free download and although the system was developed for the language acquisition field, its ability to recover frequency, context, co-occurrence and other information efficiently from large datasets (including raw text files) gives it the potential to support analyses of systematic patterns of metaphor use.

This is far from an exhaustive list of software available to assist analysis. Readers may see advantages in other software not included here. They should also refer to Chapter 9 for ideas about how specific corpus techniques can be applied to metaphor. However, the software mentioned above should be adequate for the needs of most metaphor research dealing with considerable volumes of data and using the methods set out in this volume.

## Maintaining trustworthiness with large amounts of data

The basic tenets of trustworthy analysis hold true regardless of the volume of data. Researchers must still know their data and be trained in metaphor identification; identification boundaries must be set, portions of coded transcripts checked and differences between coders ironed out; changes that result from iterative, collaborative coding need to be recorded and applied throughout the data and a final consistency check made before the analysis begins.

### Checking transcripts

As previous chapters have demonstrated, a surprising proportion of words and phrases in any discourse have the potential to carry metaphoric meaning; one quantitative study (Pragglejaz group, 2007) found an average of around 10% of words in its texts to be metaphorically used, though this varied across text types. Inaccurate transcription can therefore quite easily find its way into an analysis by including apparent metaphors in the text which were never spoken, or missing out metaphors that were. This potential mismatch between a discourse event and subsequent analysis multiplies with the volume of data and so it is very important to make time to check each transcript for accuracy against its original recording. To give an example of why this matters, a senior public official, interviewed for the PCTR research about his work liaising with Muslims in the aftermath of the 7/7 bombings, seemed to announce in a first draft transcript, *my work is Hindus really.* When the transcript was reviewed, this unexpected approach to community tensions disappeared, as he had actually said (speaking about press reporting), *my work is hindered severely.*

## Familiarity with transcripts

It is just as important to read and get to know a transcript when it is part of a large dataset as when it is the only one to be analysed. All the processes involved in identifying, coding and analysing metaphors rely on the researcher knowing the original talk well and ideally this will include a familiarity with the sound file. Researchers who have gathered and transcribed the data they analyse will have an advantage in this regard, but familiarity with recordings and texts does of course diminish with time and the salient details of several focus groups become less easy to distinguish from one another.

## Identification and coding of metaphors

Although much of the coding and analysis process takes place on screen, the identification stage, even when there are lot of transcripts to get through, might afford the researcher another opportunity to spend some time with the paper transcript. As with initially reading the text, insight gained from organic interaction with the data – a favourite chair as the birds begin to roost, the scratch of the pencil on the page – is an invaluable resource in the later stages of analysis.

Two researchers worked on each PCTR transcript, initially on paper, when time allowed. When one had selected the metaphors, the transcript was passed to the other, who checked the selection and made comments on possible changes, such as whether an item be included/excluded as a metaphor or where boundaries should be set round a particular item. Changes were discussed, and once in Excel the metaphor list was amended in line with the decision made. Decisions were recorded. Later transcripts tended to require fewer changes as the collaborative process specified more closely the criteria for identification.

The metaphor list itself was generated by specially created software, called VisDis, which can automatically create a list of selected items with additional contextual information. This list was then transferred to Excel for coding. VisDis is still in development and is not widely available, but a simple alternative is to identify metaphors in a text file by underlining, and then copy the underlined text into Excel. Metaphors could also be identified directly in Excel. Without an automatic list, metaphors need to be re-entered in a column adjacent to the relevant line of transcript text (see Figure 10.1 for the format). Transcripts not coded in intonation units would become unwieldy using this method since, if selected metaphors were to be listed adjacent to the text they appeared in, multiple copies would have to be made (vertically on the spreadsheet) of any unit of text that contained more than one metaphor. The extra effort that intonation units initially require therefore begins to pay dividends in terms of visual clarity at this point, and is more valuable the more data there are to look through.

For coding the metaphors, a separate Excel file was initially set up for each of 12 transcripts. In these, the first worksheet contained the full transcription and the second the metaphor list for coding. In this way the transcript was always available for checking that a selected item met criteria for having metaphoric potential if that was not clear from the context of one intonation unit alone (see Chapter 6).

As described in Chapter 7, vehicle categories were informed by previous research (e.g. Cameron, 2003; Semino, 2005) but were principally constructed 'bottom up' from the semantics of vehicle terms. Developing and assigning vehicle codes, like selecting metaphors, was a collaborative process. One researcher undertook the initial coding of a particular file, then passed it to a colleague for checking. Potential changes were discussed, agreed upon, applied to the data and recorded. Metaphors were also coded for topics, using the same basic approach, but from a fixed, research-specific list (see below and Chapter 7).

As the process speeds up, coders have to be conscious of interpretative bias in their own and each other's categorizations, particularly where they are dealing with multiple transcripts and speakers (96 participants, in the case of PCTR). Once again, the active presence of the text is the surest way of not straying from what is warranted by the transcription.

Since vehicle codes were refined with each new transcript, files that had been coded earlier had to be altered. To avoid the potential for inconsistencies, a master file containing the full coded metaphor list for all 12 focus groups was created, and this was used to establish the final set of vehicle codes (although the word 'final' is misleading, since categories continue to have the potential to develop). In keeping with previous practice, two coders worked together through the 12,000 plus identified metaphors. During this process, the number of vehicle groups was reduced somewhat through combining categories with complementary semantics and removing some items altogether (see Chapter 7). Although by this stage researchers were familiar with individual transcripts and speakers, it was the first point at which the source texts were not side by side with the coded lists. The researchers therefore had to be conscious of actively justifying changes to coding by reference to participants' actual talk.

The master spreadsheet provided the basic tool for subsequent analysis (see Figure 10.1). Within it, categories (columns) could be sorted dependently, which meant that various features of the data – vehicle groups, topics, focus groups and so on – could be examined together for consistencies and interesting exemplars.

Coders approaching a metaphor list for data formatted in intonation units should always be aware of the non-metaphorical language not captured by the list. It is very easy to treat the list as contiguous data and read down it as if reading a transcript. This is likely to have only a small effect on the accuracy of vehicle coding, but topic coding can be more sensitive to shifts that take place in the lines of transcript not included in the list of metaphors. Consider the following example from the PCTR data:

METAPHOR LIST

| | | | | | |
|---|---|---|---|---|---|
| CONTAINER | in | 2824 | Diane | I was <u>in</u> Tel Aviv on my way to Cyprus, |
| MOVEMENT | went off | 2826 | Diane | and a bomb <u>went off</u> in a bus stop, |
| MOVEMENT | brought it back | 2830* | Diane | that just <u>brought it back</u> to me. |
| DEPTH | up | 2840* | Cathy | who live <u>up</u> north in Israel, |
| CONTAINER | in | 2840 | Cathy | who live up north <u>in</u> Israel, |

It is reasonably clear that by Cathy's turn at line 2840 the topic has shifted since Diane's at 2830 (marked with asterisks in the extract above), but the precise nature of the new topic remains opaque from the information in the metaphor list. To know this, we have to refer to the transcript (Extract 10.1).

Extract 10.1

| | | |
|---|---|---|
| 2833 | Cathy | people who live there, |
| 2834 | Cathy | you know, |
| 2835 | Cathy | you ask them, |
| 2836 | Cathy | you talk to them, |
| 2837 | Cathy | you talk to Arabs as well, |
| 2838 | Cathy | because I-- |
| 2839 | Cathy | I knew some Arabs, |

In fact, Cathy is not speaking about Israel per se, but about how Arab Israelis respond to conflict and terrorism in Israel. This is relevant to the PCTR research but can only be recovered by checking the seven intervening lines in which no metaphor was produced. This highlights the importance of keeping the text constantly active during coding. As suggested, one way of achieving this is to use adjacent Excel worksheets for easy reference.

## Working towards findings

### Grouping metaphors

Readers will be familiar with some findings of the terrorism research from Chapter 7, which chiefly draws on data from a single transcript. Analysis of the full dataset (details of the project and abbreviations are given in the Appendix) from the master file provided evidence for systematic metaphors operating across participants from several groups. For example the systematic metaphor TERRORISM AS DEVELOPING THROUGH NATURAL GROWTH was built up from metaphors such as the following (relevant metaphors in bold font):

> *things will **evolve*** (London AB Men)
> *terrorism doesn't just **stem from** one person* (Leeds CD Men)
> *they should **look at** the **root** cause* (London Muslim Women)
> *that the community has **bred** this* (London Muslim Men)
> *in that **environment*** (London AB Women)
> *and a **virulent strain** of Islamic fundamentalism* (London AB Men).

(Total number of vehicle terms contributing to the systematic metaphor: 47.)

Another systematic metaphor conceptualized INFORMATION AS OBJECTS, a mapping familiar from previous studies (see for example Harrison *et al.*, 2008) which grew from individual metaphors such as:

> *they **give** you little **snippets*** (London CD Men)
> *you don't know whether they are **holding things back*** (Leeds AB Women)
> *and by **handing out** the **spin*** (London CD Women).

(Total number of vehicle terms contributing to the systematic metaphor: 198.)

This gives a flavour of the kind of conclusions that the master file of PCTR's extensive data made it possible to draw. Establishing these robust relationships between topics and vehicles is in many ways another beginning, of course, rather than the end of analysis. Systematic metaphors become the stepping off point for exploring the dynamics of specific discourse events (see Chapters 7 and 8), returning the researcher once again to the source.

Tables and charting

Data on the scale of the PCTR project are also amenable to a more quantitative approach to analysis. Automatically generated tables ('pivot tables' in Excel) and related visual representations can help identify potentially significant patterns which might be hard to spot in the basic metaphor list. For example, Figure 10.3 shows a chart mapping a subset of 'key topics' against focus groups in the data. Each column represents a focus group and the bands within columns represent the key topics 'responses to terrorism' (3), 'social consequences of terrorism' (4) and 'responses and consequences relating particularly to Muslims' (3M and 4M). The vertical axis measures the proportion of all the metaphors in the subset which each topic contributes within each focus group. A visual approach like this is particularly good for throwing out striking anomalies and common patterns, such as the comparative dearth of metaphorical references to Muslims (key topics 3M and 4M) in the Leeds CD Men transcript (LeCDM).

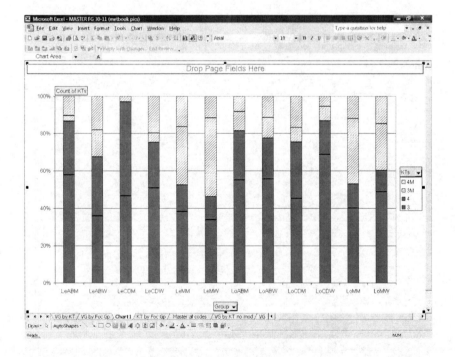

Figure 10.3. Excel 'pivot table' chart showing frequencies of different metaphorically expressed 'Key Topics' in the 12 PCTR focus groups. (Bands for key topics 3 and 4, and for 3M and 4M, are merged for ease of comparison on the page.)

The 'pivot table' in Figure 10.4 breaks down vehicle group frequencies by focus group. Vehicle groups are listed down the left of the table with focus groups running across the top. Again, this can show both general patterns (such as, everyone uses a lot of CONTAINER metaphors) and potential anomalies, such as the highly frequent use of CONNECT/SEPARATE metaphors by Leeds Muslim Men (LeMM). Of course, the question of what such patterns mean can only be answered by going back to the texts themselves.

With sufficient data, patterns can be demonstrated statistically, providing valuable support for qualitative findings. Among PCTR focus group participants, for example, men used many more NATURAL WORLD metaphors to describe terrorists and the effects of terrorism than women. Systematic metaphors expressing relationships such as GROUPS OF TERRORISTS AS NATURAL WORLD AGGREGATES, consisting of metaphors like:

> a well-known <u>bunch</u> of terrorists (London AB Men)
> a <u>cell</u> (London AB Men, London AB Women)
> an <u>element</u>

| V Group | LeABM | LeABW | LeCDM | LeCDW | LeMM | LeMW | LoABM | LoABW | LoCDM | LoCDW | LoMM | LoMW | Grand Total |
|---|---|---|---|---|---|---|---|---|---|---|---|---|---|
| ACTING / STORIES | 13 | 2 | 3 | 14 | 5 | 4 | 24 | 8 | 1 | 6 | 8 | 8 | 96 |
| ANIMALS / NATURE | 17 | 7 | 18 | 4 | 14 | 4 | 21 | 12 | 14 | 5 | 13 | 9 | 138 |
| BALANCE | 1 | 6 | 3 | 18 | 6 | 15 | 4 | 3 | 11 | 14 | 1 | 6 | 88 |
| BLOW | 26 | 1 | 15 | 11 | 2 | 5 | 5 | 6 | 10 | 8 | 6 | 4 | 99 |
| BODY | 12 | 15 | 24 | 18 | 20 | 20 | 26 | 17 | 23 | 11 | 10 | 5 | 201 |
| BUILDING | | 1 | | | | 2 | 2 | | | | 4 | | 9 |
| CIRCLE | 1 | 1 | 1 | 1 | 3 | | 3 | 1 | 2 | 1 | 1 | 1 | 16 |
| CLEAN / DIRTY | 2 | 5 | | 4 | | 6 | 5 | 6 | 6 | 1 | 1 | | 36 |
| COMMERCE | 6 | 5 | 3 | 7 | 2 | 6 | 11 | 4 | 6 | 6 | 5 | 1 | 62 |
| COMPONENT PARTS | 5 | 15 | 1 | 13 | 8 | 8 | 18 | 11 | 12 | 5 | 10 | 10 | 116 |
| CONCEALMENT | 1 | 2 | 4 | 4 | 1 | 3 | 1 | 2 | 3 | | 2 | 3 | 26 |
| CONCRETISING | 14 | 21 | 27 | 26 | 15 | 7 | 28 | 16 | 23 | 19 | 14 | 9 | 219 |
| CONNECT / SEPARATE | 28 | 29 | 20 | 19 | 69 | 19 | 34 | 35 | 14 | 28 | 28 | 22 | 345 |
| CONSTRAINT | 16 | 8 | 7 | 12 | 12 | 23 | 7 | 16 | 14 | 3 | 6 | 7 | 131 |
| CONTAINER | 138 | 179 | 199 | 166 | 230 | 115 | 228 | 151 | 177 | 139 | 116 | 102 | 1940 |
| CRAZY / WILD | 7 | 2 | 5 | 7 | 1 | 14 | 2 | 6 | 4 | 5 | 5 | 8 | 66 |
| DEPTH | 22 | 54 | 34 | 35 | 17 | 36 | 21 | 28 | 38 | 51 | 26 | 24 | 386 |
| DIMENSION | 13 | 31 | 21 | 17 | 33 | 33 | 35 | 37 | 18 | 16 | 20 | 9 | 283 |
| EXPLETIVE | 9 | 1 | 8 | | | 14 | 54 | 4 | 15 | 1 | 1 | 4 | 111 |
| FEELING | 25 | 29 | 26 | 28 | 41 | 48 | 45 | 27 | 28 | 41 | 27 | 16 | 381 |
| FINDING / LOSING | 14 | 18 | 10 | 6 | 14 | 9 | 15 | 11 | 7 | 16 | 17 | 13 | 150 |
| FOLLOWING / LEADING | 9 | 7 | 8 | 1 | 11 | 1 | 6 | 4 | 5 | 9 | 7 | 2 | 70 |
| FORM | 1 | 3 | 3 | | 1 | | | 2 | | 1 | | | 11 |
| GAME | 19 | 14 | 18 | 13 | 9 | 5 | 21 | 6 | 22 | 13 | 10 | 4 | 154 |
| GIVING / TAKING | 30 | 36 | 26 | 17 | 21 | 39 | 39 | 42 | 23 | 25 | 8 | 25 | 329 |
| HARD | 3 | 5 | 8 | 4 | 1 | 10 | 2 | 1 | 6 | 4 | | | 44 |
| HOME | 3 | 1 | 5 | | | 4 | | 2 | 1 | 7 | | | 23 |
| HORIZONTAL | 18 | 9 | 14 | 8 | 10 | 4 | 10 | 17 | 23 | 9 | 12 | 8 | 142 |
| HOT / COLD | 6 | | 2 | | 1 | 1 | 3 | 3 | | 5 | 2 | 2 | 25 |
| INCLINE | 2 | 3 | | 5 | 7 | 2 | 2 | 1 | | 9 | 3 | 2 | 36 |
| LABEL | | | | 1 | 4 | 3 | 1 | | | 1 | 4 | 7 | 21 |
| LOCATION | 75 | 108 | 95 | 123 | 108 | 91 | 126 | 101 | 71 | 98 | 70 | 74 | 1140 |

Figure 10.4. Excel 'pivot table' showing frequency mappings of focus groups and metaphor vehicle groups in PCTR data

and TERRORISTS HIDE AWAY IN DARK PLACES, with metaphors like:

> *they hide in the woodwork* (Leeds CD Men)
> and *they worm their way in* (to workplaces) (London AB Women)

were much more frequent in the male groups. This observed discrepancy (about 70%:30%) was tested statistically and found to be significant ($\chi^2 = 19.00$, df $= 1$, $p < 0.0001$).

It is important to note here that tabulated and visual data can be misleading as well as helpful. An apparent difference in vehicle categories between focus groups, for example, might represent the repeated use of one metaphor by a single participant. Speaker names in the coded data can show up this kind of effect, but it illustrates the need for researchers to be aware of potentially illusory characteristics in charts and tables and return to the transcripts to check.

## Using metaphor clusters to focus analysis

A guide to significant patterns in large volumes of metaphor data is the presence of metaphor clusters (e.g. Corts and Pollio, 1999; Corts and Meyers 2002; Chapter 1 this volume). Metaphors are not evenly distributed in talk, but tend to be produced more frequently where speakers are dealing with themes which are difficult, either conceptually or in terms of the dynamics between speakers (Cameron and Stelma, 2004). Metaphor clusters can therefore point to moments in a discourse which are worth investigating more closely. They can often be identified with little difficulty through straightforward visual inspection of a transcript, looking for sections where underlining of metaphors is particularly dense or by plotting a cumulative graph, where clusters will be marked by a steepening of the curve (Cameron and Stelma, 2004). A more quantitative approach can be taken in which a group of metaphors is deemed to be a cluster if it has a density – defined as the number of linguistic metaphors per 1,000 words of transcript – markedly greater than the transcript average. The PCTR project transcripts had a mean metaphor density of over 50 on this measure. Following Cameron and Stelma (2004) candidate clusters were first identified visually, and then checked for metaphor density. If the metaphor density was higher than 100, the segment of transcript was marked as a metaphor cluster.

As an example of using a cumulative graph, Figure 10.5 shows the cumulative total of linguistic metaphors in the Leeds CD Men focus group discussion (along the *y*-axis) plotted against time (represented by intonation unit/ line number on the *x*-axis). Each time a metaphor is used the cumulative total increases by one. When the line suddenly becomes steeper, speakers have used several metaphors in a short period of time. This happens in the segment of talk circled in the graph.

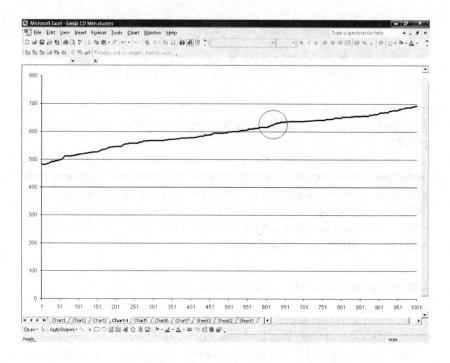

Figure 10.5. Graph of cumulative metaphor totals over time, with metaphor cluster circled. (Numbers on the *x*-axis correspond to lines 2001–3000 in the transcript.)

The graph covers intonation units 2000–3000 in the transcript; clusters are usually short-lived and do not show up clearly on a plot of a full transcript, so several plots need to be made to cover each one. An examination of the transcript at this point (Extract 10.2) shows that this cluster is no innocuous string of unrelated terms (which might be the case with any cluster), but a stretch of substantive dialogue showing coherent use of metaphor.

Extract 10.2

| 2601 | Eddie | [] the government, |
|------|-------|--------------------|
| 2602 |       | isn't actually doing <u>anything</u>. |
| 2603 |       | …they're not, |
| 2604 |       | stopping people coming <u>in</u>, |
| 2605 |       | or <u>kicking</u> people <u>out</u>. |
| 2606 | Finn  | you know, |
| 2607 |       | what's that going to do? |
| 2608 |       | …what's that going to solve? |
| 2609 |       | …not letting people <u>in</u>, |

| 2610 |       | or <u>kicking</u> people, |
|------|-------|---------------------------|
| 2611 |       | <u>out</u> of the country, |
| 2612 | Eddie | … well it [] |
| 2613 | xx    | [] <X a lot of the people X> [] |
| 2614 | Eddie | [] it'll will lessen the chances of terrorists, |
| 2615 |       | being <u>over here,</u> |
| 2616 |       | wouldn't it? |
| 2617 | Finn  | if you want to lessen the chances, |
| 2618 |       | <u>kick</u> 'em all <u>out.</u> |
| 2619 |       | … <u>get rid of</u> them all. |
| 2620 | xxx   | <XXXX> |
| 2621 | Ray   | yeah, |
| 2622 |       | I agree with, |
| 2623 |       | … that <u>thing.</u> |
| 2624 | xxx   | <XXXX> |
| 2625 | Finn  | why <u>kick</u> 'em all <u>out,</u> |
| 2626 |       | though? |
| 2627 | Ray   | you can't do that now, |
| 2628 |       | … because people, |
| 2629 |       | … X [] |
| 2630 | Finn  | [] X [] |
| 2631 | Ray   | it's marriage, |
| 2632 |       | you know, |
| 2633 |       | <u>stuff</u> like -- |
| 2634 |       | you can't do it now. |
| 2635 |       | it's impossible. |
| 2636 | Terry | <u>kick</u> 'em all <u>out.</u> |
| 2637 | Finn  | you can't do |

Thus the text relating to be sudden steepness of the cumulative curve reveals a rich, heated episode in which members of the group relate UK immigration policy to the risk of terrorism and Finn's more liberal attitudes clash with the harder line of Eddie, Ray and Terry (though it appears Ray does not recognize Finn's irony at 2618–2619). Themes (such as immigration/repatriation) and metaphors (such as the use of metaphors of VIOLENT ACTION for government policy or broader political behaviour) which emerge in significant clusters can provide inspiration for researchers looking for 'ways into' their data. Clusters such as this are also valuable resources for approaches to discourse that look at factors other than metaphor.

As mentioned above, the PCTR research included an analysis of causal attributions. Attributions are instances in talk in which a speaker expresses a cause-effect relationship. Collections of attributions can offer a powerful insight into the cognitive processes and expectations that underlie people's behaviour (Dyck and Rule, 1978; Stratton *et al.,* 1988; Satterfield 1998; Walker and Chestnut 2003). The 12,000 metaphors and 6000 attributions in the project data provided a powerful but unwieldy resource for combined study. Metaphor clusters again offered a way of targeting the close qualitative analysis of the texts.

By identifying episodes in the transcripts where metaphor clusters over-lapped with attributions it was found, for example, that metaphors were working within attributions in a way that intensified the sense of government agency in statements involving the government and terrorists. Some examples are:

1. the government *pushed* him *[Bin Laden] up* in order to *mobilize Muslim jihadi support* (in Russian-occupied Afghanistan);
2. he government should *kick [illegal immigrants] out of* the country to reduce the risk of terrorism.

The attributional and metaphorical content of examples such as these proved to be complementary: the attributions revealed a conceptualization of the government as agentive and having control, while the metaphors gave an affective quality to the idea of agency by presenting it as PHYSICAL or VIOLENT PHYSICAL ACTION (Maule *et al.*, 2007). This relationship between metaphors and attribu-tions would have been very hard to establish without first filtering the data through metaphor clusters. Other phenomena in discourse might provide a similarly productive focus, such as extended pauses, which could point to a speaker or group dealing with particularly difficult subject matter, or stretches of narrative (Bamberg, 2007).

## Conclusions

Working with large amounts of data raises particular issues for trustworthi-ness and efficiency in metaphor research. These are addressed in a variety of ways: having a clear idea of the research questions which metaphors will be used to address, choosing appropriate methods and tools for managing the data, maintaining reflective and iterative collaboration between coders and analysts, keeping a record of decision making, and using techniques to deal with data in focused ways. This chapter offers the experience of one group of researchers as an example of practical techniques and potential pitfalls. It is intended as a guide for those who may not have worked with large amounts of metaphor data before. With experience, researchers will find their own methods, some no doubt more sophisticated than those presented here. Whatever one's technical approach, however, the guiding principle remains the same: to keep in sight, like those theologians of the Renaissance, the words and intentions of one's original source. *Ad fontes!*

# 11 Multimodal metaphor analysis

## Alan Cienki

There is now a wealth of research supporting the position that metaphor is not just a matter of words; rather, it can appear in various modes of expression (see Gibbs, 2008: Part VI and Forceville and Urios-Aparisi, 2009 for recent overviews). However, if we focus on studies which involve analysis of spoken language data, researchers often start with an audio recording of the relevant talk, transcribe it in written form, and then rely largely on that transcript for the remainder of their analysis. If one is analysing the metaphors in the discourse, this will then become a question of identifying the relevant words or phrases on the page according to some set of criteria (some of which are offered in Chapter 6 of this volume). In this scenario, several levels of abstraction from the original discourse have already taken place before the metaphor analysis has even begun. First, by only recording the audio portion of the spoken interaction, the researcher is limited to the information provided via the audio channel, whereas in face-to-face spoken interaction, the (seeing) addressee is also taking in many cues visually from the speaker's behaviour (the speaker's body position, gestures, eye gaze, etc.). Second, when coding only the words as metaphoric expressions, there is often a tacit assumption that it is only in the words that one can find metaphoric expressions.

Here I would like to highlight what kinds of information may be lost in metaphor analysis through those two levels of abstraction from the original spoken context. I will focus on one type of behaviour which we perceive visually – gestures with speech that are produced by the hands and forearms, which will be referred to here simply as 'gestures'. (See Müller and Cienki (2009) for another perspective on the analysis of multimodal metaphors in spoken interaction.)

## What is lost from spoken data when gesture is not considered?

The examples below are from a series of conversations between various pairs of friends who were all students at the same American university. The students were given a series of written questions to discuss about how they take exams, and the ensuing conversations were video recorded with their permission. Each line in the transcript indicates a new intonation unit (see Chafe, 1994 on intonation units as units of analysis for spoken discourse, and Chapter 6, this volume). A full stop/period marks a final intonation unit, falling to a low pitch at the end; a comma shows the end of an intonation unit which does not go to the bottom of the speaker's pitch range, suggesting continuation; an exclamation point is used for a highly stressed emphatic unit. A longer pause by the given speaker is indicated with three dots (…), and a shorter one with two (..). First consider Example 11.1.

Example 11.1

<u>Student on the left</u>                                   <u>Student on the right</u>

I mean it's not like,

… Uhh!

I'm gonna do this,

or I'm gonna die.

                                                      Right.

It's just saying like,

I'm going to take an exam now.

                                                      An' then you usually do better.

Right!

An' you usually do better,

when you're just like nn.

…

Based on the written transcript, it is not exactly clear what the speaker on the left means at the end when she says *nn* in *you're just like nn*. In this case, even hearing them as they speak does not reveal much more information. The speaker utters *nn* in a low volume, in a low pitch, with slightly falling intonation, but almost monotone. Perhaps from hearing it one can discern that the speaker is saying this without exerting much energy. One could surmise that maybe she means something like 'relaxed' or even 'bored'.

However, at the moment of uttering *nn* the speaker makes a particular hand motion. The student is seated, and begins with her right hand closed in a loose fist, resting on her right leg (Figure 11.1). Starting when she says *nn* and continuing into the following pause, she opens her hand while keeping her wrist resting on her leg. She then extends and raises her fingers, then curls her fingers slightly (Figure 11.2) as she moves them slightly down and forward, continuing until her fingers are extended out again (Figure 11.3), at which point she raises the tips of her extended fingers slightly, and then lets her hand fall flat back onto her leg.

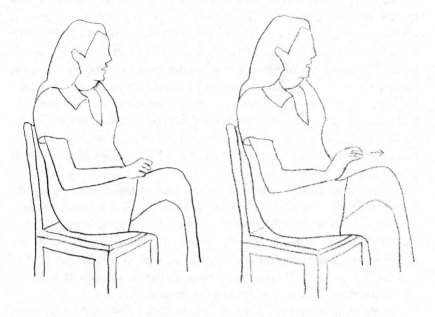

Figure 11.1. Starting position          Figure 11.2. Beginning of motion

Figure 11.3. End of motion

The entire gesture lasts only 1.0 second, but in the fast pace of the ongoing speech, this is conspicuous. The manner of motion displayed in the most emphatic part of the gesture, the so called **stroke phase** (McNeill, 1992; Kendon, 2004), is smooth and directed forward. It could be argued that this represents the manner of behaviour which the speaker is trying to describe, which perhaps could be characterized as calm and with purpose. It is particularly significant that the gesture occurs where one might normally expect to find quoted speech, given that *like* is often used by American English speakers in this age group as a way of introducing indirect speech which will also be rendered approximately in the manner in which it was first uttered (see Streeck, 2002).

If we consider the example in terms of metaphor topics and vehicles, the topic is the manner in which one behaves when one takes an exam and does well on it. The vehicle is the manual gesture, a hand shaped and moved in a specific form over a certain period of time in a delimited space. In the case of gesture, the terminological metaphor of 'vehicle' to describe the form of expression is particularly apt, as the vehicle in fact moves, and its motion is visibly controlled ('driven') by the speaker/gesturer.

The argument offered in this chapter (and in related work, such as the papers in Cienki and Müller, 2008) is that if one does not consider the gestures people produce while speaking, one may not properly interpret the metaphors they were using in words, or worse – one may miss out on some of the metaphors that the speakers were using in their thinking and reasoning at the moment, but which were not expressed in spoken words.

## Brief background on gesture analysis

In the gradual systematization of gesture research, there has been increasing awareness that some aspects of gesture analysis depend upon others. For example, to analyse the 'meaning' of a gesture, an analysis of the gesture's form is a very useful, if not essential, prerequisite. Furthermore, to analyse a gesture's form presumes that gestures have already been identified as units for analysis. Therefore the approach espoused here builds on the Method of Gesture Analysis developed in the project 'Towards a grammar of gesture' (http://www.togog. org/), directed by C. Müller, E. Fricke, H. Lausberg and K. Liebal. It involves first identifying gesture units, then characterizing their forms, then proceeding to interpret those forms. This allows one to identify metaphoric gestures and argue for one's interpretation in such a way that it can supplement the analysis of the verbal level without being circular (e.g., claiming that the gesture accompanying a given phrase was metaphoric because the words used with it were metaphoric).

## Gesture identification

Gesture production is a fluid phenomenon. How can one glean units of analysis from such behaviour? One approach that is accepted by many in gesture studies is outlined in Kendon, (2004: Chapter 7), which has its foundations in much earlier work by Kendon (e.g. 1980). In this approach, a **gesture unit** is considered to consist of the entire movement of the hands from their starting rest position, through the gesture itself, and back to a rest position. The unit begins with the initial movement of the hands, known as the **preparation**, leading to the most effortful portion of the gesture unit, the **stroke**, in which the movement dynamics and/or hand tension are the greatest. The stroke phase is the core of the gesture, the minimum required for a gesture unit. This may be followed by an optional **post-stroke hold**, in which the final image produced in the gesture, reflected in the handshape and orientation of the hand, are sustained. The final phase, in which the hand is relaxed and returns to a rest position, is the **recovery**. Performing gesture identification with the sound of the video turned off can help one focus on the forms being produced, and thus aid in producing an analysis of the gestures in their own right, not covertly guided by the word and phrase units in the co-gesture speech.

## Gesture form analysis

In addition to mentioning the hands involved (left, right, or both hands), four parameters are commonly used in analysing gestures' forms, as outlined in Mittelberg (2007: 237–240), building on work by McNeill (1992) and Webb (1996). The four are as follows:

1. Hand shape, especially with reference to the positions of the fingers, e.g., 'open hand' with all fingers extended, or 'closed fist with index finger extended', etc. Sometimes conventional descriptions of handshapes from American Sign Language are used, as in McNeill (1992: 86–88).
2. Palm orientation, indicating which way the palm of the hand is pointed, e.g., towards centre, up, down, or away from the speaker. This is often combined in descriptions with the parameter of hand shape, e.g., the characterization of a gesture as palm up, open hand (as in Müller, 2004).
3. Location in gesture space; McNeill (1992: 89) provides a model which many use as a starting point. It is based on a series of concentric squares, with the front of the speaker's torso as the centre. Squares that progressively move out from that space identify a peripheral zone (from the neck, around to shoulder width, and extending down to the

waistline), and an extreme periphery (which would include gestures made to the sides beyond shoulder width, over the head, or below one's waist). Areas of the concentric squares can also be labelled according to whether they are on the speaker's left or right sides, and/or include the upper or lower space.

4.   Movement of the hand, a description of which could include the path of movement (e.g., straight line, circular, arc shape), manner and/or speed of movement (rapid, gradual), and direction (horizontal, outward, etc.). This might be combined with the notation of gesture space (moving from the centre space straight out to the right periphery).

For a specific example of a system for transcribing gestures, one attributed to S. Duncan at D. McNeill's lab can be found at http://mcneilllab.uchicago.edu/topics/topics.html under 'coding manual.' For further specifics on the analysis of gestures' forms, note the project 'Towards a grammar of gesture', http://www.togog.org/, mentioned above, one of whose goals is the establishment of fundamental units for the analysis of gesture.

Finally, illustrations of gestures, even in a schematic form, can prove very helpful in presenting one's analysis. They do not accomplish the same goal as the identification of the parameters, described above, since description according to these parameters already involves a form of coding, and thus interpretation of the gestures' forms. However illustrations, or video captures of selected frames, provide information about the gestures' forms in a synthetic way. Use of illustrations rather than video captures may be helpful in that an illustration can highlight aspects of the gestures' forms without the distraction of additional visual information in the background. It may also be necessary to use drawings of video images if one does not have permission to publish images of video recorded research participants. This points out the fact that using video data raises additional ethical issues for one's research that need to be taken into consideration early on. Before recording the data, one should consider the ways in which one may like to use it later, e.g., in conference talks or in one's classes, in print publications, and/or in digital media. One can then give potential research participants options on different sections of a consent form they can sign to agree to have their data used as they themselves determine appropriate – either allowing the video to be used solely by the researcher, or also allowing parts or all of it to be shown publicly in various formats.

### Gesture interpretation

One can then use the form based analysis described above to ground the interpretation of the gestures. The stroke phase of the gesture is normally focused on as the part which expresses the speaker's idea which motivated the gesture in the first place, what one might call the gesture's 'meaning' (see, e.g., McNeill, 1992: 83; Kendon, 2004: Ch. 7). Particularly by approaching the video data first with the sound off, one can consider: Would someone normally do something like that with their hand(s)? If so, what, in what circumstance (e.g., holding something? moving something?)? Or might someone do that to outline, trace, or draw some thing, action, or relation? Or might someone do that with their hand(s) to have it/them stand for some thing, action, or relation? Answering these questions can help one determine what Müller (1998a) has called the mode of representation being used. To review them, they involve:

- enacting what the hands might normally do in another contexts; or
- tracing or outlining some form – either with the tip of one's finger as in two-dimensional drawing, or with the whole open hand, as if covering a three-dimensional surface; or
- embodying something, as when one explains the rotation of the earth around the sun by using two fists in the air to stand for them and show their motion.

Special mention should be made of gestures which involve pointing of some kind. As Kendon discusses (2004: Chapter 11), this seemingly simple act can take many forms: if done with the hand, different fingers can be involved, or even the whole flat hand, and the palm can have different orientations. Furthermore, the possible variations in form can be used for different purposes, such as pointing to entities with different forms, or pointing to new referents versus ones previously mentioned. (See Kita, 2003 for examples from various cultures and contexts.)

Finally, gestures used with spoken language are a dependent medium; they are not an independent semiotic system, like a sign language, but a behaviour that is a coordinated part of spoken language use. Therefore the 'meaning' of gestures, often like their forms, is schematic and underspecified. According to the categories above, this either involves depiction by reproducing (an action), drawing or tracing, standing for, or pointing to an entity, relation or action. To fully interpret gestural behaviour, one needs to consider the co-occurring speech. One can ask: in light of what the speaker is talking about in the given context, what primary function does the gesture appear to serve?

For the purposes of metaphor research, we can begin by focusing on whether the gesture appears to be used primarily to make reference to some entity/idea, relation, or process relevant in the verbal discourse or not. Reference can be made via one of the modes of representation, mentioned above, or via deixis (pointing). Note here that the term **reference** is being used here based on an interpretation of what the speaker may have had in mind when producing the gesture in light of the speech with and around it. The issue of whether the speaker meant to communicate this reference to the addressee is a separate one which is will not be treated here, but could be researched in terms of the degree to which the speaker made his/her expression **salient** in the context of its use (see Müller, 2004/2008: Ch. 6.3). Using the functional classification in Cienki (2005b), adapted from Müller (1998b: Ch. 2.3), we can distinguish between referential gestures which primarily involve concrete reference (to some physical object, person, motion, quality or relation) and those which primarily refer to the abstract (some idea, or abstract process, quality or relation). The qualifer 'primarily' is used here with the understanding that most gestures are multi-functional, but that one function comes to the fore based on the context of use, in particular the co-gesture speech.

We can say that gestures which are primarily abstract referential are the most clearly metaphoric by virtue of referring to the abstract via their physical form and motion in space. More rarely, concrete referential gestures can be metaphoric, e.g., if a person uses a gesture to imitate an animal, for example by holding one's hands to the sides of one's head to imitate donkey ears while saying that someone else is behaving like such an animal (Fricke, 2004: 180). Concrete referential gestures may also involve metaphoricity secondarily via metonymy (Cienki, 2007): e.g., if person A mentions a new idea and person B points to him and says, *That's great!* – the pointing is grounded on the person who was the source of the idea, but from the speech it is apparent that it was the idea (*that*) which was the primary referent, rather than the person (the speaker did not say *You're great!*). Gestures which primarily serve non-referential functions include discourse structuring gestures (illustrating divisions in the parts of one's argument, for example) and pragmatic gestures (e.g., indicating one's attitude towards what one is saying, such as dismissing a bad idea with a wave away). These too can be secondarily metaphoric, for example in how parts of an argument, or an idea that was dismissed, are treated as if they were objects or spatial areas which could be touched. Such ontological metaphors, simply rendering an (abstract) idea as something concrete, will be discussed further in the examples below, as they appear to constitute one of the most frequent manifestations of metaphor in gesture (Cienki, 2003).

## Expression in words and gestures – similarities and differences

There are several possible ways in which the expression of metaphor in spoken words and gestures can interrelate (Cienki, 1998). The following categories represent different ways in which these interrelations can play out, which can be relevant for research on spoken language data.

A metaphor expressed in gesture can be redundant with one expressed in words

Perhaps the most easily anticipated case (on the part of the researcher) is the one in which there is a metaphoric expression in the words uttered by the speaker, and a gesture which appears to express the same metaphoric vehicle found in the words. Consider Example 11.2, in which a student is talking about what he understands as a lack of pre-existing moral standards in life. Using additional transcription conventions from Du Bois *et al.* (1993), a long dash (--) indicates a truncated intonation unit; a caret (^) notes primary stress accent on the following syllable; and the equal sign (=) indicates lengthening of the preceding vowel or consonant. Speech during laughter is marked between 'at' signs (@) and SMILE is used to indicate words spoken while smiling.

Example 11.2

> there's ^never a situation= that is,
> ideally= r- --
> where there's--
> … an ideal,
> <@well@>,
> <SMILE at least there isn't in ^my life SMILE>,
> where there's something ^right,
> and something absolutel=y ^wro=ng.
> What you have to do is draw your line,
> and figure out on which side of it you fall.

The first verbal expression which might strike the researcher as metaphoric is 'draw your line.' Let us call this Example 11.2.1.

Example 11.2.1

> What you have to do is draw your line,

From the context we can understand it as having to do with something like making a decision about what kinds of behaviours are morally right and which ones are wrong. Precisely when he says the verb *draw* he raises his right hand in front of his torso, with the index finger extended outward from himself and other fingers slightly curled inward, and sweeps his hand and extended index finger straight downward, from shoulder height to stomach level, as shown in Figures 11.4 and 11.5.

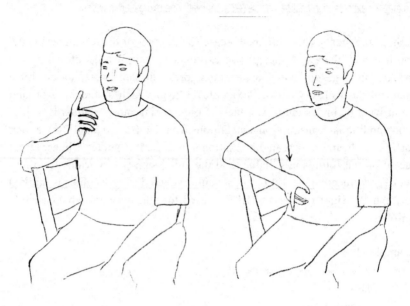

Figure 11.4. Starting point of gesture          Figure 11.5. End point of gesture

From the verbal context, *draw your line*, we can interpret the gesture as representing this process, with the extended index finger embodying a writing utensil like a pen or pencil, as if leaving a trace of a line in the air. However, why does the speaker draw the virtual line vertically, and not with some other orientation? This becomes clear if we consider the gestures which preceded it, as explained below.

### A gesture can express metaphors that are not being co-expressed in speech

One may also find gestures which may be interpreted as metaphoric in light of the co-occurring speech, even if the speech itself does not contain metaphoric expressions. Consider the first lines quoted in Example 11.2, above:

Example 11.2.2

        there's ^never a situation= that is,

        ideally= r- --

        where there's--

        … an ideal,

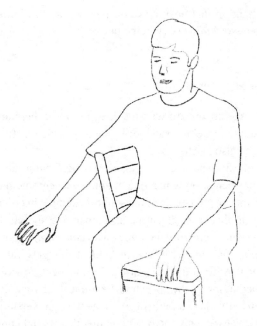

Figure 11.6. End of first gesture down in right-hand space

The speaker extends his right hand, palm down, to the extreme right-hand space and makes a downward stroke – once only down to chest level when beginning the incomplete word with an 'r' in *ideally r-*, and once down to waist level (Figure 11.6) when saying *an ideal*.

During the next two lines, when he laughs and smiles on saying *well, at least there isn't in my life*, he takes a break, as it were, and his hands return to a low rest position. He makes a quick gesture, turning the palms of both hands slightly upward and then back down again while tilting his head to the left during this side comment. From the comment, and the speech that follows, we can interpret this gesture as a pragmatic comment, an admission of not knowing what to do (cf. Müller, 2004) about this situation of lack of moral clarity in his life. But then during the following line:

Example 11.2.3

where there's something ^right,

he returns to the gestural pattern of interest. Namely on the stressed word *right*, he makes a large stroke with his open right hand, beginning up near his head, and moving down to his waist level, repeating the gesture shown in Figure 11.6.

He then holds his hand in that position (a post-stroke hold). Similarly, on the somewhat prolonged word *absolutely* in the line:

Example 11.2.4

    and something absolutel=y ^wro=ng.

he makes a large stroke downward with his open left hand, beginning at head level and moving down to below waist level, ending in the position shown in Figure 11.7, which he also briefly holds.

Both hands remain flat and open, fingers spread, and palm downward -- a handshape and palm orientation which one might use when holding down two rather wide objects, one on either side of oneself, for example in order to prevent them from moving. In this case, given the accompanying speech, the speaker is demarcating two spaces, one of which goes with *something right* and one of which with *something absolutely wrong*. In light of this gestural scenario, it even becomes clear that his original right-hand movement downward during the restarts at the beginning of the speech in Example 11.2 was setting up the spatial contrast even before he was able to articulate the right versus wrong contrast in words. What is especially interesting is that this spatial contrast, made

Figure 11.7. End of gesture in left-hand space

so saliently with the gestures is not expressed at all in words – the closest being the unspecified spatial notion of *where there's*.

It is not uncommon to see such two part contrasts accompanied by two part hand gestures, afforded by our bilateral symmetry of two-handedness (Calbris, 2008). By representing abstract ideas as physical spaces, these kinds of gestures can function on the level of the discourse itself, representing argument structure (one idea or point as this space versus another idea or point as that space), rather than the nature of the referents themselves (e.g. honesty as a 'straight' object, or honest behaviour as 'straight' movement, as described below). Given the fact that our bilateral symmetry is in the horizontal plane if we are standing or sitting upright, the two contrasting spaces that speakers often set up, including the student in this example, are adjacent to each other in the horizontal plane. This explains why the dividing line gesture in Example 11.2.1 is vertical; it serves to separate the two horizontally adjacent spaces that have been set up in the gesture sequence before it.

While we can say that all metaphoric gestures can be labelled metaphoric by virtue of expressing an idea or concept (an abstraction) via a physical form (hand-shape) or movement, the kinds of gestures mentioned in Examples 11.2.2–11.2.4 do this an extremely basic way by not characterizing much more than a meta-phor of IDEA AS ENTITY. They simply involve ontological metaphors in the sense described by Lakoff and Johnson (1980: Ch. 6), rendering ABSTRACT AS CON-CRETE. Indeed, such ontological metaphors appear to be ubiquitous in gesture (Cienki, 2003), reifying the abstract in a way which is not normally occurring in the accompanying speech. Compare McNeill *et al.*'s (1993) discussion of abstract deixis – pointing at space to represent an idea – and much earlier, Bühler's (1934/1982) characterization of this phenomenon as 'Deixis am Phantasma'.

Finally, mention should be made of beat gestures, the small rhythmic hand movements (up and down or back and forth) that speakers often use when making emphasis. Because of their simple discourse structuring function, it is usually implicitly assumed in the gesture research that they do not have any possibility for metaphoric expression. But Casasanto (2008) demonstrates that even they have the potential for metaphoricity, either in association with spe-cific words (upward beats when talking about things *getting better*, reflecting GOOD AS UP), or in connection with the overall message of a narrative, and not connected with specific 'lexical affiliates'. In the studies Casasanto reports on, there were statistically significant differences found in the use of upward beat gestures in the telling of a story about the weather getting hotter (involving the notion that MORE [degrees or quantity of heat] IS UP), and downward beat gestures in telling a story about wanting to buy a car for the cheapest price (invoking the mapping of LESS [cost] AS DOWN). Thus even the directionality of beat gestures within a spoken narrative might reflect metaphoric patterns in speaker's thinking while speaking.

Gesture can have an explicit referential function (abstract reference as metaphoric)

In certain instances, gesture can be used in place of words, and in some cases of this use, the gesture may be metaphoric. An example of this was already discussed above: Example 11.1 in which the student characterized a calm manner in which one can take a test via a smooth hand movement just after saying *like*. There was no word accompanying the gesture, just *nn* in a low voice. The word *like* draws attention to the following gesture, which in this case provides reference to the manner of action, and probably also the mood, which the speaker is trying to characterize.

Similar examples of the same phenomenon in the same type of linguistic context can be found in gesture research on other languages. In Cienki (1999: 193), a Russian student describes acting honestly (in Russian, *chestno*) as being *like this* (in Russian, *tak*), at which point he places his two hands, flat with fingers extended out straight away from his body, in the same vertical plane in the air in front of him, with his right hand above his left hand, and then moves them both slightly downward in unison, maintaining their position in the same flat, vertical plane, illustrated in Figure 11.8.

Figure 11.8. Characterization of behaving honestly as acting 'like this'

In this way he characterizes the manner of this kind of honest behaviour with a flat, straight physical form and tense movement, complementing his earlier characterization of it as an 'absolute category' with this metaphorical image of straightness and solidity. We find an example from German in Müller (2008: 235) where a woman describes an earlier love relationship as having started *like this* (in German, *so*), whereupon she begins tracing the upper arc of a large sine curve in the air with her index finger … which later becomes a progressively smaller wave, lower and off to her right side, as she tells how the relationship later *flattened out*. The initial part of the gesture shows the good beginning of the relationship as a vertical peak high up (perhaps like an emotional high-point?), but the accompanying speech only told us *like this*.

We see in all of these examples that gesture is especially useful in bearing part of the communicative burden when the expression of spatio-temporal forms, actions, or relations are in play – elements which can often be described far more economically in gesture than in lexico-grammatical constructions (Streeck, 1993: 288–289). The visuo-motoric reference produced can be integrated with the syntax of the sentence by means of words such as 'like' and 'so' and their equivalents (Müller, 2008: 236), resulting in moments when the speaker is truly taking advantage of the multimodal potential of spoken interaction.

## Gesture can express different metaphors than we find in the spoken words

In some cases, there may be a metaphoric expression in what the speaker says, yet his/her gestures may indicate something else. In some cases, the gesture may show different aspects of the metaphoric 'scene' being expressed verbally. In one example discussed in Cienki (1998: 194–196), a student comments that *Traditional morality's black and white. Today everything's just grey*. Verbally she describes the absolute nature of traditional moral categories with the opposition of black versus white, and the ambiguity of actual morality today as the mixture of the two, namely grey. However in her gestures she reflects the initial absolute opposition by dividing the space in front of her with a tense, flat right hand that makes a small, vertical chopping motion downward; but with the mention of 'grey' she changes her right hand into a loose 'claw' shape, with fingers spread and slightly curved. Thus the absoluteness versus vagueness of the contrasting source domains are rendered in words and gestures in somewhat different ways, largely because of the impossibility of depicting colours or light and dark with gestures.

Example 11.3 shows another way in which different metaphoric mappings can appear in words and the co-speech gesture. Here the student begins by saying that when it comes to academic honesty, there are no set standards because one can always rationalize one's behaviour, essentially explaining it away. She sums it up, referring to different situations as 'stuff', by stating:

Example 11.3:

> You can talk your way into stuff,
>
> or you can talk your way out of stuff.

Verbally, the speaker uses a caused motion construction (Goldberg, 1995), much as when one can describe *pushing one's way into* or *out of a crowded room*, the verb *talk* is used here in that same construction, taking on the sense of causing one's own movement. Providing verbal reasoning to justify one's behaviour is likened to moving oneself, and the situation that is ultimately either made available, or conversely for which one claims no responsibility, is likened to stuff which one can move into or out of. Based on these words, one might anticipate that the speaker would have used a gesture indicating a path of motion, first into a container or substance, and then out of it. But her gestures indicate something different. The speaker is seated and begins with her two hands resting on her lap (Figure 11.9). With the phrase *You can talk your way into stuff*, she moves her right hand outward to make a palm up, open hand gesture on her right side (Figure 11.10). Then with the phrase *you can talk your way out of stuff* she moves her left hand out to her left side, ending with it palm up, and holding it there briefly (Figure 11.11).

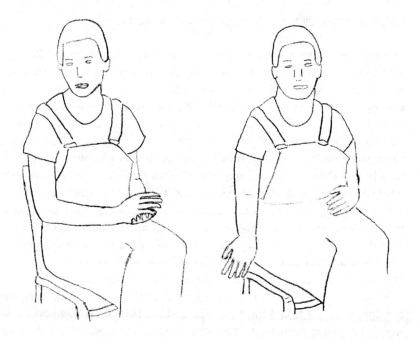

Figure 11.9. Rest position

Figure 11.10. First part of argument (*You can talk your way into stuff*)

Figure 11.11. Second part of argument (*or you can talk your way out of stuff*)

The speaker has thus set up two discourse spaces – like the speaker in examples 11.2.2–11.2.3, but here with different palm orientation of the hands (palm up). The ontological metaphors based on the argument structure of contrasting two points as separate spaces gesturally trumped the metaphor expressed in words. In addition, the differing metaphors in this speaker's words and gestures reflect different levels, namely the referential level (in words) and discourse level (in gesture). The conventional metaphor *talking one's way into things* was apparently backgrounded here by the speaker (used as what Müller 2004/2008 might call a sleeping metaphor), who instead highlighted the ontological metaphor involving ideas in discourse as separate, opposing spaces.

In sum, metaphoric gestures relate to verbal expressions (be they metaphoric or not) in various ways (Cienki, 1998; Cienki and Müller, 2008). They can therefore serve as a source of information – that is often nonredundant with the words being spoken – about what ideas the speaker is expressing.

## The importance of metaphoric gestures for metaphor theory, and thus for research on metaphor in spoken interaction

The examples discussed above have implications for the study of what metaphor itself might be. For example, if we consider what has come to be known as conceptual metaphor theory (see Chapter 3), one of the fundamental claims is that metaphoric thought gives rise to metaphoric expression. Most of the data that have been adduced in support of this theory have been linguistic expressions. They are taken as reflections of underlying patterns of metaphoric thought. The theory has been criticized for circularity, however, because the presumed conceptual metaphors are themselves deduced from patterns of linguistic expressions (see, for example, Gibbs and Colston, 1995).

But if we take conceptual metaphor theory at its word, the data can come from many different sources. Human expression takes many forms – not just words. Even with written words, the visual form they take can be highly significant. Consider the genre of visual poetry: the context in which the words are presented can be very significant for determining a metaphorical interpretation of those words.

In addition, with spoken language, the context is more often co-experienced in time and in space (that is, in a shared setting) than it is with written language. Part of this context for spoken language is the co-verbal bodily behaviour, and part is the physical (co-)location and physical setting (including what material objects are at the speaker's disposal). Taking these other factors into account cannot only help researchers in interpreting the potential metaphorical use of words, but may reveal additional expressions of metaphor in forms other than words (see Forceville, 2006).

## Some final thoughts

1.  The inclusion of gesture data provides a way out of the criticism of circularity of conceptual metaphor theory by providing an independent source of evidence of the psychological reality (on some cognitive level) of conceptual metaphors (Cienki, 1998: 190).
2.  Gestures can provide evidence of activation (on some level) of an image being used to characterize a given topic. In the case when an image is being gestured in reference to an abstract domain, we do not have a simple case of reference to a concrete object, action, or relation in the physical world. Rather we have a mapping from the concrete idea to a physical image with which it is being represented schematically in the gesture. The representation of the abstract in the form of a physical image is a process of metaphorization which the speaker

may or may not be aware of performing. But we can see evidence of highlighting of the metaphoricity of an expression in certain contexts (e.g., by production of the gesture in the speaker's and addressee's line of sight; see Müller, 2004/2008 for details), and this may be a sign of greater conceptual activation of the metaphor on the part of the speaker (and potentially by the addressee as well if s/he becomes aware of the expression due to its salience).

3. Multimodal expression and communication is the norm. Written words are seen in a specific location, often on a page in a certain layout, and they may be accompanied by relevant images. Spoken language presents words with certain intonational tunes, and speakers move more than their mouths in significant ways when they are talking. We only encounter spoken language without the visual input in specialized contexts (e.g. via certain media, such as radio or traditional telephones). For the blind, who are not relying on visual input on a regular basis, the use of multiple modalities in communicative contexts is also the norm, via hearing and touch, as well as smell. Therefore, if multimodal communication is the norm, it makes sense that metaphors can also appear in multiple modalities.

4. Note that we still do not know much about the relative frequencies of co-occurrence (or not) in natural discourse of metaphorically used words and gestures. Anecdotal evidence, for example, suggests that drawing on different metaphoric source domains in words and the co-speech gestures happens much less frequently than the use of the same source domain for metaphoric expressions in words and gestures at a given time, or the expression of a metaphor in only one mode at once (words or gestures). But it is an open empirical question as to how often some patterns occur in comparison with others, and it is an open theoretical question as to what such differences tell us about metaphoric thought processes and the functions of metaphor in spoken communication.

Approaching language use as multimodal takes us away from the tradition of studying written sentences on the page. The assumption of unimodal communication may work in the Chomskyan tradition in linguistics in which the sentence of words on the page has so often been the object of study. But once we consider spoken language, not only is the grammatically complete sentence no longer the primary unit of usage (e.g., intonation units may be considered one of the relevant forms), but – as cultural anthropologists have been telling linguists for years – the embodied communicative situation is what is in play, not words in disembodied syntactic trees.

5. *Acknowledging* the multimodal nature of interpersonal communication is one thing; *doing justice* to it in one's research is another. However, depending on one's goals, even some attempt to do so can greatly enrich one's research. Much information can be gleaned to support one's semantic analysis (particularly of metaphoric meaning) from co-verbal behaviour such as manual gesture, not to mention from description and analysis of body position, eye gaze, intonation, and so forth.

6. There are also costs of including gesture data in one's analysis. Audio-visual material is rich in information, and working with it is complex. Additional decisions need to be made in order to proceed with one's research. Some of these that were mentioned above include:

    i. How do you delimit what you are calling a gesture?

    ii. How do we decide what gestures are being used metaphorically?

An additional issue that arises is:

    iii. How do you characterize a non-verbal metaphor vehicle term (or its coordinate cognitive source domain, in conceptual metaphor theory)? Describing it in terms of words cannot only be difficult, it can also be highly inadequate (thus the old adage that a picture is worth a thousand words).

In conclusion, acknowledging the multimodal nature of face-to-face communication in one's research is indeed no easy task. However, the richness of information in video data can potentially provide great rewards to those who engage its complexity.

# Section 4

# Bringing it all together

The final section of the book complements the earlier chapters. In Chapter 12, Low and Todd bring together guidelines for good practice in doing metaphor-based research. They set out considerations for studies that require participants to make acceptability judgements about metaphoricity, studies that elicit metaphors from participants, and studies that involve the identification and coding of metaphors in discourse data.

Chapters 13 and 14 bring the previous chapters of the book together by demonstrating what can be achieved by using metaphor analysis in research projects. Chapter 13 is a report of a PhD study that was influenced by the author's attendance at our metaphor analysis workshop; it demonstrates what an individual can do with metaphor analysis in a small scale study. Chapter 14 connects to the focus group data used to exemplify procedures throughout Section 3, zooming out to the large scale social sciences project with its multiple focus groups and interviews. It demonstrates the kinds of findings available to researchers from metaphor analysis of a large dataset, answering socially important research questions.

# 12  Good practice in metaphor analysis: Guidelines and pitfalls

**Graham Low and Zazie Todd**

Earlier chapters have looked in detail at how a metaphor analysis is conducted. In particular, Chapter 2 gave examples of published studies that used metaphor analysis, while Chapters 6 and 7 showed how individual metaphors are first identified and then grouped into systematic metaphors. These chapters also introduced the concept of trustworthiness in metaphor research. Chapter 6 described several ways in which metaphors can be fuzzy: metaphors can have different meanings for different subsets of people, especially if they are technical terms; it can sometimes be difficult to decide exactly where a vehicle term begins and ends; and decisions have to be made about whether to identify all metaphors, whether to include prepositions, and whether to include very frequent words such as *put*, *do* or *have*. Chapter 7 described some of the issues that may arise when grouping metaphors systematically, such as selecting appropriate category names for the systematic metaphor, and deciding what to include and exclude. This chapter revisits issues that are potentially problematic for metaphor researchers, and considers how best to deal with them. The guidelines below are not exhaustive, and nor will they all apply to every study. They are intended to be useful when planning, conducting, or reviewing a metaphor analytic study.

The way a metaphor analysis is carried out and reported will clearly vary depending on the research question, the theories selected to underpin the work and practical aspects of the situation. In many cases, good practice will also be determined by agreed research traditions and canons in the researcher's particular field. However, researchers sometimes treat metaphor as something unproblematic and forget to apply their usual validation checks, or else they downplay the awkward fact that empirical data may not always fit how theories talk about metaphor, and again hold back from applying validation checks. The purposes of this chapter are accordingly: (1) to highlight a number of possible problems that need resolving, or at the very least, discussing in a report, and (2) to suggest for some situations a number of practical solutions. At a general level, the argument is summarized below:

Good practice in metaphor analysis involves:

- recognizing that metaphoricity can be complex, indeterminate and unstable;
- admitting the problems and treating one's solutions as compromises;
- knowing what the compromises entail;
- telling the reader how/why one arrived at conclusions; and
- admitting the limitations of one's conclusions.

Our suggestions relate to two areas: issues when eliciting judgements about metaphors from research participants, and issues when analysing and identifying metaphors.

## Issues when eliciting judgements about metaphors

Try and avoid mental overload for participants with large numbers of similar judgements

When researching mental (or cognitive) models which involve metaphor, researchers frequently need to elicit subtle judgements from participants at numerous points in order to establish the limits of what is acceptable or appropriate. The judgements required of participants may involve deciding whether or not given phrases are metaphorical, or they may involve rating metaphors on various scales, such as aptness or beauty. The result can rapidly spiral into a need for participants to make hundreds of minimally different judgements. For example, in Low (1999a), the aim was to examine the acceptable limits, for markers, of personification in university assignments. It was hypothesized that all sorts of language and contextual phenomena might affect the acceptability of, say, an essay *thinking*, but just three noun phrase subjects (*This essay/paper/ The Guardian*), nine verbs and two types of context resulted in 54 statements for participants to judge. This was just for one very small part of the study. Even though 'motivating' pile sorts were used and these were constructed so as to limit cognitive overload (e.g. a choice was given between just two categories, then two more, making no more than four options in all), one participant reported that the cards all looked the same by the end and another reported being tired half way through. It is hard to know what the answer is, and the difficulty may well account for why there are so few comprehensive elicitation-based studies of underlying metaphors and metaphoric mental models.

Pilot work can help to ensure that participants are not given unrealistic numbers of judgements to make. It may also be helpful to group the judgements into blocks so that some participants receive them in one order (block 1, then block 2), while others receive them the other way round (block 2, then block 1). This will at least ensure that any effects of practice or fatigue are balanced across the study.

Try and avoid serious delayed halo effects – and report if they are found or not

A halo effect (Thorndike, 1920) occurs when participants' ratings or opinions are influenced by ratings they gave, or opinions they formed, earlier on in a study. For example, in a small follow-up study to the one mentioned above, using ESL students, Risiott (1997) found that several students treated the per-sonification judgements as a learning experience, even though the task was to judge unacceptability as much as acceptability, and they reported increasing their use of personification after 5–6 weeks. The following two quotes illustrate the point:

> *When I wrote my introduction, I remembered this essay thinks ... I have now adapted my views;*

> *Can you really say that in English? I thought not, obviously I was wrong.*

The solution in this sort of situation would seem to be to debrief participants at the end, when all the data have been collected, and discuss the applicability of the phrases with them.

Ensure that alternative choices given to participants are unbiased alternatives

What we mean here is that if researchers explore or make use of the differences between different figurative forms, like metaphor and simile, they need to be careful to make sure the reactions they elicit are not biased. In other contexts, one would take care to establish that experimental choices functioning as alter-natives in, say, a multiple choice item, were functionally equivalent, or equally representative of the topic/genre; the point is simply that the same thing needs to be done for figurative language. To illustrate the need to think about these two related areas, we note some problems with respect to *occurrence, form* and *interpretation*.

Occurrence

If asking for reactions to linguistic metaphors and similes, one needs to check whether both are equally frequent (and thus expected) in the discourse genre being studied. They may well not be. In a study of 20 book reviews in 19 aca-demic journals, Low (2008) found that on average, 10.5% of the words were metaphorically used, but there was not one figurative simile. A later study com-paring four UK university lectures found one or two, but still very few and most of those were conventional, such as *like hell* (Low, under review). Simile may be relatively frequent in contexts like novels and poems and in primary class-rooms (Cameron, 2003), but not in other contexts.

## Form

If using the A *is (like) B* format to present figurative language, researchers should also check whether it is as representative for linguistic metaphors as for similes. It has repeatedly been found in studies of metaphor in discourse that metaphors are rarely found in the canonical A IS B form, whereas similes frequently are. Researchers might therefore wish to be careful before present-ing their metaphors in this way, as they may be treated by readers as particu-larly emphatic, or particularly unsubtle, or as having a particular function, like explanation.

## Interpretation

Similes have been found to elicit a number of different interpretations from metaphors. We focus here on just one from Littlemore and Low (2006a, 2006b): the fact that simile may well make the listener think of attributes central to the source domain, whereas the equivalent metaphor may require one to restructure the domain and make peripheral detail become central. We give examples of metaphors and similes relating to: (i) a fixed idiom, (ii) a creative poem ('Love is…' by Adrian Henri) (Henri, 1983) and (iii) an invented maxim.

### 1. Idiom
*Life is a joke ~ Life is like a joke*

### 2. Poem
*Love is a fan club with only 2 fans ~ Love is like a fan club with only 2 fans.*

### 3. Invented maxim
*Love is a Catholic priest getting married ~ Love is like a Catholic priest getting married*

In *life is a joke* (and other variants on the theme, like *you're having a laugh*) there is no reference to humour, bonhomie or social bonding: quite the opposite in fact. The simile *life is like a joke* does not, however, background humour in the same way. Fan clubs normally (by definition) have members who idolize a third-party hero. In the poem, however, (with the metaphor) the reader must restructure the notion of a fan club so that it excludes the hero and has the two fans reciprocally idolizing each other. The simile requires no such revision and seems harder to interpret. In the maxim, love can be seen as something power-ful, positive and heroic. In the simile, however, the evaluation seems far more negative: the priest should not marry. Recent developments in the Catholic

Church's approach to universal celibacy of priests may lead us to modify this interpretation a little, but the basic idea holds good.

To illustrate the problematic nature of assuming functional equivalence of metaphors and similes, we give an example where discourse analysis can highlight a problem with a quantitative approach. Todd and Clarke (1999) gave readers short conversations and asked them to estimate the age and intelligence of the child speaking. There were three versions of each passage: each version contained a metaphor, a simile or a literal phrase (bold, below). One of the passages is given below with the three alternatives:

| Mother: | Look at the cat in the garden | |
|---|---|---|
| Paul: | Where? … Oh yeah | |
| Mother: | He's hunting | |
| **Paul:** | **A tiger** | **(metaphor)** |
| | **Like a tiger** | **(simile)** |
| | **Cat!** | **(literal version)** |
| Mother: | He wants to catch the bird | |
| Paul: | Oh! | |
| Mother: | Oh it's flown away | |

In the versions with *a tiger* and *like a tiger,* the Mother's response supports and praises the child's clever utterance. However, the literal response *Cat!* could imply that the child has not understood *hunting* and is not 'being relevant' to the interaction. The Mother's response can then be understood as her feeling the need to explain hunting, as if the child is very young or dim. This interpretation might influence participants' judgements about the child. Judgements of age and intelligence may thus derive as much from implications of discourse structure as from whether the words are figurative or not. Carrying out a discourse analysis can hence often aid validation work.

## Avoid priming effects and researcher bias

This guideline relates particularly to studies in which metaphors are elicited in the context of an interview or focus group discussion. All we are suggesting here is that researchers remember to apply the checks for researcher bias suggested in every research handbook on interviewing. So, not only should interviewers or moderators check transcripts for their own impact on the interview, but they should also take preliminary precautions, such as not starting an interview with explicit mention of metaphor e.g. *Think of a metaphor for cancer/a company/ the foreign exchange market*, if they are trying to find out how far metaphor is used 'naturally' in the rest of the interview.

Researchers spend a lot of time devising interview questions that are not leading or biased; see for example Berg (2001) or Robson (2002). If one is planning to conduct interviews or focus groups for metaphor analysis, then one also needs to consider whether or not to include metaphors in the interview questions, as these may influence the metaphors that the participants use. Similarly, if one is analysing data that has already been collected, then the analysis should include a consideration of any metaphors that were used by the interviewer.

## Issues when identifying and analysing metaphors

### Establish whether reliability is relevant

It is becoming common these days to find reliability checks applied to empirical studies of metaphor in discourse, and quite appropriately so (Pragglejaz group, 2007), but it is worth bearing in mind the following three points.

1.  The same persons may code the same phrase differently on two occasions – for very valid reasons. For example, the more they read a text, the more metaphor they see (Gibbs, 1994). Or else, the second time an analyst reads a text, he or she knows a metaphor is coming and may interpret the language ahead of it in a way that fits the metaphor (what Cameron and Low (2004) and Low (2005) called 'resonance'). Texts and interpretive situations vary, but researchers may find this becomes a serious enough problem to limit the types of reliability they wish to report.

2.  Reliability indices, for say intercoder reliability, rely heavily on agreed protocols/exclusion lists and because metaphor identification contains so many grey areas and arguable examples, the inclusion/exclusion lists can get extremely long. (By protocol, we simply mean that coders agree beforehand to exclude, say, *make* in *make a noise* and so on; some examples of these kinds of decision were given in Chapter 6). In order to interpret a reliability index, it is necessary to know what items the exclusion lists contained. Publishers rarely like publishing this sort of detail in journal articles, but researchers can easily create coding books and make them easily available to interested readers of their articles.

3.  An index of 0.9 can equal a happy convergence of expert opinion, or it might just equal the mechanical implementation of a fixed procedure. The moral is simply to tell the reader about how the raters interacted before the index was calculated.

Qualitative researchers in particular may feel uneasy about including reliability estimates in their studies, with all their implications of variable-based enquiry and ideal solutions being somewhere 'out there in the aether'. We would argue, however, that most qualitative studies include coding and transcribing activities, and readers of the papers describing those studies need some indication that both have been achieved systematically and consistently. In many cases, there is no problem with applying more qualitative notions, like Lincoln and Guba's (1985) 'trustworthiness', when it is a question of interpreting the data coded or transcribed.

### Ensure your discourse sample is appropriate, and explain to readers how it is appropriate

For those who are not linguists or corpus analysts, it is easy to forget to check on the nature of the sample. However, we would urge researchers to check its appropriateness for the task in hand.

1. If exploring foreign language teaching metaphors, it is better not to include reports of L1 (first language) classes, journalism classes, or the L1 literature as primary data – however tempting (see Low, 2003).
2. If comparing data against a large reference corpus (like the Bank of English, see Chapter 9), it is important to check how the corpus data were generated. Thus, if one is researching metaphor in conversation, one should exclude subcorpora of novels or newspapers, and establish that the spoken examples were not in fact from, say, formal speeches or news reports. Achieving this is not always straightforward; one sometimes has to read the small print to find the information. Deignan (1999) emphasizes how researchers can easily get carried away in a large corpus and simply forget to make this sort of check.

### Have and report a decision procedure

It is important to develop a consistent procedure for identifying metaphors and to report the procedure when one writes up the study. Both are equally important. If one simply says that metaphors *emerged* from reading 35 published articles (e.g. Schlesinger and Lau, 2000), the reader does not know whether there was a procedure but it is not being reported, or whether there was no decision procedure in the first place. The important questions are then (1) what did *not* emerge? and (2) how systematic were the researchers? No decision procedure is perfect, but it is still important to develop one. Describing the procedure that was used is one way to demonstrate transparency in research (Yardley, 2000).

The decision procedure should also explain how the decision was made to stop identification. With a large dataset, how does one decide that enough is enough? i.e. that one has identified all the relevant or interesting metaphors, and does not need to analyse further? This is similar to the issue of saturation in grounded theory. There aren't any standard rules, and different authors have taken different approaches. Sometimes the whole dataset isn't analysed in full. Oberlechner *et al.* (2004) stopped analysing after 26 interviews (out of 52 collected) when the metaphors that they were finding seemed to be quite stable. Sopory (2005) stopped identifying metaphors after reading 60% of the transcripts, and just did a search on the remaining 40% to find instances of these metaphors. So as well as reporting the procedure for identification, researchers need to explain and justify how it was applied to the data.

### Make identification decisions relevantly data based, and make sure your choice of underlying (systematic or conceptual) metaphor is appropriate

This guideline relates to the grouping of metaphors into 'systematic' or 'conceptual' metaphors, and to the choice of appropriate labels. Chapter 7 considered the need to use imagination and creativity in order to come up with the best groupings of metaphors, but at the same time to ensure rigour; it is important that the groupings are appropriate and based securely on the data. Here, we highlight the issues that can arise in light of two published studies. In Labbo's (1996) study of the development of screen-based literacy in children, a semiotic analysis was used. The assumption was made explicitly that observed behaviour *must* be metaphorical and the metaphors (or metaphoric levels) **must** be organizable into a hierarchy with a top-level 'overarching' metaphor (p. 363).[1] Our interest here is not semiotic theory, but the problems that such a position poses for the researcher. The researcher's job changes from one of needing to be convinced that there is any metaphor around, to that of simply locating suitable metaphors; that is to say, the need to justify identifications using the data is markedly reduced – because he or she assumes there must be an underlying metaphor there somewhere. The temptation becomes very strong to identify a particular metaphor purely on the grounds that the data is 'consistent' with it. Consistency is an extremely weak basis for identification, as many phrases are consistent with many different metaphors and there is frequently no strong linguistic or discourse reason for invoking any of them. If researchers do decide to use consistency, this should be reported as such. In our experience, over-identification from a desire for consistency is one of the commonest problems in published studies. We give two examples of where it can prove problematic.

1.  Labbo admitted inventing an overarching metaphor *Screenland* based on her working assumptions, 'it cannot be assumed that screenland is a metaphor the children would sanction' (p. 380). More relevant to the present discussion are the lower-level metaphors, of which we take one as an illustration. Children's literal play in class was taken as an instantiation of the metaphor SCREEN AS PLAYGROUND. Had the children been transferring the rules of a playground game to the classroom task at hand, the justification would have been clear, but with no evidence given of meaningful transfer, the decision to invoke metaphor seems guided more by the requirements of the theory. It may be that there was in fact good evidence for both identifications, but our point is that cases like this need to be argued and the grounds for the identification reported to the reader.

2.  In a study of metaphor in three UK university lectures from the BASE corpus (Low *et al.*, 2008),[2] one of the lectures, on the European Community and the Economic and Monetary Union (EMU), contained a series of metaphoric phrases about playing (*major world player, major player, to play on X*), about fighting (*battle, conflict*) and about winning and losing. The question was, should we treat them all as manifestations of THE EMU IS A GAME? The answer would appear to be no. There is no reference to a game, or elaboration in game terms; winning and losing are never collocated with fighting or gaming, and indeed winning is relexicalized as *benefit* and *gain*. However much we might have hoped to find evidence to pull together the diverse phrases into an overarching metaphor of the sort suggested by Ponterotto (2003), we could find no linguistic justification for doing so.

As a final rider to this argument, we would note that the need to avoid identifying on the grounds of consistency alone is even stronger where visual, gestural or behavioural metaphor is involved. The reason is simply that when studying linguistic metaphor, there is at least a huge base of interconnecting data and support from reference manuals, like corpora and dictionaries, that can be used as evidence to support or reject the identifications. We would suggest that in non-linguistic cases, researchers need to set up particularly strict and explicit criteria for recognizing metaphor; if in doubt, err on the side of caution.

State how one is managing to count what is essentially uncountable

There are so many occasions where the metaphoricity of a phrase is either not clear-cut, or varies with the situation, that the only valid conclusion is that the occurrence of metaphor is essentially uncountable in a cross-sectional study.

However, as a social scientist, one is often going to have to impose countability. The result will inevitably be a compromise; the key factors are: (a) to be honest about having a compromise; and (b) to think hard about where one needs to take classification or procedural decisions. We note a few useful points below:

1. Researchers need to create a procedure for coping with words that seem to become more metaphoric when they are near a salient or clear cut metaphor – what we earlier called resonance (Cameron and Low, 2004; Low, 2005: 136). This is inevitably very subjective, can vary with the number of readings made of a written text, and thus makes accurate coding almost impossible. Such resonances may be unintended and accidental, but they might equally well be intended and calculated by the speaker.

2. It is important to note that resonance can impact on an exclusion policy; a resonant *give* can, for example, undermine a universal decision that was made to exclude the verb in instances of *Give an answer*.

3. Technical and non-technical readers may identify the same phrase in quite different ways (as can in-group and out-group members, as mentioned in Chapter 6). A technical term may have little metaphorical impact on the technical reader, but be treated consistently as metaphor by the non-technical one. Even when experts and non-experts are using the same technical term metaphorically, there may still be differences in understanding. For example, when talking about pain, general practitioners use the term *burning* in quite a specific sense, to refer to acid reflux or to pain in the urinary tract. However, patients have been observed to use *burning* much more widely (Skelton *et al.*, 2002). Thus the metaphor is being used differently by expert and lay people. Researchers need to decide on a policy with respect to technical terms, which matches their own needs as analysts and takes account of the fact that writers will often 'play' with technical terms, by 'activating' or 'foregrounding' (and backgrounding) the metaphoricity.

4. We have noted in passing several times that people read a text differently the second or third time and will thus process the metaphors differently (including identifying different words as metaphoric). In a crude sense, one can often control the number of readings, but without eye-tracking devices, it is not possible to control the extent to which readers review sentences or phrases within the same reading 'session'.

### Establish that metaphor is actually involved: consider the alternatives

Metaphor and metonymy are often linked in complex ways and can be hard to disentangle. This is especially the case where the speaker emphasizes and foregrounds one aspect of, say, their job. We illustrate this with three example 'conceptual metaphors' (of many) in the literature about language teaching and learning.

- THE TEACHER IS A CONTRACTED PROFESSIONAL
- TEACHER AS DELEGATOR
- USING THE FOREIGN LANGUAGE AS TRANSLATING

Clearly most teachers *are* contracted professionals and, even though the role carries expectations about honesty, determination and skill ('association of ideas' metonymy), the overriding sense of the words and the utterance is quite literal. Similarly, probably most teachers delegate as part of their teaching (part-whole metonymy) and learners do quite genuinely translate from their first language, amongst other activities. Oxford *et al.* (1998) infer the metaphor TEACHER AS FRIEND from their data, which is perhaps more interesting, as it highlights the greyness of the situation: the teacher isn't really the learners' friend like other friends, and remains a partial friend, or else the teacher creates the illusion of being a friend, though of course genuine friendship can result from a professional, simulated, partial friendship or friendlike behaviour.

### Justify that metaphors are 'real' and try and establish what they mean

The reality of metaphor is a huge topic and cannot be covered in depth here. We limit ourselves to noting three important points.

1. Metaphors are often used to mark boundaries between different sections of a text or discourse. In speech, Drew and Holt (1998) have shown that one aspect of this can be to flag requests by the speaker to change the topic of conversation. Boundary demarcating can become quite complex and subtle, especially in written text, with the use of multiple interconnected frames (see for example the account in Low (1997) of Braddick's (1986) review in *Nature* of *Functions of the Brain*). However, despite the complexity that can be involved, one needs to be careful not to over-interpret boundary framing metaphor, and be prepared to accept that the primary role is just that: to demarcate and foreground or background a discourse boundary.

2. Establishing deliberate or intentional use of metaphor can be quite hard and researchers do need to argue the case. It may be that the speaker uses several related phrases, or else makes an interpretable accompanying gesture. In spoken discourse, there may well be a marker indicating a degree of conscious awareness, such as a longish hesitation, a filled pause (*erm*), one or more hedges (*sort of ... as it were*), a speech

rate change, or even a direct assertion (*sorry about the metaphor*) (see Cameron and Deignan, 2003). One may not need to create the sort of detailed transcript used for Conversation Analysis, but the implication is that pauses are frequently worth transcribing.

3. We end with a reminder to try not to read more into utterances than one can justify from the data. The temptation remains strong for us all. The difficulty is illustrated in Extract 12.1, a brief passage from Gurney (1999) in an excellent study based on interviews about home ownership. CMG is the interviewer.

Extract 12.1

| Mrs Miller: | Well, the house, it's something lasting that you can pass on to them. It's also for the future of the family, and *an Englishman's* or an English family's *home is their castle*, isn't it? |
| CMG: | An Englishman's home – why? |
| Mrs Miller: | [pause] I don't know really. It's, erm, well [pause] it's just the best way to explain it really, it's just the way I'd sum it up. I know it's a cliché but it's true. I don't know what else I can say really. Sorry. |

(Gurney, 1999: 1712, italics in original)

Gurney says of the phrase *an Englishman's home is (his) castle*:

It is so common that it is seldom given a second thought. However, the imagery conveyed – of impregnable ramparts, familial heraldry and a secured drawbridge – vividly underpins the ideologies of independence, identity and security so frequently associated with home ownership. (Gurney, 1999: 1813)

Clearly Gurney infers the rich associations, but it is hard to say on the evidence presented in the paper that **all** of his participants feel the same, since one of them was unable to explain any of it. Of course, researchers don't often ask participants what they mean by the metaphors they use. Gurney's example serves as a cautionary reminder that we must be careful not to over-interpret.

## Conclusion

Metaphor is not an easy topic to research empirically; it frequently seems to become increasingly elusive, the more you try and pin things down. Our aim is not to stop people researching it, as the process is almost always fascinating and the results are often incredibly rewarding. All we are saying is develop a consistent and explicit identification procedure, do not specify an inferred underlying or overarching metaphor (whether linguistic, systematic or conceptual) unless there are good grounds for both the metaphoricity and the formulation, and check, as part of the validation procedures, that the data is not linguistically biased or unrepresentative. And admit where things go wrong, or identification and classification are less clear-cut than one might wish. Problems are inevitable in metaphor analysis, but the more they are discussed openly, the more other researchers can benefit from one's work. This, we have to admit, is easily said, but can be hard to realize in practice.

## Acknowledgements

We would like to thank Lynne Cameron, Alice Deignan, Simon Harrison, and participants at the MetNet workshops for their comments on an earlier version of this chapter. Thanks too to Ruth Risiott for permission to quote from her BA study.

## Notes

1. Labbo's exact words were: 'The final step [of analysis] seeks an overarching metaphor that work on the computer had across all classroom contexts' (p. 363). Metaphor itself is not defined, but seems roughly to correspond to conceptual metaphor. While Ponterotto (2003) used 'overarching metaphor' as a grouping notion *within* a discourse, used by the speaker consciously or unconsciously to structure it, Labbo applied the term *across* a small corpus of episodes and interactants, as a way of describing a general context. We should perhaps highlight here the seemingly paradoxical directional labelling system that is found in parts of the literature (on conceptual metaphor in particular), where 'underlying' metaphors are 'below' the linguistic surface of a text, but 'overarching' ones, which connect them thematically or inferentially, are somehow 'above' the text!

2. The transcriptions and recordings used in Low *et al.* (2008) come from the British Academic Spoken English (BASE) corpus project. The corpus was developed at the Universities of Warwick and Reading under the directorship of Hilary Nesi and Paul Thompson. Corpus development was assisted by funding from BALEAP, EURALEX, the British Academy and the Arts and Humanities Research Council.

# 13  Bringing it all together: Applying metaphor analysis to online discussions in a doctorate study

## Sue Rivers

Metaphors are frequently used by teachers and other professionals to link concepts familiar to learners with concepts which are new or less familiar. Metaphor is defined here as the application of a name or descriptive term or phrase to an object or action to which it is imaginatively but not literally applicable (see also Chapters 1 and 6). The essence of conceptual metaphor is expressed by Lakoff and Johnson (1980: 5) as understanding and experiencing one kind of thing in terms of another. An example is the term *learning journey*, where the concept of learning is associated with that of a journey, although, of course, learning is not literally a journey.

The use of vivid language by participants was a feature of the online talk which forms the subject of this chapter, with metaphor particularly striking. For example:

Extract 13.1

... we do after all <u>have to steer</u> the group <u>towards a destination</u> we have in mind. Hopefully we are all <u>along for the ride</u> <u>to the same destination</u> (providing we have made it clear <u>where we are going prior to departure</u>) but if we are not all <u>trying to go the same way</u> then we must be prepared for certain ones <u>to jump overboard</u> rather than trying <u>to steer us away from our intended target</u>.

(Male student 3, Conference 4)

It became increasingly apparent that there were possible links between metaphor use and learning and between metaphor use and emotion. In a learning environment which relied on use of the written word and where metaphor was very noticeable, it was important to consider why participants communicated with each other in this way.

## The researched programme

The researched programme was an online distance learning programme about online learning, aimed at educational professionals who were, or would be, implementing e-learning projects in their workplace. It was available to learners anywhere in the world, but the particular cohort studied were based in the United Kingdom. The programme took place for 9 months between 2002 and 2003. It was a prerequisite that students had either previously completed a specific online programme run by the same institution or an equivalent programme or have experience in e-learning.

In this chapter, the terms 'online learning' or 'e-learning' (electronic learning) are used interchangeably, as generic terms to mean learning through materials and/or learning experiences provided via the Internet (which includes sites on the World Wide Web and email). The terms 'networked learning' or 'online networked learning' are used to mean:

> Learning in which information and communications technology (ICT) is used to promote connections; between one learner and other learners; between learners and tutors; between a learning community and its learning resources. (based on Goodyear, 2001; Banks *et al.*, 2003; Goodyear *et al.*, 2005)

Two other relevant terms are collaborative and co-operative learning. Collaborative learning occurs when participants mutually engage in a co-ordinated effort to solve a problem together and this may be distinguished from co-operative learning where each person is responsible for a portion of the problem solving (Roschelle and Teasley, 1995: 70). The researched programme used a form of networked learning, which could possibly amount to networked collaborative learning, although the only task the learners had was to take part in discussions.

There were originally seven students in the cohort studied (four women and three men), but this was reduced to six part way through the programme, leaving three women (including myself) and three men. In addition, there was one male tutor.

The programme used minimal online learning materials and the main focus was a combination of online conferences, compiling and sharing of progress reports on the students' individual implementation projects, and, at the end, submission of a portfolio which formed the sole summative assessment. The conferencing took place on a discussion board using relatively basic computer conferencing software.

The research focused on a four month period of intensive asynchronous online conferencing when students participated in a series of seven discussions on subjects of their choice connected with implementing e-learning, such as Virtual Learning Environments, motivating learners and presenting materials online. Students were required to post a message at least once per month and to lead at least one conference. No other roles (such as scribe or summarizer) were allocated. There was a separate social area ('the café') where students and the tutor could post messages freely on social issues as well as e-learning or education matters. Prior to the start of the conferences the group was asked to compile collaboratively a set of rules for the conduct of the conferencing but failed to do so.

This study aimed to explore how and what people learn through online learning, in order to establish whether this can be a rewarding learning experience. The aims were underpinned by the principle that text which distance learners create themselves, collaboratively through dialogue, has the capacity to be educationally valuable, in that it uses the potential of the Internet for 'mindweave', as Kaye (1989: 3–4) puts it, in a way that simply putting existing text onto a Virtual Learning Environment (VLE) does not. This acknowledges the view of Goodyear *et al.* (2005: 474) that, at the heart of networked learning, lies the human-human connection, whereas the interaction between people and online materials is not a sufficient characteristic to define networked learning.

## The theoretical basis of the study

### The essence of metaphor

One of the key tenets of cognitive linguistics is that metaphor is not just a surface ornamentation of language but a phenomenon of human thought processes (Cameron, 2003: 2). Conceptual metaphors are claimed to be among our principal vehicles for understanding (Lakoff and Johnson, 1980: 159).

It has been asserted that language is what sets humans apart from animals by enabling a sharing of mental resources and a combining of mental capacities (Mercer, 2000) and that communication is at the heart of all forms of educational interaction (Garrison and Anderson, 2003: 2). A cognitivist view of writing sees text production as a dynamic process that occurs in the writer's mind (Johnson-Eilola, 1998: 21). In the case of online discussions, it therefore seems significant that the very word 'discussion' is metaphorical: communication is actually by the written word (text) rather than by talk.

Lakoff and Johnson (1980: 115) claim that because so many of the concepts that are important to us are either abstract or not clearly delineated in our experience (such as emotions, ideas and time) we need to get a grasp on them by means of other concepts that we understand in clearer terms (such as spatial orientations and physical objects). This claim may be supported to some extent by the fact that key theorists themselves have relied on metaphor to describe (and presumably enable understanding of) their concepts. These include Plato (1882)[1] (the cave), Vygotsky (1986) (Zone of Proximal Development), Bloom *et al.* (1956) (levels of learning), and arguably Wenger (1998) ('communities' of practice). The concept of learning, as an abstract process, may itself need to be understood by being related to something concrete.

Metaphors have potential educational value; according to Cortazzi and Jin (1999: 161), they invite interaction and organize concepts. Ortony (1993: 5, 13) suggests that something new is created when a metaphor is understood, and that metaphors afford a different way of viewing the world. Petrie and Oshlag (1993: 580–584) conclude that metaphors are not just ornamental, but necessary to provide a basic way of passing from the well known to the unknown, i.e. an aid to acquiring new knowledge. Petrie and Oshlag argue (1993: 580, 583) that metaphor use enables transfer of understanding from what is well known to what is less known ('leaping the epistemological chasm') in a vivid and memorable way. Indeed, Cameron suggests (2003: 36) that the vivid use of language may aid recall. On these bases, it would appear that metaphor use may aid cognition.

## Metaphor and emotion

According to Kövecses (2000: 192) language is not only a reflection of experiences but it also creates them: we say what we feel and we feel what we say. In postmodern cyberspace, even if words are 'disembodied', they can still hurt, as anyone who has experienced email 'flaming' will know. It is possible to feel tangible anger from offensive words whether emanating from a computer screen or from the mouth of someone materially present (Sanchez, 1998: 99). According to Stone (1995), in face to face communication there is 'wide bandwidth' in the sense that many different modes of communication and expression are conveyed at the same time (such as speech, gestures, facial expression and tone). Arguably, emotions may be heightened online as 'narrow bandwidth' (i.e. relatively low amount of information exchange in unit time) is experienced as communication by text alone. Participants may therefore be forced to raise their level of interpretive engagement, creating and absorbing maximal meaning from minimal symbology and the situation may be ripe for misinterpretation and misunderstandings (Stone, 1995).

It is feasible that metaphor is used to make up for the lack of body language online, especially in the case of emotions such as anger, which could provoke a strong reaction if not tempered by the use of a euphemistic metaphor. Cameron (2003: 23) suggests that metaphor may have an affective function; for example, in giving negative feedback to a learner in such a way as not to impact on their confidence by suggesting publicly that they have given a wrong answer (e.g. *you are on the right track* as opposed to *you are wrong*). Drew and Holt's research (1988) shows that metaphors are frequently used when making complaints (e.g. *it was like banging my head against a brick wall*).

## Methodology and methods

### Virtual autoethnography

The research was conducted by virtual autoethnography. Ethnography is a way of studying cultures in their natural state. It involves participating in people's daily lives for an extended period of time, watching what happens, listening to what is said, asking questions, in fact collecting whatever data are available to throw light on the issues that are the focus of the research (Hammersley and Atkinson, 1995: 1). It is an appropriate and well-established approach within educational settings as a means of understanding the culture of learning and social environments, since it examines the nature and meaning of patterns of behaviour (Anderson, 1990: 148).

A virtual ethnography is ethnography conducted in an online setting. It can be used to develop an enriched sense of the meanings of technology and the cultures which enable it and are enabled by it (Hine, 2000: 8). There are a number of precedents for its use in important studies of cyberspace (such as Turkle, 1995; Hine, 2000). In the case of the researched programme it was a particularly useful way to study group dynamics, an aspect of e-learning which may be missing when researchers only analyse the content of scripts of online conferences in which they may not have taken part and which have already taken place. It was an opportunity to experience at first hand what it is like to be a user of this form of communication for education and to engage in this in a highly reflective way (Markham, 1998). The term autoethnography is used in this context to indicate that the researcher participated fully in the online programme researched as a student, including taking the assessment, and her own experiences were included in the text of her doctoral thesis.

### Interviews

Once the programme was over, 14 semi-structured interviews were conducted with fellow students on the researched programme, the tutor and Course Director. These incorporated the Critical Event Recall (CER) technique (Tuckwell, 1980; Kagan, 1984; Kagan and Kagan, 1991; Lally, 2002; Steeples, 2004; Carr *et al.*, 2006). This is a method of stimulating recall of an occurrence. It is based on the premise that humans store up large amounts of information about events which they have participated in, much of the detail of which may be soon forgotten but can be recalled with appropriate stimulation. The original events may have occurred months or even years previously. In the case of group of learners, it may even enable previously unexpressed aspects of the learning experience to be recalled and verbalized; for example, the interviewee is able to reflect upon and analyse the transcript extracts, and, in so doing, verbalize what was not directly observable from them (De Laat and Lally, 2003). A core part of this technique is to enable interviewees to remain focused on the thoughts and feelings they experienced at the time of the event rather than subsequently (Kagan, 1984; Kagan and Kagan, 1991; Lally, 2002).

Accordingly, after preliminary warm up questions, the first part of the interview was based around Critical Event Recall, with interviewees being asked about their recollections of three particular online conferences that they had been involved in. They had been sent written copies of the transcript of these in advance of the interview so that they could familiarize themselves with the text (De Laat and Lally, 2003, 2004). The remainder of the interview was a more open time for them to raise issues of importance from their own perspective rather than in response to questions (De Laat and Lally, 2004).

The rationale for using this technique, apart from its inherent value, was to complement other forms of analysis (Lally, 2002), in the case of this study, content analysis and metaphor analysis. The inclusion of interviews was motivated by the desire to capture the complexity of the learning processes involved in online networked learning and to gain a fuller understanding of learning processes than might be possible by using content analysis alone, including the need to probe the 'thinking behind the text' (Lally, 2002).

## Data analysis

### The data
The data consisted of transcripts of the seven online conferences which had taken place during the 4 month research period, one particular exchange from the social ('café') area and transcripts of 14 interviews. In total this comprised 191 individual online postings by the conference participants, amounting to over 31,000 words, and around 30 hours of interviews.

### Content analysis
Content analysis is frequently used to examine the transcripts of online conferences (Garrison and Anderson, 2003; Henri, 1992; Lally and De Laat, 2002). However, purely analysing the content of conference scripts or only using one technique to do so may result in oversimplification. There was therefore scope in this study to complement these approaches with other techniques, such as metaphor analysis, to investigate the nature and significance of the language used by participants in a way that goes beyond a straightforward analysis of content.

A preliminary analysis of the conference transcripts was undertaken using categories emerging from the messages themselves, without detailed reference to the literature, drawing upon grounded theory (Glaser and Strauss, 1967; Strauss and Corbin, 1998). Further data analysis was carried out in the light of the literature review. This approach is particularly suited to research in new or under-researched fields, such as those in which there are significant gaps in theory, as is the case with online networked learning. In this case it enabled important themes to be identified, like the use of metaphor online, which might not otherwise have been given the prominence they deserved. It also gave added rigour. The usefulness of this approach has been acknowledged by researchers in this field (De Laat and Lally, 2003; Lally and De Laat, 2002; McConnell, 2000; McConnell, 2006: 150–151; Steeples, 2004).

In the initial analysis, various grids and frameworks for analysis were considered, taking into account the work of Henri (1992) and Garrison and Anderson (2003). The framework used was derived by listing the research questions, breaking them down into component parts and using these directly as the headings for analysis. The content of the online conferences and interviews was analysed against these headings, allowing new themes and theory to emerge from the data. One such theme was metaphor, and it eventually formed the basis of a new, additional research question. The original column headings were:

- Learning; other activities in the silence
- Kind and quality of learning
- Learning styles
- Community, behaviour and culture.

A meta-analysis of the 'kind and quality of learning' and 'community, behaviour and culture' columns was conducted to seek evidence of issues raised following completion of the literature review. A new grid was created for this purpose based on Henri (1992) and Bloom *et al.*'s taxonomy (1956). The revised sub-headings for the 'learning' column were:

- Knowledge, understanding or surface learning (detailed approach)
- Application
- Analysis, synthesis or reflection
- Evaluation or deep learning (holistic approach)
- Metacognition.

When determining the units of analysis, the approach favoured by Chi (1997), Henri (1992) and De Laat and Lally (2003) was used: the messages were split into 'units of meaning' by using semantic features such as ideas, arguments or discussion topics. A protocol was devised which set out the principles for conducting the analysis. These principles included a rule that units of meaning were only to be recorded under one heading to which they were relevant to avoid double counting. Where they could relate to more than one heading, they were to be recorded under the higher or highest level. For example, if a unit of meaning from the text of an online conference showed evidence of both knowledge and analysis, it would be recorded only under analysis.

At one point during this process, a new column heading was added (metaphor and language) because the metaphorical use of language online became particularly striking. A theory was formed that complex language such as metaphor might occur at times of heightened emotion and possibly at times of deeper learning. This aspect was highlighted and set aside as a theme for particular further attention. Having received training, metaphor analysis (Cameron and Low, 1999; Cameron, 2003) was carried out of the full set of conference transcripts.

## Metaphor analysis

Metaphor analysis identifies and examines metaphors, considers their occurrence, density, and, indeed, absence. Researcher subjectivity can be problematic in identifying metaphor, leading to a danger of over-analysis and lack of rigour (Low, 1999b: 49). In this study, these problems were addressed by setting clear criteria, using double blind data analysis to check reliability of the analysis and triangulating metaphor analysis with other methods (in this case content analysis and Critical Event Recall), in accordance with good practice (Cameron, 2003; Chapter 12, this volume).

In this study, the striking use of metaphor by participants was apparent from conference transcripts in the preliminary content analysis. However, this technique revealed insufficient detail and little about the significance of metaphor use. Cameron (2003: 30) advises caution in claiming to find evidence of thinking as well as speaking by examining discourse. To address this, metaphor analysis was used to complement content analysis, and interviews were conducted with the students and the tutor on the researched programme. As stated earlier, Critical Event Recall was used in the interviews to provide additional evidence of what the participants intended and learned through metaphors. The researcher was also interviewed by her supervisor, giving her an opportunity to examine her own mental and emotional processes.

In the metaphor analysis, the conference transcripts were examined again and all metaphors identified and marked by underlining. This revealed four principal types or occurrences of metaphors being used, which were categorized as follows:

- **deliberate metaphor**: prominent and clear metaphor, likely to have been intentional and clearly distinguishable from normal conventionalized metaphors (Cameron, 2003);
- **conventionalized metaphor:** less prominent, possibly unintentional metaphor use, difficult to distinguish from normal idiomatic expression e.g. *put in place*;

- **metaphor clusters:** where two or more metaphors were used in a short space of time within the same posting by an individual, but where the vehicles did not come from the same domain;
- **narrative metaphor:** where two or more metaphors were used in a short space of time within the same posting by an individual, where the vehicles were from the same domain and the effect was a story-like (narrative) feel (called 'metaphorical stories' in Chapter 7).

Further analysis was conducted of the incidence and nature of the deliberate metaphors and narrative metaphors used. Conventionalized metaphors were not analysed further (except where they occurred as part of a narrative). Examining metaphor clusters was beyond the scope of the current study but could be an area for future research.

## Findings

### General

The single most common subject matter for deliberate metaphor use overall was TIME, which was generally viewed in a negative way (e.g. *time is an enemy, pressures of time*) or as a valuable commodity (e.g. *time is spent, saved, a premium*). This is perhaps indicative of the importance of time to professional adult distance e-learners juggling work, home and study commitments. Other commonly occurring deliberate metaphor source domains were TRAVEL, CONTAINERS, CONSTRUCTION, CREATIVITY, MOVEMENT, TRANSMISSION, RICHNESS and VALUE.

### Metaphor and cognition

There appeared to be co-occurrence of metaphor use with critical incidents, and a hypothesis was formed that there might be a link between use of metaphor online and learning which went beyond the cognitive effort used in creating the metaphor. In analysing the occurrence and type of metaphor used in the researched programme, the researcher sought to examine whether there was any correlation between occurrence of metaphor and of learning, especially higher level learning, such as analysis, synthesis and evaluation (Bloom *et al.*, 1956).

Conferences 1, 3, 4 and 7 had the highest number of recorded instances of higher level learning and also showed the highest use of deliberate metaphors (as shown in Table 13.1).

Table 13.1. Occurrence of deliberate metaphors

| Person | C1[1] | C2 | C3 | C4 | C5 | C6 | C7 | Total |
|---|---|---|---|---|---|---|---|---|
| Male 1 | 4 | 2 | 10 | | | | 2 | 18 |
| Male 2 | 2 | 3 | 1 | | | | | 6 |
| Male 3 | 39 | 13 | 11 | 27 | 8 | 11 | 16 | 125 |
| Female 1 | 28 | 1 | | 7 | 1 | | | 37 |
| Female 2 | 10 | 0 | 4 | 9 | 1 | | | 24 |
| Female 3 | 14 | 3 | 16 | 67 | 11 | 25 | 31 | 167 |
| Tutor | 14 | 4 | 10 | 6 | 11 | 16 | 15 | 76 |
| **Total** | **111** | **26** | **52** | **116** | **32** | **52** | **64** | **453** |

[1] C = Conference

Since the analysis shown in Table 13.1 did not take into account the relative size of the conferences, a corpus approach was adopted, in addition, in which the number of metaphors per 100 words was calculated as shown in Table 13.2.

Table 13.2. Number of metaphors per 100 words

| | C1[1] | C2 | C3 | C4 | C5 | C6 | C7 | Total |
|---|---|---|---|---|---|---|---|---|
| Number of words | 7,775 | 3,321 | 3,870 | 5,515 | 1,499 | 4,194 | 4,192 | 30,334 |
| Metaphors per 100 words | 1.43 | 0.78 | 1.34 | 2.1 | 2.13 | 1.23 | 1.52 | 1.49 Average |

[1] C= Conference

Table 13.2 reveals more of what happened, in that Conference 5, which showed a relatively small amount of higher level learning, had the highest count of metaphors per 100 words, whereas Conference 3, which had a relatively high amount of higher level learning, had the second lowest count of metaphors per 100 words. This seems to shed some doubt on whether there was a direct correlation between use of deliberate metaphor and occurrence of higher level learning in the researched programme.

Similar analysis was carried out of the occurrence of narrative metaphors during the conferencing period. The results are shown in Table 13.3. The highest occurrence was in Conferences 1 and 4, two of those with the greatest incidence of higher level learning.

Table 13.3. Occurrence of narrative metaphors

| Person | C1[1] | C2 | C3 | C4 | C5 | C6 | C7 | Total |
|---|---|---|---|---|---|---|---|---|
| Male 1 | 0 | 0 | 0 | 0 | 0 | 0 | 0 | 0 |
| Male 2 | 0 | 0 | 0 | 0 | 0 | 0 | 0 | 0 |
| Male 3 | 0 | 0 | 0 | 2 | 1 | 1 | 1 | 5 |
| Female 1 | 2 | 0 | 0 | 1 | 0 | 0 | 0 | 3 |
| Female 2 | 1 | 0 | 0 | 0 | 0 | 0 | 0 | 1 |
| Female 3 | 0 | 0 | 1 | 10 | 2 | 1 | 0 | 14 |
| Tutor | 2 | 0 | 0 | 0 | 0 | 1 | 0 | 3 |
| **Total** | **5** | **0** | **1** | **13** | **3** | **3** | **1** | **26** |

[1] C= Conference

This was also cross-checked, using a corpus approach, against the number of incidences per 100 words as before. The results are shown in Table 13.4.

Table 13.4. Number of narrative metaphors per 100 words

| | C1[1] | C2 | C3 | C4 | C5 | C6 | C7 | Total |
|---|---|---|---|---|---|---|---|---|
| Number of words | 7,752 | 3,321 | 3,870 | 5,515 | 1,499 | 4,194 | 4,192 | 30,334 |
| Narrative metaphors per 100 words | 0.06 | 0 | 0.025 | 0.235 | 0.2 | 0.07 | 0.024 | 1.49 Average |

[1] C= Conference

This again tells a different story, in that Conference 5, which, as stated previously, showed a relatively small amount of higher level learning, had the highest count of narrative metaphors per 100 words. Conference 4 was the next highest, and that did have a relatively large amount of higher level learning.

However, examining only the numbers of metaphors may not give the whole picture; for example, the impact of particularly powerful metaphor use in Conference 7 does not register. There was therefore a need to examine the researched programme in a more qualitative way to consider whether the use of such metaphors had educational value.

There is evidence from the researched programme that metaphors may have been useful in the learning process, for example by inviting interaction and organizing ideas (Cortazzi and Jin, 1999:161) as well as assisting with reflection. In Extract 13.2, from Conference 4, one of the learners reflects back on her earlier online participation, using (and developing upon) animal metaphors suggested by her reading of Salmon (2002) to help her categorize this behaviour and organize her thoughts:

Extract 13.2

On reflection I wondered if I had <u>been a bit wolf-like</u> in this course in the past (albeit for genuine reasons such as <u>competing</u> priorities and <u>time pressures</u>.) I felt surprised and rather guilty when I checked the [name] bit of this site and found that I seemed to be making quite a lot of postings but wasn't logging on very much, comparatively. I have therefore decided to become more of <u>an</u> <u>'elephant'</u> (steady – visits most days) by getting up earlier and trying to log on in the morning before going to work ... does this mean that the optimum on-line team is composed entirely of <u>elephants</u> or is a bit of variety helpful?

(Female 3, Posting 4.10)

Two postings later, Extract 13.3, it is clear that another participant has learned about the relevant (learner activity tracking) section of the Virtual Learning Environment from Female 3's comments above. This learner also picks up on the same metaphor to add humour and it is as if the use of this metaphor has aided her reflection and provoked or encouraged her to respond to Female 3's posting:

Extract 13.3

I didn't know about the [name] section and now don't feel quite so bad about my slow start & lack of contribution but the thought of being compared to an elephant would really depress me ...!

(Female 1, Posting 4.13)

The data analysis also appears to give some support to the views of Petrie and Oshlag (1993: 580–584) that metaphors provide a basic way of passing from the well known to the unknown, i.e. they are an aid to acquiring new knowledge and moving from what is well known to what is less known in a vivid and memorable way, and therefore have potential as a teaching tool. In 42.3% of narrative metaphor occurrences the user was adopting a tutoring role (such as facilitating or moderating) and 70% of these involved a student adopting a tutoring role rather than the tutor himself doing so (see Table 13.5). For example, referring to the extract above, Female 3 made it clear in interview that she was deliberately trying to shame others into participating at a time when there was a lull in contributions and when the tutor did not seem to be successful in doing so. She felt she was fulfilling a tutor's role.

At the very least, metaphors afforded a different way of viewing the world (per Ortony, 1993: 5, 13). For example, in Conference 3, on the topic of student motivation, the leader started with a very wide opening posting. One participant later put forward a series of three headings, all of which were phrased as deliberate metaphors and explicated, by way of a suggested structure for the conference as *a LONG JOURNEY*:

Table 13.5. Narrative metaphor use and tutoring role

| Conference | Number of narrative metaphors | Using a tutoring role |
|---|---|---|
| C1 | 5 | 2 |
| C2 | 0 | 0 |
| C3 | 1 | 1 |
| C4 | 13 | 7 |
| C5 | 3 | 0 |
| C6 | 3 | 1 |
| C7 | 1 | 0 |
| **Totals** | **26** | **11 (42.3%)** |

Extract 13.4

I agree with those who have pointed out that this is a huge subject. Would it help to consider it in terms of:

Getting started

Keeping going - what happens during a course

Staying the 'distance' - ensuring that learners finish the course.

(Female 3, Posting 3.8)

This metaphor was taken up and used by subsequent participants as a way of narrowing down a wide subject and a useful way of expressing themselves.

Whatever the exact subject matter of an online course, it is important for all participants to learn how to behave and how to learn online. In Conference 4, on the subject of team working online, there was the greatest incidence of narrative metaphors. In this conference, the complexity of language used seemed to be matched by a positive cognitive turning point in the programme. For example, Extract 13.5 shows students reflecting on the previous behaviours of themselves and others and learning from them:

Extract 13.4

Looking back, I do feel guilty that at the beginning poor [name of student] was logging on loads and posting like fury and I just wasn't out there in support…

(Female 3, posting 4.14)

In Extract 13.4, Female 3 uses a number of metaphors to express her reflection on a period of time when she felt she had not participated enough. The metaphors she uses in this passage have different vehicle domains (see Table

13.6); but there are some links between them. For example, physical/spatial presence (*I wasn't out there*) and physical movement backwards (*looking back*) give the idea of cyberspace as a place. It is also interesting that emotion is expressed literally (I am feeling guilty) but then an emotion (anger) is used metaphorically to express frequency and speed of someone else's contributions (*posting like fury*).

Table 13.6. Metaphor groups, Extract 13.4

| Metaphor used | Vehicle domain | Topic |
| --- | --- | --- |
| *Looking (back)* | VISION/SEEING | Mental/cognitive reflection |
| *(Looking) back* | PHYSICAL MOVEMENT BACKWARDS | The past |
| *Logging on loads* | WEIGHT | Quantity/frequency (many times) |
| *Posting like fury* | ANGER | Quantity/speed/frequency/urgency of contributions |
| *I wasn't out there* | PHYSICAL AND/OR SPATIAL PRESENCE | Lack of participation/support for other team member |

## Metaphor and emotion

The link between emotion and learning is acknowledged, for example, by the inclusion of an affective (emotional) domain in Bloom *et al.*'s taxonomy (1956). Lakoff and Johnson's view (1980: 115) is that one way of expressing and understanding abstract concepts such as emotions, ideas and time is to consider them in terms of concepts that we understand more clearly, such as spatial orientations and physical objects. This is borne out by the fact that, in the text-only world of the researched programme, emotions were often expressed through the device of metaphor, especially narrative metaphor as shown in Table 13.7. In nearly 70% of cases where narrative metaphors occurred, they were used to express emotion, and, of these, 83% of the emotions expressed were negative feelings such as frustration, anger or guilt.

Table 13.7. Narrative metaphor use and emotion

| Conference | Number of narrative metaphors | Number of these expressing emotion | Negative emotions | Positive emotions |
|---|---|---|---|---|
| C1 | 5 | 1 | 1 | 0 |
| C2 | 0 | 0 | – | – |
| C3 | 1 | 0 | – | – |
| C4 | 13 | 12 | 11 | 1 |
| C5 | 3 | 2 | 0 | 2 |
| C6 | 3 | 2 | 2 | 0 |
| C7 | 1 | 1 | 1 | 0 |
| **Totals** | **26** | **18 (69%)** | **15 (out of 18)** | **3 (out of 18)** |

These findings tend to support Stone's view (1995) that emotions may be difficult to express or even heightened due to the relatively low amount of information exchange in unit time ('narrow bandwidth'), so that participants may be faced with interpreting and drawing maximum meaning from minimal symbology (Stone, 1995). This may also partly explain why part-way through Conference 4 the group began to use text messaging symbols or 'emoticons' for a while.

Apart from the noticeable use of visual metaphors such as emoticons, Conference 4 was clearly the one with the highest occurrence of narrative metaphors (see Table 13.7). Considering such figurative language and modes of expression does indeed, in Kövecses' terms (2000: xi), reveal a lot about the emotions the participants experienced, the dominant feelings at this time being frustration and anger at the non-participation or 'silence' of peers:

Extract 13.5

At one point I felt as if I was doing a ballet solo – fortunately [the tutor] joined in and then it became a 'Pas de Deux' but it didn't feel quite right. You don't know where everyone else has gone. Where's the 'corps de ballet'? You put down what you hope are a few cue lines but no-one comes on stage.

(Female 3, Posting 4.14)

Craig *et al.* (1998: 124) suggest that online learners may feel freer to express disagreement: freed from the constraints of real life social norms. However, this was not generally true of the researched programme, which was characterized by a culture of 'no critique'. Participants rarely challenged the views others expressed and disagreements tended to be over behaviour rather than opinion. That is not to say that there was no emotional engagement. In this respect a key area for strong emotion and cognitive conflict was that of peer-peer and tutor-learner feedback.

The most notable narrative metaphors tended to occur during 'critical incidents': times of heightened emotion which also seemed to be key moments in the learning process. Such metaphors were used to express negative emotions (like anger, frustration or loneliness) in a socially acceptable way. They were particularly used, as in Extract 13.6, as euphemisms when giving negative feedback, such as criticizing fellow students for non-participation:

Extract 13.6

I'm feeling a bit lonely <u>out here</u> at the moment. ... If you <u>are back</u> folks do let us know what you think before I become a <u>mouse</u> (visits once a week, reads but doesn't contribute) or even a <u>mole</u> (posts dissembodied [sic] comments in a random way)!

(Female 3, Posting 4.12)

It is feasible therefore, that metaphor was being used to make up for the lack of body language online, especially in the case of emotions such as anger, which could provoke a strong reaction if not tempered by the vehicle of a euphemistic metaphor. This is in line with Drew and Holt's research (1988) that metaphors are frequently used to express feelings when making complaints (e.g. *like banging my head against a brick wall*). On the researched programme those criticizing their fellow learners used metaphor at least partly to spare their feelings, and adds to Cameron's claim (2003: 23) that metaphor may be used in classroom contexts to give negative feedback to learners in such a way as to avoid publicly saying that they have made a mistake.

A highly memorable critical incident of conflict occurred in Conference 7 in which a student overtly criticized the tutor in an online conference, shown in Extract 13.7. This marked a break from covert to overt criticism of the tutor and built on previous comments which the student had made about lack of tutor feedback:

Extract 13.7

I remember stating this point before regarding that we don't seem to get any feedback during this course so it is hard to know <u>how we are doing</u>. It is a bit like <u>sailing at night</u> <u>with no stars for naviga-tion! Forget "longitude" we need "[Tutor's name]-itude" but our digital sail journey appears to take place before this was invented</u>. I know we are supposed to get feedback from our peers but <u>let's face it</u> (certainly in <u>my case</u>) this is about as often as we get told we are doing a good job by our manager - not often enough.

(Male 3, Posting 7.3.3)

When interviewed, the student explained:

Extract 13.8

With something as ambiguous as this … you've not no visual clues you can't pick anything up from what's been said you can't see anything … you need more either direct feedback via email from him to you or indirect onto the message board.

(Male 3, interview 10.8)

I thought I'll send that and see what happens and he replied and he did and he stood up there and he explained why he'd done it and I was quite happy that what he'd said was a reasonable justification.

(Male 3, interview 10.2)

Asked why he put this into a 'public' conference rather than emailing the tutor privately, the student said:

Extract 13.9

I would have emailed him about it but it was better off on the discussion thread 'cos everybody could see it. I'm quite happy to say anything in front of everybody … I didn't know whether people would agree or disagree.

(Male 3, interview 10.4)

The tutor's reaction to this posting confirms that it is possible to have tangible feelings from words emanating from a computer just as from the words of someone physically present (Sanchez, 1998: 99):

Extract 13.10

Researcher:     What did you think about all that?

Tutor:          I was - a mixture of being baffled and a little bit angry.

(Interview 11.1)

The fact that this incident was regarded as highly memorable by the participants supports Cameron's view (2003: 36) that the vivid use of language may aid recall. It is clear that is likely to influence participants' own e-learning practice, as a number mentioned giving feedback as one of the things they would include in their own online courses as a result of completing the researched programme. Cognitive conflict can clearly be useful for learning.

Metaphor and online identity

There appeared to be a link between choice of metaphor vehicle and the gender of the person using the metaphor. Overall, men tended to use metaphors connected with POWER, VEHICLES and TIME, whilst women tended to use those connected with CATERING, CREATIVITY and THE ARTS. This was especially noticeable in the case of major narrative metaphors (SAILING and ASTRONOMY versus BALLET). This is in line with those who claim that writing can transmit the body (Argyle and Shields, 1996) and that, when we write, our words embody ourselves in significant ways (Miller, 1991). It tends to contrast with the views of those who believe that gender is socially constructed and that, in the virtual world you are who you pretend to be (for example, Turkle, 1995). In the researched programme, the self was revealed and identified by language rather than made and transformed by it.

If gender is more visible than this medium would at first suggest this could pose a threat to the democratizing nature of such discussion (Brookfield and Preskill, 2005: 3) and may go against the claim that computer supported co-operative learning allows women more equality of opportunity (McConnell, 2000: 105). Detailed examination of this issue was beyond the scope of the current study but is an area that would merit further research.

## Summary and conclusions

This study demonstrates that, in the researched programme, metaphor was more than 'frilly speech': there was coincidence between deliberate metaphor use and incidences of emotion and cognition. It is feasible that metaphor was being used to make up for the lack of body language online, especially in the case of emotions such as anger, which could provoke a strong reaction if not tempered by metaphor use. Metaphor analysis has therefore proved its worth as a useful tool for complementing other approaches to analysing data from online conferences and ultimately for providing an insight into how people learn through online discussions.

Note
1. The year cited refers to the edition actually used in the research study rather than the year in which the work was first written or published

# 14   Using metaphor analysis to compare expert and public perceptions of the risk of terrorism

## Lynne Cameron and Robert Maslen

Throughout the book, we have used data from a focus group discussion involving members of the public that was collected as part of a large social sciences research project, Perception and Communication of the Risk of Terrorism (details in the Appendix). In this closing chapter, we zoom out to the closing stages of the research project and describe the outcomes of using metaphor analysis to compare the perceptions of members of the public with those of experts.

## Metaphor analysis and the project aims

Metaphor analysis was used[1] to answer the following research question:

> Do factors such as location, gender, social class, whether Muslim or non-Muslim, and expertise affect how people conceptualize and respond to the threat of terrorism?

The patterns of metaphors found in elicited discourse data were used as one source of evidence for people's ideas and attitudes about risk and terrorism.

## Participants and data

The influence of the factors mentioned in the above question was evaluated by collecting data from different sets of people. As described in the Appendix, to address the influence of religion, and gender, separate focus groups were organized for men and for women, and for Muslim and non-Muslim participants. Location was examined by having groups in Leeds and in London, and social class was operationalized using social grade definitions. Twelve focus groups, involving members of the public recruited to these criteria, were held.

To address the influence of expertise, we compared metaphors generated by the general public with metaphors generated by 'experts'. Experts in the topic of the research – risk, security, terrorism – were contacted and invited to take part in one-to-one interviews with a researcher. The experts were UK-based specialists or high-level professionals in the various areas covered by the research project. Thirteen interviews were carried out and transcribed, but because of project time constraints, just eight of these were used for further analysis. The eight expert participants, most of whom cannot be identified by name for security reasons, came from the following fields:

| | |
|---|---|
| Expert 1 | News media (print and online) |
| Expert 2 | Muslim community organization |
| Expert 3 | UK Security Service (MI5) |
| Expert 4 | Political 'think tank' |
| Expert 5 | Government communications |
| Expert 6 | News media (television, radio and online) |
| Expert 7 | Politics |
| Expert 8 | Police |

An expert interview schedule was drawn up that included some of the questions in the focus group schedule, together with questions to elicit participants' expert opinions. As with the focus groups, care was taken to avoid using metaphors in the interview questions and thus influencing participants' metaphor use through priming. The interviews were carried out by members of the research team, usually in the expert's place of work, and lasted between 45 minutes and 90 minutes. They were audio recorded.

## Method

### Preparation for analysis

The focus group and interview recordings were transcribed into intonation units and linguistic metaphors were underlined in the transcripts, as described in Chapters 6 and 10.

The focus group data provided approximately 190,000 words of transcription, in which 12,363 linguistic metaphors were identified. The expert interview data produced 69,918 words of transcription, in which 6,299 linguistic metaphors were identified.

### Metaphor analysis

The metaphor analysis of focus group data has been fully described in earlier chapters. Metaphor analysis of the expert interviews proceeded in a similar fashion: it began with an analysis of each interview to produce systematic metaphors, and then proceeded to comparisons across expert interviews, and to comparisons between experts and focus groups.

As described in Chapter 7 for the focus group data, systematic metaphors in the expert data were produced by working with each interview in turn and assigning linguistic metaphors to vehicle groupings. By this stage in the project, stable groupings had emerged from the focus group analyses, and these were used for the expert data wherever possible.

After allocating metaphors to vehicle groupings, the key discourse topics developed in the focus group analyses (Chapter 7) were used to group linguistic metaphors into the following sets:

1.   systematic metaphors about terrorism;
2.   systematic metaphors about communication, by the authorities and by the media;
3.   systematic metaphors about responses to terrorism, by the authorities and affecting Muslims;
4.   systematic metaphors about groups in society.

For each expert interview, a list was produced of the systematic metaphors together with the linguistic metaphors included in each systematic metaphor. For example, some of the linguistic metaphors produced by expert 8 (Police) were grouped into systematic metaphors about terrorism (key topic 1) as follows:

*DEATH IS LOSS OF LIFE*

| 2522 | because it *involves massive **loss*** *of life* |
| 2534 | ***loss*** *of loved ones* |
| 2570 | *people **lost** their lives* |

*DEALING WITH TERRORISM IS A KIND OF (BALL) GAME*

| 344 | *we are **in a different ball game** here now* |

*BELIEFS ARE POSITIONS ON A LANDSCAPE*

| 1450 | *for a person to **move**,* |
| 1473 | *for **moving from** radical views **to** extremism,* |
| 1475 | *it is something very different **going on**.* |

To compare across the experts, each discourse topic was taken in turn. The systematic metaphors about, for example, terrorism (topic 1) used by each expert were put together and compared for similarities and differences. This stage produced both a composite 'expert perspective', where similarities were evidenced by the data, together with contrasts reflecting differences between individual experts.

The outcome of the expert comparisons was then compared with the summary of focus groups' systematic metaphors to answer the research question about the effect of expertise on conceptualizations of and responses to terrorism. Examples of findings from this process of comparison are presented in the next section.

The metaphor analysis process is one of successive condensations of the data. However, condensation or reduction of data does not mean that we lose sight of the detail that has been condensed into summary documents. The point we have repeatedly emphasized throughout the book, that metaphors cannot be separated from their discourse context and thus that our analytic methods need to retain the connection, was addressed in this work in the following ways: by knowing the transcripts through numerous readings, and in some cases through participation in the interview; by keeping the transcripts close by to refer to constantly; and by using the intonation unit of each metaphor in lists, rather than just the metaphor vehicle term. The final stages of analysis and subsequent interpretation that are highlighted in this chapter require imagination and creativity alongside the rigour that we have tried to incorporate throughout. Thorough knowledge of the data and of the analytic outcomes inform the generation of findings and implications, and of accessible and motivating dissemination to research users.

## The effect of expertise on conceptualizations of and responses to terrorism

Comparing and contrasting the use of metaphors by members of the general public in focus group discussions with the experts in interviews revealed differences with implications for official communication about and responses to terrorist risk. In some cases, the same systematic metaphor or metaphor scenario was used with quite different implications. In other cases, a set of systematic metaphors was used more by one group or the other. In all cases, we attended to the affective content of the patterns of metaphor use (or the secondary simulations, to use Ritchie's term from Chapter 4). Implications for official communication include suggestions as to how metaphors might be employed to create more positive feelings and attitudes in the general public, such as counteracting felt helplessness in the face of terrorist risk or constructing more positive perceptions of official action. In this final section, we have selected four findings about comparative use of metaphors to present, and briefly discuss their implications.

### RESPONSE TO THE RISK OF TERRORISM AS THEATRE

Both experts and focus groups made use of systematic and linguistic metaphors that together form a metaphor scenario[2] labelled RESPONSE TO THE RISK OF TER-

*RORISM AS THEATRE*. However, as we show below, the scenario presented very differently.

The experts (particularly experts 3 and 4) produced systematic and linguistic metaphors such as those below, which contributed to the larger scenario:

| | |
|---|---|
| *ACTING* | they *perform* a very important *role* |
| | they've created such a *drama* |
| | there's more than one *audience* |
| *BALANCE* | that difficult *balancing act* |
| *GIVING OUT* | if you *give out* a reasonable amount of information |
| *LOCATION* | that public debate is *out there* |
| *MOVEMENT* | then you're just *straight into* the *realm* of |
| *PHYSICAL ACTION* | to *stand up* and say |
| *SEEING* | relatively *clear* who the bad guys are |
| | however his public *image* is *portrayed* |
| *SPEAKING/LISTENING* | you can't *talk* to one *audience* |
| *STORIES* | some *magic wand* I would *wave* |
| | he and his *merry men* |

In this expert *THEATRE* scenario, Government ministers and other authority figures are seen as actors playing *roles* on the stage, *addressing the issues of terrorism*, advised by the security services and others *behind the scenes*, with scenarios, *stories* and *narratives* constructed for the public as audience, scripted and stage-managed without much improvisation. Experts are sometimes *trotted out* to make statements to the audience. The power and control of authorities is represented by control over the 'drama' and by their position on the stage, in front of and above the *audience* who is *Joe public*. In the experts' use of the *THEATRE* metaphor, the public are positioned as receivers of information not as participants in a joint effort, and are not usually allowed to join the actors, i.e. the experts, on stage. There is a danger that the audience is seen as a single group rather than as multiple audiences since all members of the audience are, relative to the stage placed in similar positions, at distance and separated from the actors.

The focus groups also made use of *THEATRE* metaphors, but from their position as audience. They use these metaphors to evaluate the performance of the authorities, speaking of it as a *farce*, *pantomime* or tragi-comedy in which the government is seen to act inappropriately or to make fools of themselves. They speak of key players as having roles in these kinds of dramas: Bush/Blair as *Billy the Kid*; the extremist Islamic cleric Abu Hamza as *Captain Hook*; racists in their community are *a lot of Alf Garnets* (British television character, adapted in the US as Archie Bunker). The government slogan used to encourage the public to be 'alert but not alarmed' is evaluated by focus groups as lightweight and glib, as a *catch phrase* or *tag line*, more suited to popular light entertainment than serious theatre. An important implication of the negative affect of focus group THEATRE metaphors is that the public want to see the authorities taking real action that goes beyond a performance or show.

For the focus groups, CONCEALMENT metaphors also contribute to the scenario. The authorities conceal and restrain information, and, while focus group members accept that a certain amount of secrecy is necessary, they feel they are being unnecessarily *kept in the dark*.

We chose THEATRE as a broad label to capture different kinds of spectacle seen on a stage or a screen by an audience. A similar metaphor scenario, 'POLITICS-AS-SPECTACLE', appears in a list compiled by Beer and De Landtsheer (2004: 19) of metaphorical sources for political target domains, and incorporates domains including Carnival, Circus, Drama, Fairytale, Science Fiction, Theatre and Wild West. In our data, the target or topic domain is not just politics but includes responses to terrorism by politicians, the authorities, the media and the general public.

As we often find in researching metaphors, language use slips between the metaphorical and the literal, and the THEATRE metaphor scenario reflects and slips into people's actual experience of watching terrorism events and their aftermath play out on their television screens.

The metaphor scenario RESPONSE TO TERRORISM AS THEATRE neatly summarizes two versions of the same experience; it captures the difference felt in agency and control by experts and by the general public. From the authorities' point of view, this metaphor suggests potential dangers: their actions could be interpreted by the public as fictitious or as entertainment, rather than as serious honest efforts; positioning the public as audience may be felt as removing agency in a situation where the authorities need commitment and participation.

As implications of the research, we can suggest that overuse of the THEATRE metaphors be avoided by the authorities, and that a combination of LANDSCAPE and MOVEMENT metaphors might offer a less evaluative, more neutral metaphorical scenario for talking about positions in respect of terrorism and responses to it. We would certainly suggest that experts and people in authority put themselves in the position of the general public watching their performance, and adjust what they do and say in public to better connect with their multiple audiences.

## BODY, ANIMAL, PHYSICAL ACTION metaphors and personification to describe official responses to the risk of terrorism

The metaphor analysis showed that the general public, but not experts, used BODY, ANIMAL, PHYSICAL ACTION metaphors and personification in thinking and talking about official responses to terrorist risk, and that this was mostly negative in affect.

The focus groups used *BODY* metaphors, *ANIMAL* metaphors and personification (speaking of the government as if it were a person) that carry mainly negative affective content about government and authority responses to terrorism. The government was seen as a timid animal: *pussy footing, chicken;* or as a person who *bends over backwards,* has *no balls,* is *spineless,* has *knee jerk reactions* and will *bow down to what America does.*

Metaphors of physical closeness are used by the focus group in talking about political alignment: Blair as *sleeping with Bush*; and metaphors of physical power and strength are used to talk about political power, or its absence: *strong leaders, nobody's strong enough, they need to stick their neck out.*

In contrast, experts do not use these kinds of *BODY, ANIMAL* or *PHYSICAL ACTION* metaphors that convey a sense of weakness about the government and authorities. The multiple use of *face* metaphors in talk about terrorism, such as *the biggest threat we face* (mainly by security services expert 5), positions the authorities as standing in front of terrorism, resolutely rather than weakly. Society is personified as weak in the metaphorical technical term used by the security services: *vulnerability.*

*BODY, PHYSICAL ACTION* metaphors and personification metaphors take their power from people's everyday physical experience and from cultural conventions about the meaning of physical activity or stance. The metaphors are powerful because they key directly into people's embodied experience, and again there is likely to be slippage between the metaphorical and literal thinking about the people involved in official responses to terrorist risk. As an implication of the research, we might suggest that experts and people in authority use more *BODY* metaphors, in particular metaphors of *POSITION* and *PHYSICAL ACTIVITY*, to convey a positive sense of power, control and determination in the face of terrorism. Not only that, but physical appearance and stance, on television and in person, may have a more profound influence on public opinion about the capability of authorities to respond to terrorist risk than is assumed.

### *BALANCE* metaphors and terrorist risk

Both experts and the focus groups use metaphors of *BALANCE* but use them in talk about different topics. Experts make most use of *BALANCE* metaphors in talk about how authorities make difficult decisions about how much information to share with the public. They have to balance panicking the public and encouraging them to provide information; warning people in time and not too soon; warning and then finding an attack does not happen. The *BALANCING* is described as *balance, tension, the see-saw tipped, thin blue line, a balancing act* (meshing with *THEATRE* metaphor). The media also have to balance people's right to know about risks with giving a realistic measure of risk: *tight rope, line to tread, not an easy path to walk, equation.*

Expert 5 speaks of *the disruption of social/technical networks* and seems to understand how people respond: *a shock to their system; the more it shakes them the more terror it arouses.*

In focus groups, the normal state of social and individual (emotional) life is described as *balanced, harmonious,* with terrorism acting to disturb this equilibrium: *on edge, out of balance, stir it up, upset.* After a while, equilibrium is restored: *settles down.* Women across the focus groups make more use than men of BALANCE metaphors, and 'working class' speakers use more than 'professional' participants.

Once again, the comparison showed expert BALANCE metaphors involving skilled, agentive performance, such as tight rope walking, whereas focus groups' metaphors featured less agency and disturbance from the actions of terrorists.

Official communication that used BALANCE metaphors with agency or to suggest how equilibrium may be restored might empower recipients.

## GAME metaphors: Chance or skill

Systematic GAME and TEAM metaphors were mentioned in Chapter 7. Focus groups conveyed a sense of helplessness in the face of terrorism through frequent use of metaphors about GAMES OF CHANCE: *a poker game, pawns in a game, lottery, odds, my number's up.* In this metaphor, terrorists are seen to be in control of the game and ordinary people must take their chance in unpredictable situations.

GAME metaphors were hardly used by the experts, although they did talk about uncertainty in terms of balance. Only expert 8 (Police) used GAME metaphors in talking about dealing with terrorism: *a different kind of ball game.* In this metaphor, the game is a matter of skill rather than chance. In talking about the police and 7/7, he says *we lost that trick* (as in a card game) and that they are *playing catch up.* These metaphors do not convey the sense of helplessness of the public's GAME OF CHANCE metaphors, but have more sense of power and the possibility of 'winning'.

Implications for official communicators might be to work with GAME metaphors and restructure them from games of chance into games of skill that can be won, to make the public feel less helpless. People might also be encouraged through these metaphors to *play their part* in supporting police and authorities in preventing terrorist attacks. However, it will be important to remember that comparisons showed that GAME metaphors are gender-preferred, used in the focus groups significantly more by men than by women. As above, communicators need to choose and use metaphors with multiple audiences in mind.

## Conclusion

Throughout the book, we have been concerned to open up and discuss research practice in metaphor analysis, sharing our concerns about potential difficulties in the various steps. In closing the book with results and implications from a large scale research project, we hope to have shown something of the power of metaphor analysis when applied to real world situations.

### Notes

1   Metaphor analysis was one of three methods used to address the project research questions. The other methods were attribution analysis (described briefly in Chapter 10), and field experiments that tested qualitative findings.

2   In Chapter 7, we differentiated 'metaphorical stories', which occur in single discourse events, from 'metaphor scenarios', which are put together across multiple discourse events or corpora. We use 'scenario' here because it derives from multiple discourse events and people, and because it appropriately suggests a schematic structure.

# 15  Concluding remarks

## Lynne Cameron and Robert Maslen

We set out in this book to illustrate how metaphor can offer insights into people's ideas, attitudes and beliefs, and to demonstrate research methodology that builds on this premise. In presenting various aspects of metaphor analysis we have tried to show both the possibilities and the limitations of metaphor as a research tool. The discourse dynamics theoretical framework has been elaborated as suitable for supporting research that uses naturally occurring or elicited discourse as data. We have explained how this departs from the cognitive approach of conceptual metaphor theory, which essentially concerns metaphor at the level of a speech community. Metaphor here is held to be, not just cognitive, but also a dynamic and discourse phenomenon. The language of metaphor has been consistently treated as an inherent aspect of the phenomenon, crucial rather than 'mere expression'.

Further, we accept that language is only one of the modalities of metaphor that come into play when people express their ideas and feelings. The important work on gesture and metaphor introduced in the book gives an indication of the rich possibilities of multimodal perspectives to expand and deepen both our understanding and our methodological toolkit. The next few years are likely to bring technological innovations that will assist the analysis of gesture and extend its applicability from today's pioneers to the mainstream of discourse research. As we have also seen in the book, developments already enabled by technology have made the use of corpora and corpus linguistic techniques not just important but almost indispensable in metaphor analysis, enabling understandings of the relation of individual choices to larger levels of metaphor use across speech communities.

We have used two main data samples across the chapters – a political speech and a focus group discussion – to exemplify methodological steps; the empirical findings that we have reported as outcomes of the analysis give new insights into how people employ metaphor in their communication with others, and support our claims for the effectiveness of metaphor analysis. Readers who wish to do so will be able to continue and develop the metaphor analysis using the transcripts in the appendix, and are sure to find yet more of interest in the data.

The real test of the book's usefulness will come when it is applied in readers' own work. We cannot guarantee there will not be difficulties – in fact, we can probably guarantee that metaphor analysis applied to discourse data will always present problems – but we have tried to provide guidelines and techniques for dealing rigorously and sensitively with those problems. We can certainly guarantee a fascinating experience in which the metaphors that people use continue to surprise, delight and intrigue.

# Appendix

## Data source 1: Perception and Communication of Terrorist Risk (PCTR) project

This project (ESRC RES 228250053) was funded by the UK Economic and Social Research Council under its New Security Challenges research programme, from 2005–2007, and was based at the University of Leeds. The overall aims of the project were to investigate people's perceptions about the risk of terrorism and the consequences for official risk communications. The project included three phases and types of methodology: focus group discussions; expert interviews; field experiments. The experimental data are not used here. Focus group and expert data were subjected to metaphor analysis and attribution analysis.

### Focus group data collection

Twelve focus groups were organized, and used to investigate differences in perceptions about terrorism across location, gender, religion and socioeconomic status.

Location was examined by having six groups in London and six in Leeds (in the north of England). Separate focus groups were held for men and women, and for Muslims and non-Muslims. This latter group was not further divided by religion. Socioeconomic status was operationalized using social grade definitions from the UK National Readership Survey (http://www.businessballs.com/demographicsclassifications.htm accessed 20 January 2008). Two categories were created using these grade definitions: AB, corresponding approximately to 'professional', and CD, corresponding approximately to 'working class'.

Ethical approval for the study was given by the Institute of Psychological Sciences, University of Leeds. Participants gave informed consent in line with British Psychological Society guidelines, and all names used are aliases.

## Data source 2: The Blair speech

This version of the speech is divided and numbered by paragraphs based on the text as published (http://www.guardian.co.uk/politics/2005/feb/14/labour. speeches. Accessed 12 July 2009).

A fight we have to win

Sunday 13 February 2005. Speech by Tony Blair, Prime Minister and Leader of the Labour Party to Labour's Spring Conference, Sage Centre, Gateshead.

1    What a wonderful Centre this is. I would like to thank all the staff who have looked after us so brilliantly and a particular thank you to the police and security, who have done a great job.

2    And say thank you to the people of Gateshead and Tyneside, with apologies for disruption. But it's been a great place to come to. Just four years ago a derelict industrial land. Now one of the finest concert halls in the world. And before it even opened, it had already benefited more than a million people through its education work.

3    Just along from this magnificent Centre is the Baltic Exchange, one of Britain's newest galleries for contemporary visual art.

4    Along the waterfront, once derelict – are houses, businesses, galleries, restaurants. Joining Gateshead to Newcastle is the Millennium Bridge designed by Wilkinson Eyre, and along that waterfront too, once a place of empty factories and ghosts of times past, the new housing, hotels and business park.

5    Here in Gateshead, in 1997, primary schools had only half of their 11 year olds with the proper reading skills. Now it's 78%. Less than half with the proper maths skills. Now nearly 70%. Only 40% of 16 year olds got five good GCSEs. Now it's over 60%.

6       Long term unemployment was over two and a half thousand. Now it's about 400. And long-term youth unemployment has virtually been eliminated.

7       There is still poverty. There is still hardship. There are still too many lives untouched by change.

8       But to anyone who doubts Britain has got better since we took over from the Tories in 1997, I say: come to Gateshead; see what the people here have achieved; and then understand why we, in the New Labour Government, who have worked with them, are so passionate about winning that historic third term so that never again are people as talented as this, who can achieve so much, neglected and left behind by an uncaring Tory Government.

9       I had a tremendous time on Friday touring the country. Loved every moment of it. Enjoyed the Q&A yesterday, and anyone who texted or e-mailed a question – and there were a lot – will get a reply from me.

10    I'm back. And it feels good.

11    Back in the North East, to thank the people from Sedgefield who gave me the chance to serve in Parliament, and have given me strength and support every day that I've been there.

12    Back with the Labour Party that has given me the honour of leadership, first of the party and then, more important of course, of the country.

13    Back with a relentless focus on the job of delivering better lives for Britain's hard working families, because that is my job, and I never forget it.

14    In this second term, in particular after September 11th, events have sometimes taken me far from home.

15    But no matter how far, I have never forgotten the top line of my job spec – to work for

Britain, and the British people. They are the
boss. Always have been. Always will be. And
none of us, not me, not any of us, should
ever forget it.

16    It is good to be back in a fight with the
Tories. And make no mistake – this is a
fight. A fight for the future of our country.
A fight that for Britain, and the people
of Britain, we have to win.

17    The polls can tell one story, but the story
that counts is the one unfolding in the minds
of millions of people around the country as
they face up to the fundamental choice facing
the country – forward or back.

18    And that story will not be told until the
only poll that matters – the general
election.

19    The Tories may be a mess. Their policy
incoherent. Their tax and spending plan an
economic disaster waiting to take our
prosperity away. Their leader a
representative of everything the country
voted in 1997 to get rid of.

20    But they have a strategy: not power by the
front door but by the back. Spread
disillusion and cynicism. Tell everyone the
country's hopeless, the NHS can't work, the
education system is in tatters, the
investment all wasted, hope to depress our
vote and get out their own through a hard
right agenda. Don't underestimate it.

21    What it means to us is this: we take nothing
for granted. Not one vote. Not one seat. We
go out and earn every vote, every seat as we
work towards earning a majority. I said no
complacency in 1997. I said no complacency in
2001. I say it again now.

22    Where we have lost support, we go out and try
to win it back.

23    Where we have lost old friends, we try to
persuade them to come back to the fold.

24    Where we have made mistakes, we say so.

25    Where we have done well, we shout it out with
pride and passion and energy.

26    Where we know we can make a difference in the
future, we set out our stall for the people
with confidence.

27    Because now they are thinking, reflecting –
do we go forward with Labour, or back to the
Tories.

28    Our task is to persuade them to go forward.

29    To vote for us not as a rejection of the
others but as an endorsement of what we are
trying to do for the country.

30    I understand why some people feel angry – not
just over Iraq but many of the difficult
decisions we have made.

31    And, as ever, a lot of it is about me.

32    I think a lot about my relationship with the
country. Everyone thinks they know you.
Everyone has a view. Sometimes the view is
settled. You're a good thing. Sometimes it's
settled the other way. You're a bad thing.
And sometimes people change their mind
according to their mood, according to what's
happening in the country, in the world, in
their own lives, in the swirl of what passes
for political debate.

33    And it's not a bad idea to think of it in
terms of it being like any relationship: you,
the British people and me, the person you
chose as your Prime Minister.

34    When I first became leader of the Labour
Party, everywhere I went, I could feel the
warmth growing, the expectations rising.

35    Then came the euphoria surrounding our
victory. I remember saying at the time it was
all a bit unreal, because people would expect
miracles. We have delivered a lot, but no
miracles. Politicians don't deliver miracles.
And life is not about euphoric moments. It's
about steady change for the better.

36     So after the euphoria, came the steady hard
       slog of decision-making and delivery.

37     And the events that tested me. And the media
       mood turning, and friends sometimes being
       lost as the big decisions mounted, and the
       thousand little things that irritate and
       grate, and then all of a sudden there you
       are, the British people, thinking: you're not
       listening and I think: you're not hearing me.
       And before you know it you raise your voice.
       I raise mine. Some of you throw a bit of
       crockery.

38     And now you, the British people, have to sit
       down and decide whether you want the
       relationship to continue. If you decide you
       want Mr Howard, that is your choice. If you
       want to go off with Mr Kennedy, that's your
       choice too. It all ends in the same place. A
       Tory Government not a Labour Government.

39     Going back not moving forward.

40     But for me, I believe in you, the British
       people as much as ever.

41     I have learnt some lessons in these past
       years. This job is a harsh teacher but a wise
       one.

42     As we sought power, reached out for new
       support, fought to establish ourselves on
       fresh political terrain, the accusation was
       of 'all things to all people'.

43     And I soon learnt that however pleasant
       popularity is, 'all things to all people'
       never lasts for long.

44     Then as I struggled with the levers of power,
       saw with a genuine urgency the challenges a
       new world was thrusting on Britain, I was
       determined to do the right thing.

45     But for a political leader, 'doing the right
       thing' in reality is only ever 'doing what I
       think is the right thing'.

46     And if you're not careful, 'doing the right
       thing' becomes 'I know best'.

47 So, starting with the Big Conversation, I
went back out, and rather than talking at,
talked with people.

48 And I learnt.

49 I learnt that when I'm working hard, trying
my damnedest and wondering, frustrated, why
people can't appreciate the delivery, it's
easy to forget life is still so tough for so
many people, a real life daily struggle, not
for a life of luxury but just to get by.

50 And I learnt that the best policy comes not
from courting popularity or mere conviction,
but comes from partnership between politics
and people, from the blend of listening and
leading; that people don't expect miracles,
but they do demand dialogue; that they aren't
disinterested in politics or even disengaged
but they do feel disempowered.

51 So we developed ASB laws because that is what
real people in real communities told us
blighted their lives.

52 We made after school clubs and nursery
education our third pledge because that is
what hard-working families told us they
needed.

53 We faced up to the toughening of our asylum
and immigration rules because like it or not,
decent people, a million miles from the BNP,
told us it mattered to them.

54 I learnt that on some issues, sometimes you
just have to agree to disagree, like Iraq,
though hopefully now, with 8 million people
in Iraq coming out to vote, we can all agree,
however we got here, we should stay as long
as the Iraqis want us to help ensure
democracy not terror determines their future.

55 I learnt that the best policy comes from a
true partnership between Government and
people.

56 And I learnt that no matter how powerful the
position you hold, no matter how powerful

others think you are, you can achieve very
little alone.

57     More together than we achieve alone – the
heart of our party's new constitution and as
true for the country.

58     We can take some credit for the strong
economy but it would not have been possible
without the hard work of the people who work
for and run our businesses. I don't ask for
their thanks. We give them ours, and ask them
to keep working with us to keep our economy
growing.

59     We can take some credit for the strength of
our reputation and image abroad. But if we in
Britain have a lot going for us it is because
of the work, the strength, the creativity and
the decency of our people.

60     This is a country with a lot to be proud of,
and we should be proud above all of the
people we are.

61     This is especially so in our public services.
We as a government can take some credit for
the investment plans that have seen the
thousands of extra teachers, nurses and
doctors but the real credit for improvements
in public services goes to them and their
colleagues. Governments can spend. We can
exhort. We can legislate. But we cannot cure
the sick. We cannot be inside every
classroom. We cannot police the streets. So I
have learned with every passing day, month
and year to value and respect the work of the
real deliverers, the people who can do those
things, and do do those things – every hour
of every day.

62     So this journey has gone from 'all things to
all people' to 'I know best' to 'we can only
do it together'. And we all know which is
best of those three.

63     A partnership.

64     Forward together.

65    It's your choice.

66    I'm still the same person. Older. A little
      wiser, I hope. But still with the same
      commitment and belief.

67    And I believe together we still make the best
      team for Britain and its future.

68    Indeed throughout, my values never changed.

69    My political insight is the same – that a
      modernized Labour Party is the route to a
      Britain modernized in a way that benefits the
      many and not the few.

70    I have the same passion and hunger as when I
      first walked through the door of 10 Downing
      Street.

71    Because I have seen what our progressive
      values applied to the modern world can do.

72    This country had the courage to move forward
      in 1997; and it got better.

73    In 2001 it kept going forward; and got better
      still.

74    And now it can go yet further still.

75    And the hunger and passion is there for me
      because though I can see change happening, I
      know it's not nearly enough.

76    So when I opened a new school down in Bexley
      in one of the poorest estates of the country,
      the kids in new school uniforms, the
      classrooms buzzing, the teachers committed,
      the results in a few short months several
      times better than the miserable pass rates
      before, and the young girl showing me round
      says: 'you know, I never thought this type of
      school was for people like me'. I felt such a
      mixture of humility and pride, but then anger
      because I suddenly thought: how many wasted
      lives had passed through this school before
      and how many other schools still wait for
      such change, whilst their children under-
      achieve and the poverty of expectations pass
      from one generation to another?

77    So we have Pledge 2: Your child achieving

more. Modern schools for all, strong
discipline, and a guaranteed place in
training, sixth-form or an apprenticeship.

78    What does it mean?

79    The Building Schools for the Future programme
      – rebuilding or renewing every secondary
      school in England within a generation. Every
      secondary school able to become a specialist
      school and 200 Academies.

80    Since 1997 places in Pupil Referral Units
      almost doubled and headteachers now with the
      powers and the guaranteed budgets to expand
      provision in and out of school for
      disruptive pupils.

81    And 100,000 extra sixth form places by 2008
      and up to 300,000 apprenticeships every year
      - four times the number in 1997.

82    And what is the Tory response? To give a
      voucher for a few of the parents tospend at
      a private school. Can you imagine anything
      more typical and more backward? We must never
      let them put back the notion that high
      standards in education are for the few not
      the many. Not now. Not ever.

83    On Friday in Kettering, I talked to a patient
      suffering from cancer and he told me how
      under the new arrangements he had been seen,
      diagnosed and started treatment within weeks,
      how wonderful his care was, how dedicated the
      staff; and I saw the new equipment, the new
      ambulatory care centre being built and I
      thought: how dare these Tories say the money
      is all wasted. It's there in bricks and
      mortar, in new nurses and doctors, in new
      scanners and wards, making a difference
      literally to people's lives.

84    And then the same night, back in my own
      constituency, a woman came over to me,
      limping badly and explained how many months
      she had been waiting to be treated for a knee
      operation, not life-threatening, but the

difference between a life worth leading and
one in pain, and I felt anger that even with
all the progress, the best we could offer at
present was a 6 month wait. Six months. Yes,
better than the 18 months we inherited, but
too long for any person to wait in pain.

85  That is why Pledge No 4: Your family treated
better and faster. No one waiting more than
18 weeks, guaranteed, for hospital treatment
- with choice over where and when – in an NHS
free at the point of need.

86  And what does that mean. In 1997, 119,000
patients waiting over 9 months, today 306.

87  Look at our progress on heart surgery. By the
end of this March, 2005, no one will wait
more than three months – a goal originally
scheduled for 2008.

88  In 1997 maximum waits over 18 months, by 2008
no one waiting more than 18 weeks, from door
of GP surgery to operating theatre. For the
first time since the 1970s, spending up to
the EU average and on a par with France and
Germany.

89  And the Tory response? To give her a voucher
for half the cost of a private operation, and
if she can't afford the other half, which she
couldn't, then tough.

90  How backward, how typical. I never want that
philosophy in charge of our NHS, not now, not
ever.

91  A couple of months ago, I visited Falconwood
where I saw police officers, community
support officers, local council staff, local
people working together, using the new ASB
legislation, rejoicing – not too strong a
word – that at long last they had the power
and the people to stop the law-breaking
minority making life hell for the law-abiding
majority; but as I was going out, feeling
very pleased, a man stopped me and said: 'I
didn't want to say this with the media

present, but I live in the next ward and we
don't have these neighbourhood police teams
because they say there isn't enough money and
our life is still hell' and I know that we
can tell people crime is down not up till we
are blue in the face, but they won't believe
it until every community has its visible
uniformed presence out on the street and the
legal system of our country finally puts the
decent law-abiding citizen at the centre of
it.

92   So Pledge No 5: Your community safer. Local
policing teams cracking down on graffiti,
gangs and drug-dealers. This means 12,750
more police since 1997 and plans now to
create a dedicated neighbourhood policing
team in every community including an
additional 25,000 CSOs and Neighbourhood
Wardens by 2008.

93   New powers will deal with anti-social
behaviour and alcohol related violence
including Drink Banning Orders, Alcohol
Disorder Zones and shutting pubs which sell
to under age drinkers.

94   And the Tory response? To freeze the police
budget. Not surprising from a Tory leader who
when Home Secretary cut the number of police
to save money. But we should not go back to
those days. Not now. Not ever.

95   And I've seen the two sides of the refugee
issue. I've visited a school in Manchester,
in one of the poorest parts, in a classroom
full of the children of asylum seekers; some
could barely speak English. I said to the
teacher: 'it must be a terrible problem – how
do you manage'. He said to me: 'You know, Mr
Blair, I've only one problem, at the end of
each day, I have to force these children to
leave; I've never seen such motivation; such
desire to learn; such a will to succeed. This
country won't ever regret these kids being
here'.

96     But I've also sat around a table with
frontline immigration officers as they told
me of the scams, the fraud, the criminal
gangs, trafficking in human beings and their
sense of anger and frustration because they
know too many people play the system not play
by it.

97     And I realize that we will never maintain the
tolerant, diverse nation of which we can be
so proud, unless we have the strict controls
that keep it so.

98     So Pledge No 6: Your country's borders
protected. ID cards and strict controls that
work to combat asylum abuse and illegal
immigration.

99     And the Tory response: a crude quota and
becoming the only nation in the world to
withdraw from the UN Convention on Refugees;
and a halving, yes a halving of the
immigration service budget, the stupidest
most backward policy you could think of.

100     And I've visited Sure Start in every part of
Britain, and before Christmas I was in
Hackney at Millfields Primary School seeing
the breakfast club, talking to parents,
hearing how it had transformed their ability
to juggle family and work.

101     I saw the new computers and the extra staff
and knew it was our investment that made
their dedication count. But then one parent
said to me: 'what a pity this is the
exception not the rule'; and I thought there
is still so much to do, so many lives still
not what they could be, so many opportunities
for happiness and security not delivered
when, with time and effort and will, they
could.

102     So: Pledge No 3: Your children with the best
start. More choice over parental leave for
mums and dads, more childcare for under-5s,
and after school care for over 5s.

103    Look what we've done – maternity leave up
from 14 to 28 weeks and now we  pledge up to
9 months by 2007; a guaranteed free part time
nursery place for every 3 and 4 year old,
rising in our third term to 15 hours a week.
1.2 million new child care places and now we
pledge to create a Sure Start Children's
Centre in every community and every school
age child up to 14 years old with access to
out of school care and activities between
8.00 a.m. and 6.00 pm.

104    And the Tory response? You have it, more cuts
in spending, more of anything that doesn't
mean we ever accept there are some things we
have to do together, we hold in common, that
sometimes we should care about helping even
when it's others that benefit from the help.

105    But all of it depends on one thing: a stable
economic foundation. Let me quote you
directly from one family's experience under a
different Government: '15% interest rates,
sky high mortgage arrears, negative equity,
bankruptcies, entrepreneurs giving up the
ghost on private run companies and a lot of
people losing their jobs. I don't think there
was a family in the country that didn't
experience at least one of those anguishes.
My parents lost their jobs in the recession.'

106    That's not someone I met. It's John Redwood
speaking, the one they put back on the Tory
front bench to show how they'd changed.

107    Why did 15% interest rates happen? Because
the Tories tried pledging tax cuts, spending
cuts and spending promises all at the same
time, lost control of the economy and the
rest is their history and millions of others'
misery.

108    What is their policy now? You have it: £4 bn
tax cuts; £35 bn spending cuts and £15 bn
spending promises all at the same time.

109    Plus eliminating the New Deal for young

people, the unemployed, and lone parents.
Plus cutting the housing programme for key
workers and first-time buyers.

110    I do not want this country to go back to
those failed Tory policies. Not now. Not
ever.

111    So Pledge No 1: Your family better off. Low
inflation, and mortgages as low as possible,
more people off benefit and into work, a
rising minimum wage and more help for first
time buyers.

112    Forward not back.

113    The 1997 pledges met and more.

114    The 2001 pledges met and more.

115    Now these for 2005.

116    More ambitious. But deliverable because of
the foundations laid.

117    The Tory leadership said on Friday our
pledges were worthless.

118    Look at Pledge No 1. Low inflation and the
lowest mortgage rates possible. Worthless? It
may be to the purveyors of the boom and bust
of Tory years, Mr Howard; but not to the
British people.

119    A rising minimum wage – worthless? It may be
to Michael Howard when he led the Tory
opposition to the minimum wage and told us it
would wreck the economy, but it is worth
something to the millions of women in low
paid industries who need it to survive.

120    More people off benefit and into work.
Worthless? Yes to the Tory Employment
Secretary who put one million people on the
dole but not to the two million extra in jobs
today. More help for first time buyers.
Worthless? Well, it's a damn sight better
than negative equity and housing repossession
he gave us.

121    Are these things worthless? No, Mr Howard,
they're just worth nothing to you because
you're a right-wing Tory who never delivered

them in the past and can't deliver them for
the future.

122    We can't promise paradise. But we can make
progress.

123    We haven't relinquished our idealism but now
it is tempered by realism.

124    Forward not back.

125    The biggest choice in politics.

126    For the country.

127    For us, the Labour Party.

128    Ten years ago, we created New Labour, not in
defiance of our values; but in defiance of
the refusal to modernize their application.

129    It was painful, even distressing for some,
but it also showed something. It showed we
cared more about getting it right for our
country than getting it comfortable for our
Party.

130    The true reason why the Conservative Party
does not deserve to win is that they have
conducted no such self-analysis, no soul-
searching, no painful reconsideration and
reconstruction. They just think the public
will eventually come to their senses and re-
elect them.

131    They don't understand the public were in full
possession of their senses when they threw
them out.

132    But we must never forget how we got here.

133    We got here only by being New Labour. We will
stay only by being New Labour. Traditional
values in a modern setting. Values as old as
time. Renewed for each time.

134    Forward not back.

135    For us.

136    For Britain.

# References

Anderson, G. (1990) *Fundamentals of Educational Research*. Lewes, East Sussex: Falmer Press.

Argyle, K. and Shields, R. (1996) Is there a body in the net? In R. Shield (ed.) *Cultures of Internet: Virtual Spaces, Real Histories, Living Bodies*, 58–69. London: Sage.

Archer, D., Culpeper, J. and Rayson, P. (2009) Love – a familiar or a devil? An exploration of key domains in Shakespeare's comedies and tragedies. in D. Archer (ed.) *What's in a Word List? Investigating Word Frequencies and Keyword Extraction*, 137–177. London: Ashgate.

Baker, P., Gabrielatos C., Khosravinik, M., Krzyzanowski, M., McEnery, T. and Wodak, R. (2008) A useful methodological synergy? Combining critical discourse analysis and corpus linguistics to examine discourses of refugees and asylum seekers in the UK press. *Discourse and Society* 19 (3): 273–305.

Bakhtin, M. M. (1981) *The Dialogic Imagination*. Austin, TX: University of Texas Press.

Bamberg, M. (2007) *Narrative: State of the Art*. Amsterdam: John Benjamins.

Banks, S., Goodyear, P., Hodgson, V. and McConnell, D. (2003) Introduction to the Special Issue on advances in research on networked learning. *Instructional Science* 31 (1–2): 1–6.

Barcelona, A. (2000) On the plausibility of claiming a metonymic motivation for conceptual metaphor. In A. Barcelona (ed.) *Metaphor and Metonymy at the Crossroads. A Cognitive Perspective* 31–58. Berlin and New York: Mouton de Gruyter.

Barr, D. (2004) Establishing conventional communication systems: Is common knowledge necessary? *Cognitive Science* 28: 937–962.

Barr, D. J., and Keysar, B. (2005) Making sense of how we make sense: The paradox of egocentrism in language use. In H. L. Colston and A. N. Katz (eds) *Figurative Language Comprehension: Social and Cultural Influences* 21–42. Mahwah, NJ: Lawrence Erlbaum.

Barsalou, L. W. (1989) Intraconcept similarity and its implications for interconcept similarity. In S. Vosniadou and A. Ortony (eds) *Similarity and Analogical Reasoning* 76–121. Cambridge: Cambridge University Press.

Barsalou, L. (1999) Perceptual symbol systems. *Behavioral and Brain Sciences* 22: 577–609.

Barsalou, L. W. (2008) Grounded cognition. *Annual Review of Psychology* 59: 617–645.

Bateson, P. (2005). The role of play in the evolution of great apes and humans. In A. D. Pellegrini and P. K. Smith (eds) *The Nature of Play: Great Apes and Humans* 13–26. New York: The Guilford Press.

Beer, F. and De Landtsheer, C'l. (eds) (2004) *Metaphorical World Politics*. East Lansing, MI: Michigan State University Press.

Berg, B. L. (2001) *Qualitative Research Methods for the Social Sciences*. 4th edition. Needham Heights, MA: Pearson Education.

Bialostok, S. (2008) Using critical metaphor analysis to extract parents' cultural models of how their children learn to read. *Critical Inquiry in Language Studies* 5 (2): 109–147.

Block, D. (1992) Metaphors we teach and learn by. *Prospect* 7 (3): 42–55.

Bloom, B. S., Englehart, M. D., Furst, E. J., Hill, W. H. and Krathwohl, D. R. (eds) (1956) *Taxonomy of Educational Objectives: The Classification of Educational Goals. Handbook 1: Cognitive Domain.* New York: David McKay.

Braddick, O. (1986) Inside the working of the brain. A review of C. W. Coen (ed.), *Functions of the Brain. Nature* 320: 223.

Brennan, S. and Clark, H. (1996) Conceptual pacts and lexical choices in conversation. *Journal of Experimental Psychology: Learning, Memory, and Cognition* 22 (6): 1482–1493.

Brewster Smith, M. (2002) The metaphor (and fact) of war. *Peace Psychology* 8 (3): 249–258.

Brookfield, S. and Preskill, S. (2005) *Discussion as a Way of Teaching: Tools and Techniques for Democratic Classrooms,* 2nd edn. San Francisco, CA: John Wiley and Sons.

Brown, B., Nerlich, B., Crawford, P., Koteyko, N, and Carter, R. (2009). Hygiene and biosecurity: The language and politics of risk in an era of emerging infectious diseases. *Sociology Compass* 3 (5): 811–823.

Bühler, K. (1934/1982) *Sprachtheorie: Die Darstellungsfunktion der Sprache.* Jena. Reprinted by Fischer (Stuttgart).

Burke, K. (1945) *A Grammar of Motives.* New York: Prentice Hall.

Calbris, G. (2008). From left to right …: coverbal getures and their symbolic use of space. In A. Cienki and C. Müller (eds), *Metaphor and Gesture* 27–53. Amsterdam/Philadelphia, PA: John Benjamins.

Cameron, L. (1999a) Identifying and describing metaphor in spoken discourse data. In L. Cameron and G. Low (eds) *Researching and Applying Metaphor* 105–132. Cambridge: Cambridge University Press.

Cameron, L. (1999b) Operationalising metaphor for applied linguistic research. In L. Cameron and G. Low (eds) *Researching and Applying Metaphor* 3–28. Cambridge: Cambridge University Press.

Cameron, L. (2003) *Metaphor in Educational Discourse.* London: Continuum.

Cameron, L. (2007a) Confrontation or complementarity: Metaphor in language use and cognitive metaphor theory. *Annual Review of Cognitive Linguistics* 5 (1): 107–135.

Cameron, L. (2007b) Patterns of metaphor use in reconciliation talk. *Discourse and Society* 18 (2): 197–222.

Cameron, L. (2008a) Metaphor and talk. In R. Gibbs (ed.) *Cambridge Handbook of Metaphor* 197–211. Cambridge: Cambridge University Press.

Cameron, L. (2008b) Metaphor shifting in the dynamics of talk. In M. S. Zanotto, L. Cameron and M. Cavalcanti (eds) *Confronting Metaphor in Use; An Applied Linguistic Approach* 45–62. Amsterdam: John Benjamins.

Cameron, L. (2009) *Metaphor and Reconciliation.* New York: Routledge.

Cameron, L. (in press a) Metaphor in prosaic and poetic creativity. In J. Swann, R. Pope and R. Carter (eds) *Language and Creativity: The State of the Art.*

Cameron, L. (in press b) Metaphor in physical-and-speech action expressions. In A. Deignan, L. Cameron, G. Low and Z. Todd (eds) *Researching and Applying Metaphor in the Real World.* Amsterdam: John Benjamin.

Cameron, L. and Deignan, A. (2003) Combining large and small corpora to investigate tuning devices around metaphor in spoken discourse. *Metaphor and Symbol* 18 (3): 149–160.

Cameron, L. and Deignan, A. (2006) The emergence of metaphor in discourse. *Applied Linguistics* 27 (4): 671–690.

Cameron, L. and Low, G. (2004) Figurative variation in episodes of educational talk and text. *European Journal of English Studies* 8 (3): 355–373.

Cameron, L. and Low, G. (eds) (1999) *Researching and Applying Metaphor.* Cambridge: Cambridge University Press.

Cameron, L., Maslen, R., Todd, Z., Maule, J., Stratton, P. and Stanley, N. (2009) The discourse dynamics approach to metaphor and metaphor-led discourse analysis. *Metaphor and Symbol* 24 (2): 63–89.

Cameron, L. and Stelma, J. (2004) Metaphor clusters in discourse. *Journal of Applied Linguistics* 1 (2): 7–36.

Carlin, G. (1972) *Seven Words You Can Never Say on Television. Lyrics of* Class Clown. Los Angeles, CA: Atlantic.

Carolan, Michael S. (2006) The values and vulnerabilities of metaphors within the environmental sciences, *Society and Natural Resources,* 19 (10): 921–930.

Carr, T., Lally, V., De Laat, M. and Cox, G. (2006) Computer supported collaborative learning and the central research question: two illustrative vignettes. In E. Sorensen and D. Murchú (eds) *Enhancing Learning Through Technology* 203 226. London: Information Science Publishing.

Carter, R. (2004) *Language and Creativity: The Art of Common Talk.* London: Routledge.

Casasanto, D. (2008) Conceptual affiliates of metaphorical gestures. Paper presented at the conference Language, Communication and Cognition, Brighton, UK, August.

Chafe, W. (1994) *Discourse, Consciousness and Time*. Chicago, IL: University of Chicago Press.

Charmaz, K. (2001) Grounded theory: Objectivist and constructivist methods. In N. Denzin and Y. Lincoln (eds) *Handbook of Qualitative Research* 2nd edn, 509–536. Thousand Oaks, CA: Sage.

Charteris-Black, J. (2004) *Corpus Approaches to Critical Metaphor Analysis*. Basingstoke: Palgrave Macmillan.

Charteris-Black, J. (2005) *Politicians and Rhetoric: The Persuasive Power of Metaphor*. Basingstoke: Palgrave Macmillan.

Chi, M. T. H. (1997) Quantifying qualitative analysis of verbal data: a practical guide. *Journal of the Learning Sciences* 6 (3): 271–315.

Chilton, P. (1996) *Security Metaphors: Cold War Discourse from Containment to Common European Home*. Berne and New York: Peter Lang.

Cienki, A. (1998) Metaphoric gestures and some of their relations to verbal metaphoric expressions. In J.-P. Koenig (ed.) *Discourse and Cognition: Bridging the Gap* 189–204. Stanford, CA: CSLI.

Cienki, A. (1999) Metaphors and cultural models as profiles and bases. In R. W. Gibbs, Jr. and G. J. Steen (eds), *Metaphor in Cognitive Linguistics* 189–203. Amsterdam/Philadelphia, PA: John Benjamins.

Cienki, A. (2003) Ontological metaphors prevail in gesture with speech (and image schemas provide handy source domains). Paper presented at the Eighth International Cognitive Linguistics Conference, La Rioja, Spain, July.

Cienki, A. (2005a) Metaphor in the 'Strict Father' and 'Nurturant Parent' cognitive models: Theoretical issues raised in an empirical study. *Cognitive Linguistics* 16: 279–312.

Cienki, A. (2005b) Image schemas and gesture. In B. Hampe (ed.), *From Perception to Meaning: Image Schemas in Cognitive Linguistics* 421–442. Berlin/New York: Mouton de Gruyter.

Cienki, A. (2007) Reference points and metonymic sources in gesture. Paper presented at the Tenth International Cognitive Linguistics Conference, Kraków, Poland, July.

Cienki, A. and Müller, C. (eds) (2008) *Metaphor and Gesture*. Amsterdam: John Benjamins.

Clark, H. (1996) *Using Language*. New York: Cambridge University Press.

*Collins Cobuild Advanced Learners Dictionary* (2003) London: HarperCollins.

Cook, G. (2000) *Language Play, Language Learning*. Oxford: Oxford University Press.

Cooper, D. (1986) *Metaphor*. Oxford: Blackwell.

Cortazzi, M. and Jin, L. (1999) Bridges to learning: Metaphors of teaching, learning and language. In L. Cameron and G. Low (eds) *Researching and Applying Metaphor* 149–176. Cambridge: Cambridge University Press.

Corts, D. and Meyers, K. (2002) Conceptual clusters in figurative language production. *Journal of Psycholinguistic Research* 31 (4): 391–408.

Corts, D. and Pollio, H. (1999) Spontaneous production of figurative language and gesture in college lectures. *Metaphor and Symbol* 14 (1): 81–100.

Craig, T., Harris, L. and Smith, R. (1998) Rhetoric of the contact zone: Composition on the front lines. In T. Taylor and I. Ward (eds) *Literacy Theory in the Age of the Internet* 122–145. New York: Columbia University Press.

Damasio, A. (2003) *Looking for Spinoza: Joy, Sorrow and the Feeling Brain*. New York: Harcourt, Inc.

de Guerrero, M. C. M. and Villamil O. S. (2000) Exploring ESL teachers' roles through metaphor analysis. *TESOL Quarterly* 34 (2): 341–351.

de Guerrero, M. C. M. and Villamil O. S. (2002) Metaphorical conceptualizations of ESL teaching and learning. *Language Teaching Research* 6 (2): 95–120.

De Laat, M. and Lally, V. (2003) Complexity, theory and praxis: Researching collaborative learning and tutoring processes in a networked learning community. *Instructional Science* 31: 7–39.

De Laat, M. and Lally, V. (2004) It's not so easy, researching the complexity of emergent participant roles and awareness in asynchronous networked learning discussions. *Journal of Computer Assisted Learning* 20 (3): 165–71.

Deignan, A. (1999) Corpus-based research into metaphor. In L. Cameron and G. D. Low (eds) *Researching and Applying Metaphor* 177–199. Cambridge: Cambridge University Press.

Deignan, A. (2005) *Metaphor and Corpus Linguistics*. Amsterdam: John Benjamins.

Drew, P. and Holt, E. (1988) Complainable matters: The use of idiomatic expressions in making complaints. *Social Problems* 35 (4): 398–417.

Drew, P. and Holt, E. (1998) Figures of speech: Figurative expressions and the management of topic transition in conversation. *Language and Society* 27 (4): 495–522.

Du Bois, J., Schuetze-Coburn, S., Cumming, S. and Paolino, D. (1993) Outline of discourse transcription. In J. Edwards and M. Lampert (eds) *Talking Data: Transcription and Coding in Discourse Research* 45–90. Hillsdale, NJ: Lawrence Erlbaum Associates.

Dyck, R. J. and Rule, B. G. (1978) Effect on retaliation of causal attributions concerning attack. *Journal of Personality and Social Psychology* 36 (5): 521–529.

Edwards, D. (1997) *Discourse and Cognition*. London: Sage Publications.

Elliott, R., Fisher, C. T. and Rennie, D. L. (1999) Evolving guidelines for publication of qualitative research studies in psychology and related fields.
*British Journal of Clinical Psychology* 38 (3): 215–229.

Erasmus, D. (1511/1941) *The Praise of Folly*. Princeton, NJ: Princeton University Press.

Fauconnier, G. and Turner, M. (2002) *The Way We Think: Conceptual Blending
and the Mind's Hidden Complexities*. New York: Basic Books.

Feldman, J. (2006) *From Molecule to Metaphor. A Neural Theory of Language*.
Cambridge, MA: MIT.

Forceville, C. (2006) Non-verbal and multimodal metaphor in a cognitivist
framework: Agendas for research. In G. Kristiansen, M. Achard, R. Dirven
and F. J. Ruiz de Mendoza Ibáñez (eds) *Cognitive Linguistics: Current
Applications and Future Perspectives* 379–402. Berlin/New York: Mouton
de Gruyter.

Forceville, C. and Urios-Aparisi, E. (eds) (2009) *Multimodal Metaphor*. Berlin:
Mouton de Gruyter.

Fricke, E. (2004) Origo, Geste und Raum: Lokaldeixis im Deutschen. PhD dissertation, Technische Universität Berlin, Germany.

Garrison, D. R. and Anderson, T. (2003) *E-learning in the 21st Century, a
Framework for Research and Practice*. Abingdon: Routledge Falmer.

Gernsbacher, M. A., Keysar, B., Robertson, R. W., and Werner, N. K. (2001)
The role of suppression and enhancement in understanding metaphors.
*Journal of Memory and Language* 45: 433–450.

Gibbons, P. (2002) *Scaffolding Language, Scaffolding Learning: Teaching
Second Language Learners in the Mainstream Classroom*. Portsmouth, NH:
Heinemann.

Gibbs, R. W. (1994) *The Poetics of Mind: Figurative Thought, Language and
Understanding*. Cambridge: Cambridge University Press.

Gibbs, R. W. (1998) The fight over metaphor in thought and language. In A. N.
Katz, C. Cacciari, R. W. Gibbs and M. Turner (eds) *Figurative Language
and Thought (Counterpoints, Cognition, Memory and Language)* 88–118.
Oxford: Oxford University Press.

Gibbs, R. W. (1999) Taking metaphor out of our heads and putting it into the
cultural world. In R. W. Gibbs and G. Steen (eds) *Metaphor in Cognitive
Linguistics* 145–166. Amsterdam: John Benjamins.

Gibbs, R. W. (2000) Making good psychology out of Blending Theory. *Cognitive Linguistics* 11: 347–358.

Gibbs, R. W. (2006a) *Embodiment and Cognitive Science*. New York: Cambridge University Press.

Gibbs, R. W. (2006b) Metaphor interpretation as embodied simulation. *Mind
and Language* 21 (3): 434–458.

Gibbs, R. W. (ed.) (2008) *The Cambridge Handbook of Metaphor and Thought*. Cambridge: Cambridge University Press.

Gibbs, R. W., Bogdanovich, J., Sykes, J. and Barr, D. (1997) Metaphor in idiom comprehension. *Journal of Memory and Language* 37: 141–154.

Gibbs, R. W. and Cameron, L. (2008) The social-cognitive dynamics of metaphor performance. *Journal of Cognitive Systems Research* 9 (1–2): 64–75.

Gibbs R. W. and Colston, H. L. (1995) The cognitive psychological reality of image schemas and their transformations. *Cognitive Linguistics* 6 (4): 347–378.

Gibbs, R. W. and Matlock, T. (2008) Metaphor, imagination, and simulation: Psycholinguistic evidence. In R. W. Gibbs (ed.) *The Cambridge Handbook of Metaphor and Thought* 161–176. Cambridge: Cambridge University Press.

Glaser, B. G. and Strauss, A. L. (1967) *The Discovery of Grounded Theory: Strategies for Qualitative Research*. Chicago, IL: Aldine.

Goatly, A. (1997) *The Language of Metaphors*. London: Routledge.

Goldberg, A. (1995) *Constructions: A Construction Grammar Approach to Argument Structure*. Chicago, IL: University of Chicago Press.

Goodyear, P. (2001) Psychological foundations for networked learning. In C. Steeples and C. Jones (eds) *Networked Learning: Perspectives and Issues* 49–75. London: Springer.

Goodyear, P., Jones, C., Arensio, M., Hodgson, V. and Steeples, C. (2005) Networked learning in higher education: students' expectations and experiences. *Higher Education* 50 (3): 473–508.

Goossens, L. (1995) Metaphtonymy: The interaction of metaphor and metonymy in expression for linguistic action. In L. Goossens, P. Pauwels, B. Rudzka-Ostyn, A-M. Simon-Vandenbergen and J. Vanparys (eds) *By Word of Mouth. Metaphor, Metonymy and Linguistic Action in a Cognitive Perspective* 159–174. Amsterdam: John Benjamins.

Grady, J. (1999) A typology of motivation for conceptual metaphor: Correlation vs. resemblance. In R. W. Gibbs and G. Steen (eds) *Metaphor in Cognitive Linguistics* 101–124. Amsterdam: John Benjamins.

Graumann, C. (1990) Perspective structure and dynamics in dialogue. In I. Markova and K. Foppa (eds) 105–126. *The Dynamics of Dialogue*. London: Harvester Wheatsheaf.

Gurney, C. M. (1999) Lowering the drawbridge: A case study of analogy and metaphor in the social construction of home-ownership. *Urban Studies* 36 (10): 1705–1722.

Gwyn, R. (1999) 'Captain of my own ship': Metaphor and the discourse of chronic illness. In L. Cameron and G. D. Low (eds) *Researching and Applying Metaphor* 203–220. Cambridge: Cambridge University Press.

Hammersley, M. and Atkinson, A. (1995) *Ethnography: Principles in Practice,* 2nd edn. London: Routledge.

Hardie, A., Koller, V., Rayson, P. and Semino, E. (2007) Exploiting a semantic annotation tool for metaphor analysis. *Proceedings of Corpus Linguistics 2007,* University of Birmingham.

Harrison, S. J., Todd, Z. and Lawton, R. J. (2008) Talk about terrorism and the media: communicating with the conduit metaphor. *Communication, Culture and Critique* 1 (4): 378–395.

Haser, V. (2005) *Metaphor, Metonymy, and Experientialist Philosophy: Challenging Cognitive Semantics.* Berlin: Mouton de Gruyter.

Henri, A. (1983) Love is … In A. Henri, R. McGough and B. Patten, *The Mersey Sound* (revised edition) 21. Harmondsworth: Penguin.

Henri, F. (1992) Computer conferencing and content analysis. In A. R. Kaye (ed.) *Collaborative Learning Through Computer Conferencing, the Najaden Papers* 117–136. New York, Springer.

Hine, C. (2000) *Virtual Ethnography.* London: Sage.

Holmgreen, L-L. (2008) Biotech as 'biothreat'?: Metaphorical constructions in discourse. *Discourse and Society* 19 (1): 99–119.

Howe, J. (2008) Argument is argument: An essay on conceptual metaphor and verbal dispute. *Metaphor and Symbol* 23 (1): 1–23.

Hunston, S. (2002) *Corpora in Applied Linguistics.* Cambridge: Cambridge University Press.

Jackson, R. (2005) *Writing the War on Terrorism: Language, Politics, and Counter-Terrorism.* Manchester: Manchester University Press.

Johnson, M. (1987) *The Body in the Mind: The Bodily Basis of Meaning, Imagination and Reason.* Chicago, IL: University of Chicago Press.

Johnson-Eilola, J. (1998) Negative spaces: from production to connection in composition. In T. Taylor and I. Ward (eds) *Literacy Theory in the Age of the Internet* 17–33. New York: Columbia University Press.

Kagan, N. (1984) Interpersonal process recall: Basic methods and recent research. In D. Larsen (ed.) *Teaching Psychological Skills* 229–244. Monterey, CA: Brooks Cole.

Kagan, N. and Kagan, H. (1991) IPR – A research/training model (offprint). In P. N. Dewrick (ed.) *Practical Guide to Using Video in the Behavioural Sciences.* Canada: Wiley.

Kasperson, R. E. (1992) The social amplification of risk: progress in developing an integrative framework. In S. Krimsky and D. Golding (eds) *Social Theories of Risk* 3–22. Westport, CT: Praeger.

Kasperson, J. X., Kasperson, R. E., Pidgeon, N. and Slovic, P. (2003) The social amplification of risk: assessing fifteen years of research and theory. In N. Pidgeon, R. E. Kasperson and P.Sloveic (eds) *The Social Amplification of Risk* 13–46. Cambridge: Cambridge University Press.

Kaye, A. (1989) Computer-mediated communication and distance education. In R. Mason and A. Kaye *Mindweave: Communication, Computers and Distance Education* 3–21. Oxford: Pergamon Press.

Kendon, A. (1980) Gesticulation and speech: two aspects of the process of utterance. In M. R. Key (ed.) *The Relation between Verbal and Nonverbal Communication* 207–227. The Hague: Mouton.

Kendon, A. (2004) *Gesture: Visible Action as Utterance*. Cambridge: Cambridge University Press.

Keysar, B. and Bly, B. M. (1999) Swimming against the current: Do idioms reflect conceptual structure? *Journal of Pragmatics* 31 (12): 1559–1578.

Kintsch, W. (1998) *Comprehension*. New York: Cambridge University Press.

Kita, S. (ed.) (2003) *Pointing: Where Language, Culture, and Cognition Meet*. Mahwah, NJ: Lawrence Erlbaum Associates.

Kittay, E. F. (1987) *Metaphor: Its Cognitive Force and Linguistic Structure*. Oxford: Oxford University Press.

Koller, V. (2004) *Metaphor and Gender in Business Media Discourse: A Critical Cognitive Study*. Basingstoke: Palgrave Macmillan.

Koller, V. (2009) Missions and empires: religious and political metaphors in corporate discourse. In A. Musolff and J. Zinken (eds) *Metaphor and Discourse* 116–134 Basingstoke: Palgrave.

Koller, V., Hardie, A., Rayson, P. and Semino, E. (2008) Using a semantic annotation tool for the analysis of metaphor in discourse. *Metaphorik.de* retrieved on 17 July 2009 from http://www.metaphorik.de/15/koller.pdf

Kövecses, Z. (2000) *Metaphor and Emotion*. Cambridge: Cambridge University Press.

Kövecses, Z. (2002) *Metaphor: A Practical Introduction*. Oxford: Oxford University Press.

Kövesces, Z. (2005) *Metaphor and Culture*. New York: Cambridge University Press.

Labbo, L. (1996) A semiotic analysis of young children's symbol making in a classroom computer center. *Reading Research Quarterly* 31 (4): 356–385.

Lakoff, G. (1991) Metaphor and the war: The metaphor system used to justify war in the Gulf. Paper presented at the University of California, Berkeley, 30 January 1991. Retrieved on 16 July 2009 from http://www2.iath.virginia.edu/sixties/HTML_docs/Texts/Scholarly/Lakoff_Gulf_Metaphor_1.html

Lakoff, G. (1993) The contemporary theory of metaphor. In A. Ortony (ed.) *Metaphor and Thought* 2nd edn, 202–251. New York: Cambridge University Press.

Lakoff, G. (1996) *Moral Politics: What Conservatives Know That Liberals Don't*. Chicago, IL: University of Chicago Press

Lakoff, G. (2001). *Metaphors of Terror*. Retrieved on 27 July, 2008 from http://www.press.uchicago.edu/News/911lakoff.html

Lakoff, G and Frisch, E. (2006) *Five Years after 9/11: Drop the War meta-phor.* Retrieved on 4 August 2008 from http://www.rockridgeinstitute.org/research/rockridge/fiveyearsafter911/view

Lakoff, G. and Johnson, M. (1980) *Metaphors We Live by.* Chicago, IL: University of Chicago Press.

Lakoff, G. and Johnson, M. (1999) *Philosophy in the Flesh.* New York: Cambridge University Press.

Lakoff, G. and Turner, M. (1989) *More than Cool Reason: A Field Guide to Poetic Metaphor.* Chicago, IL: University of Chicago Press.

Lally, V. (2002) Squaring the circle: Triangulating content and social network analysis with critical event recall. In S. Banks, P. Goodyear, V. Hodgson and D. McConnell (eds) *Networked Learning 2002: A research based conference on e-learning in higher education and lifelong learning: Proceedings of the third international conference.* Sheffield: University of Sheffield.

Lally, V. and De Laat, M. (2002) Deciphering individual learning processes in virtual professional development. In S. Banks, P. Goodyear, V. Hodgson, V. and D. McConnell (eds) *Networked Learning 2002: A research based conference on e-learning in higher education and lifelong learning: Proceedings of the third international conference.* Sheffield: University of Sheffield.

Landauer, T. K. and Dumais, S. T. (1997) A solution to Plato's problem: The latent semantic analysis theory of acquisition induction, and representation of knowledge. *Psychological Review* 104 (2): 211–240.

Larsen-Freeman, D. and Cameron, L. (2008) *Complex Systems and Applied Linguistics.* Oxford: Oxford University Press.

Lemke, J. L. (1990) *Talking Science: Language, Learning and Values.* Norwood, NJ: Ablex.

Lincoln, Y. and Guba, E. (1985) *Naturalistic Inquiry.* Thousand Oaks, CA: Sage Publications.

Lincoln, Y. and Guba, E. (2000) Paradigmatic controversies, contradictions, and emerging confluences. In N. Denzin and Y. Lincoln (eds) *Handbook of Qualitative Research: Second Edition* 163–188. Thousand Oaks, CA: Sage Publications, Inc.

Linnell, P. (1998) *Approaching Dialogue: Talk, Interaction and Contexts in Dialogical Perspectives.* Amsterdam: John Benjamins.

Littlemore, J. (2001) The use of metaphor in university lectures and the problems that it causes for overseas students. *Teaching in Higher Education* 6 (3): 333–351.

Littlemore, J. (2003) The effect of cultural background on metaphor interpretation. *Metaphor and Symbol* 18 (4): 273–288.

Littlemore, J. (2005) The functions of different types of figurative language in spoken academic discourse: a case study. In P. Durán Escribano, G. Aguado de Cea and A. M. Roldán Riejos (eds) *Reflections on Language Use in the Academic Context* 17–28. Madrid: Departamento de Lingüística Aplicada UPM.

Littlemore, J. and Low, G. D. (2006a) Metaphoric competence and communicative language ability. *Applied Linguistics* 27 (2): 268–294.

Littlemore, J. and Low, G. D. (2006b) *Figurative Thinking and Foreign Language Learning.* London: Palgrave Macmillan.

Low, G. D. (1997) *Celebrations and SQUID Sandwiches: Figurative Language and the Manipulation of Academic Writing.* Unpublished project report, University of York, UK. Retreived on 15 May 2009 from http://www.york. ac.uk/depts/educ/Staff/gdl_Celebration.pdf

Low, G. D. (1999a) 'This paper thinks …': Investigating the acceptability of the metaphor AN ESSAY IS A PERSON. In L. Cameron and G. D. Low (eds) *Researching and Applying Metaphor* 221–248. Cambridge: Cambridge University Press.

Low, G. D. (1999b) Validating metaphor research projects. In L. Cameron and G. D. Low (eds) *Researching and Applying Metaphor* 48–65. Cambridge: Cambridge University Press.

Low, G. D. (2003) Validating metaphoric models in applied linguistics. *Metaphor and Symbol* 18 (4): 239–254.

Low, G. D. (2005) Explaining evolution: The use of animacy in an example of semi-formal science writing. *Language and Literature* 14 (2): 129–148.

Low, G. D. (2008) Metaphor and positioning in academic book reviews. In M. Zanotto, L. Cameron and M. Cavalcanti (eds) *Confronting Metaphor in Use: An Applied Linguistic Approach* 79–100. Amsterdam: John Benjamins.

Low, G. D. (under review) Wot, no similes? The non-occurrence and function of simile in educational discourse. In A. Deignan, L. Cameron, G. Low and Z. Todd (eds) *Researching and Applying Metaphor in the Real World.* Amsterdam: John Benjamins.

Low, G. D., Littlemore, J. and Koester, A. (2008) Metaphor use in three UK university lectures. *Applied Linguistics* 29 (3): 428–455.

Lu, L.W-L. and Ahrens, K. (2008) Ideological influence on BUILDING metaphors in Taiwanese presidential speeches. *Discourse and Society* 19 (3): 383–408.

MacWhinney, B. (1991) *The CHILDES project: Tools for analyzing talk.* Hillsdale, NJ: Lawrence Erlbaum Associates.

Markham, A. (1998) *Life Online: Researching Real Experience in Virtual Space.* Walnut Creek, CA: Altamira.

Markova, I., Linell, P., Grossen, M. and Orvig, A. S. (2007) *Dialogue in Focus Groups.* London: Equinox.

Maule, A. J., Cameron, L., Stanley, N. and Todd, Z. (2007) Perception and

Communication of the Risk of Terrorism. Full Research Report, ESRC End of Award Report, RES-228-25-0053. Swindon: ESRC.

McConnell, D. (2000) *Implementing Computer Supported Co-operative Learning,* 2nd edn. London: Kogan Page.

McConnell, D. (2006) *E-learning Groups and Communities.* Maidenhead: Society for Research into Higher Education, Open University Press.

McNeill, D. (1992) *Hand and Mind: What Gestures Reveal about Thought.* Chicago, IL: University of Chicago Press.

McNeill, D., Cassell, J. and Levy, E. T. (1993) Abstract deixis. *Semiotica* 95 (1/2): 5–19.

Mercer, N. (2000) *Words and Minds, How we use Language to Think Together.* Abingdon: Routledge.

Miller, S. (1991) *Textual Carnivals: The Politics of Composition.* Carbondale, IL: Southern Illinois University Press.

Mittelberg, I. (2007) Methodology for multimodality: one way of working with speech and gesture data. In M. Gonzalez-Marquez, S. Coulson, M. J. Spivey and I. Mittelberg (eds), *Methods in Cognitive Linguistics* 225–248. Amsterdam/Philadelphia, PA: John Benjamins.

Müller, C. (1998a) Iconicity and gesture. In S. Santi, I. Guaïtella, C. Cavé and Konopcznski (eds), *Oralité et Gestualité: Communication Multimodale, Interaction* 321–328. Paris: L'Harmattan.

Müller, C. (1998b) *Redebegleitende Gesten. Kulturgeschichte – Theorie – Sprachvergleich.* Berlin: Berlin Verlag A. Spitz.

Müller, C. (2004) Forms and uses of the Palm Up Open Hand: a case of a gesture family? In C. Müller and R. Posner (eds), *The Semantics and Pragmatics of Everyday Gestures* 233–256. Berlin: Weidler.

Müller, C. (2004/2008) *Metaphors Dead and Alive, Sleeping and Waking.* Habilitationsschrift, Freie Universität Berlin/Chicago, IL: University of Chicago Press.

Müller, C. (2008) What gestures reveal about the nature of metaphor. In A. Cienki and C. Müller (eds), *Metaphor and Gesture* 219–245. Amsterdam: John Benjamins.

Müller, C. and Cienki, A. (2009) When speech and gesture come together: forms of multimodal metaphor in the use of spoken language. In C. Forceville and E. Urios-Aparisi (eds), *Multimodal Metaphor.* Berlin/New York: Mouton de Gruyter.

Musolff, A. (2000) *Mirror-Images of Europe. Metaphors in the Public Debate about Europe in Britain and Germany.* Munich: Ludicium.

Musolff, A. (2004) *Metaphor and Political Discourse: Analogical Reasoning in Debates about Europe.* Basingstoke: Palgrave Macmillan.

Musolff, A. (2006) Metaphor scenarios in public discourse. *Metaphor and Symbol* 21 (1): 23–38.

Musolff, A. (2007) What role do metaphors play in racial prejudice? The function of antisemitic imagery in Hitler's Mein Kampf. *Patterns of Prejudice* 41 (1): 21–43.

Nerlich, B., Dingwall, R. and Clarke, D. D. (2002) The book of life: How the completion of the human genome project was revealed to the public. *Health* 6 (4): 445–469.

Nerlich, B. and Halliday, C. (2007) Avian flu: the creation of expectations in the interplay between science and the media. *Sociology of Health and Illness* 29 (1): 46–65.

Nerlich, M. S. (2006) The values and vulnerabilities of metaphors within the environmental sciences. *Society and Natural Resources* 19: 921–930.

Nikitina, L. and Furuoka, F. (2008) 'A language teacher is like …': examining Malaysian students' perceptions of language teachers through metaphor analysis. *Electronic Journal of Foreign Language Teaching* 5 (2): 192–205.

Norrick, N. R. (1993) *Conversational Joking: Humor in Everyday Talk*. Bloomington, IN: Indiana University Press.

Oberlechner, T., Slunecko, T. and Kronberger, N. (2004) Surfing the money tides: Understanding the foreign exchange market through metaphors. *British Journal of Social Psychology* 43: 133–156.

Obst, P. (2003) *Grief is a Journey*. Retrieved on 7 September 2006 from http://www.helphorizons.com/care/search_details.htm?id=455

Ortony, A. (ed.). (1993) *Metaphor and Thought* (2nd edn). New York: Cambridge University Press.

Oxford, R., Tomlinson, S., Barcelos, A., Harrington, C., Lavine, R. Z., Saleh, A. and Longhini, A. (1998) Clashing metaphors about language teachers: toward a systematic typology for the language teaching field. *System* 26 (1): 3–50.

Petrie, H. and Oshlag, R. (1993) Metaphor and learning. In A. Ortony (ed.) *Metaphor and Thought,* 2nd edn 579–609. Cambridge: Cambridge University Press.

Pidgeon, N., Kasperson, R. E. and Slovic, P. (eds) (2004) *The Social Amplification of Risk*. Cambridge: Cambridge University Press.

Plato (1882) *The Republic.* Translated by J. Davies and D. Vaughan. London: Macmillan

Ponterotto, D. (2003) The cohesive role of cognitive metaphor in discourse and conversation. In A. Barcelona (ed.) *Metaphor and Metonymy at the Crossroads* 283–298. Berlin: Mouton de Gruyter.

Pragglejaz group (2007) MIP: A method for identifying metaphorically-used words in discourse. *Metaphor and Symbol* 22 (1): 1–40.

Quinn, N. (1991) The cultural basis of metaphor. In J. Fernandez (ed.) *Beyond*

*Metaphor: The Theory of Tropes in Anthropology* 56–93. Stanford, CA: Stanford University Press.

Quinn, N. (2005) How to reconstruct schemas people share from what they say. In N. Quinn (ed.) *Finding Culture in Talk: A Collection of Methods* 35–82. New York: Palgrave Macmillan.

Rayson, P., Archer, D., Piao, S., McEnery, T. (2004) The UCREL semantic analysis system. *Proceedings of the Workshop 'Beyond Named Entity Recognition. Semantic Labelling for NLP Tasks', in association with the 4th International Conference on Language Resources and Evaluation (LREC 2004)*, 7–12.

Rees, C. E., Knight, L. V. and Wilkinson, C. E. (2007) Doctors being up there and we being down here: A metaphorical analysis of talk about student/doctor-patient relationships. *Social Science and Medicine* 65 (4): 725–737.

Reddy, M. (1979) The conduit metaphor: A case of frame conflict in our language about language. In A. Ortony (ed.) *Metaphor and Thought* 164–201. New York: Cambridge University Press.

Risiott, R. (1997) Can you really say that in English? University of York, Dept. of Language and Linguistic Science: BA assignment (ms).

Ritchie, D. (2003a) 'ARGUMENT IS WAR' - Or is it a game of chess? Multiple meanings in the analysis of implicit metaphors. *Metaphor and Symbol* 18 (2): 125–146.

Ritchie, D. (2003b) Categories and similarities: A note on circularity. *Metaphor and Symbol* 18 (1): 49–53.

Ritchie, L. D. (2006) *Context and Connection in Metaphor*. Basingstoke: Palgrave Macmillan.

Ritchie, L. D. (2008) Gateshead revisited: Perceptual simulators and fields of meaning in the analysis of metaphors. *Metaphor and Symbol* 23 (1): 24–49.

Ritchie, L. D. (2009) *Metaphor, narrative, and social reality in a conversation about homelessness*. Presented to the annual meeting of the International Communication Association. Chicago, IL.

Ritchie, L. D. and Dyhouse, V. (2008) Hair of the frog and other empty metaphors: The play element in figurative language. *Metaphor and Symbol* 23 (2): 85–107.

Ritchie, J. and Spencer, L. (1994) Qualitative data analysis for applied policy research. In A. Bryman and R. G. Burgess (eds) *Analysing Qualitative Data* 173–194. London: Routledge.

Robson, C. (2002) *Real World Research,* 2nd edn. Malden, MA: Wiley Blackwell.

Roschelle, J. and Teasley, S. (1995). The construction of shared knowledge in collaborative problem solving. In C. O'Malley and E. Heidelberg (eds)

*Computer Supported Collaborative Learning* 69–97. Berlin, New York: Springer-Verlag.

Russell, B. (2005) Blair admits he must win back voters' trust' in *The Independent* retrieved on 17 July 2009 from http://www.independent.co.uk/news/uk/politics/blair-admits-he-must-win-back-voters-trust-483361.html

Salmon G, (2002) *E-tivities the Key to E-learning.* London: Kogan Page.

Sanchez, R. (1998) Our bodies? Our selves? Questions about teaching in the MUD. In T. Taylor and I. Ward (eds) *Literacy Theory in the Age of the Internet* 93–106. New York: Columbia University Press.

Sandikcioglu, E. (2000) More metaphorical warfare in the Gulf: Orientalist frames in news coverage. In A. Barcelona (ed.) *Metaphor and Metonymy at the Crossroads: A Cognitive Perspective* 299–320. Berlin: Mouton de Gruyter.

Santa Ana, O. (1999) 'Like an animal I was treated': Anti-immigrant metaphor in US public discourse. *Discourse and Society* 10 (2): 191–224.

Satterfield, J. M. (1998) Cognitive-affective states predict military and political aggression and risk taking. *Journal of Conflict Resolution* 42 (6): 667–690.

Schlesinger, M. and Lau, R. R. (2000) The meaning and measure of policy metaphors. *The American Political Science Review* 94 (3): 611–626.

Schiffrin, D., Tannen, D. and Hamilton, H. (eds). (2001) *The Handbook of Discourse Analysis.* Oxford: Blackwell.

Schmitt, R. (2005) Systematic metaphor analysis as a method of qualitative research. *The Qualitative Report* 10 (2): 358–394.

Schön, D. (1979) Generative metaphor: A perspective on problem-setting in social policy. In A. Ortony (ed.) *Metaphor and Thought* 137–163. Cambridge: Cambridge University Press.

Scott, M. (2008) *WordSmith Tools 5.* Oxford: Oxford University Press.

Searle, J. (1979) Metaphor. In A. Ortony (ed.) *Metaphor and Thought* 83–111. New York: Cambridge University Press.

Semino, E. (2005) The metaphorical construction of complex domains: the case of speech activity in English *Metaphor and Symbol* 20 (1): 35–70.

Semino, E. (2008) *Metaphor in Discourse.* Cambridge: Cambridge University Press.

Semino, E., Heywood, J. and Short, M. (2004) Methodological problems in the analysis of metaphors in a corpus of conversations about cancer. *Journal of Pragmatics* 36 (7): 1271–1294.

Sherzer, J. (2002) *Speech Play and Verbal Art.* Austin, TX: University of Texas Press.

Sinclair, J. (1991) *Corpus, Concordance, Collocation.* Oxford: Oxford University Press.

Sinclair, J. (2004) *Text and Technology.* Amsterdam: John Benjamins.

Skelton, J. R., Wearn, A. M. and Hobbs, F. D. R. (2002) A concordance-based study of metaphoric expressions used by general practitioners and patients in consultation. *The British Journal of General Practice* 52 (475): 114–118.

Skorczynska, H. and Deignan, A. (2006) A comparison of metaphor vehicles and functions in scientific and popular business corpora. *Metaphor and Symbol*, 21: 87–104.

Slobin, D. (1996) From 'Thought and Language' to 'Thinking for Speaking'. In J. Gumperz and S. Levinson (eds) *Rethinking Linguistic Relativity* 70–96. New York: Cambridge University Press.

Sopory, P. (2005) Metaphor in formative evaluation and message design: An application to relationships and alcohol use. *Health Communication* 17 (2): 149–172.

Sperber, D. and Wilson, D. (1986) *Relevance*. Oxford: Blackwell.

Spivey, M. (2007) *The Continuity of Mind*. New York: Oxford University Press.

Steen, G. (2007) *Finding Metaphor in Grammar and Usage*. Amsterdam: John Benjamins.

Steen, G. (2008) The paradox of metaphor: Why we need a three-dimensional model of metaphor. *Metaphor and Symbol* 23 (4): 213–241.

Steen, G. (in press) Pragglejaz in practice: finding metaphorically used words in natural discourse. In A. Deignan, L. Cameron, G. D. Low and Z. Todd (eds) *Researching and Applying Metaphor in the Real World*. Amsterdam and Philadelphia: John Benjamins.

Steeples, C. (2004) Using action-oriented or participatory research methods for research on networked learning. In S. Banks, P. Goodyear, V. Hodgson, C. Jones, V. Lally, D. McConnell and C. Steeples, C. (eds) *Networked Learning 2004: Proceedings of the Fourth International Conference* 113–118. Networked Learning 2004. Lancaster: Lancaster University.

Stelma, J. and Cameron, L. (2007) Intonation units in research on spoken interaction. *Text and Talk* 27 (3): 361–393.

Stone, A. R. (1995) *The War of Desire and Technology at the Close of the Mechanical Age*. Cambridge MA: MIT Press.

Stratton, P., Munton, A., Hanks, H., Heard, D. and Davidson, C. (1988) *Leeds Attributional Coding System (LACS) Manual*. Leeds: Leeds Family Therapy Research Centre.

Strauss, A. and Corbin, J. (1998) *Basics of Qualitative Research. Grounded Theory Procedures and Techniques,* 2nd edn. Thousand Oaks, CA: Sage.

Streeck, J. (1993) Gesture as communication I: its coordination with gaze and speech. *Communication Monographs* 60: 275–299.

Streeck, J. (2002) Grammars, words, and embodied meanings: on the use and evolution of *so* and *like. Journal of Communication* 52 (3): 581–596.

Sutton-Smith, B. (1995) Conclusion: The persuasive rhetorics of play. In A. Pellegrini (ed.) *The Future of Play Theory: A Multidisciplinary Inquiry into the Contributions of Brian Sutton-Smith* 275–296. Albany, NY: SUNY Press.

Thelen, E. and Smith, L. (1994) *A Dynamic Systems Approach to the Development of Cognition and Action.* Cambridge, MA: MIT Press.

Thorndike, E. L. (1920) A constant error in psychological ratings. *Journal of Applied Psychology* 4 (1): 25–29.

Todd, Z. and Clarke, D. (1999) When is a dead rainbow not like a dead rainbow? A context-sensitive method for investigating differences between metaphor and simile. In L. Cameron and G. D. Low (eds) *Researching and Applying Metaphor* 49–268. Cambridge: Cambridge University Press.

Tuckwell, N. B. (1980) *Stimulated Recall: Theoretical Perspectives and Practical and Technical Considerations.* Occasional Paper Series 8-2-3. Alberta, Canada: Centre for Research in Teaching.

Turkle, S. (1995) *Life on the Screen, Identity in the Age of the Internet.* New York: Simon and Schuster.

Vervaeke, J. and Kennedy, J. M. (1996) Metaphors in language and thought: Falsification and multiple meanings. *Metaphor and Symbol* 11 (4): 273–284.

Vygotsky, L. (1986) *Thought and Language.* Translated by A. Kozulin. Cambridge, MA: MIT Press.

Walker, K. L. and Chestnut, D. (2003) The role of ethnocultural variables in response to terrorism. *Cultural Diversity and Ethnic Minority Psychology* 9 (3): 251–262.

Wan, W. (2007). An Examination of Metaphorical Accounts: L2 Writers Tell about their Writing Processes. Unpublished MA dissertation: Dept. of Educational Studies, University of York.

Webb, R. (1996) Linguistic features of metaphoric gestures. PhD dissertation. University of Rochester, New York.

Wenger, E. (1998) *Communities of Practice, Learning, Meaning and Identity.* Cambridge: Cambridge University Press.

Wheeler, B. (2005) Rekindling the Labour love affair. *BBC News website.* Retrieved on 17 July 2009 from http://news.bbc.co.uk/1/hi/uk_politics/426 2333.stm.

Yardley, L. (2000) Dilemmas in qualitative health research. *Psychology and Health* 15: 215–228.

Zapata, G. C. and Lacorte, M. (2007) Preservice and inservice instructors' metaphorical conceptions of second language teachers. *Foreign Language Annals* 40 (3): 521–534.

# Index

as metaphor trajectory, 129
emergence of, 128–130
importance of, 129
use across speakers, 14
*See also* discourse dynamics framework, metaphor analysis, topic, vehicle, vehicle grouping

talking-and-thinking, 78, 80, 82, 84, 88, 93, 120
teachers' use of metaphors, 6, 148
Teasley, S., 231
Thelen, E., 83
Thorndike, E., 219
Todd, Z., 11, 35, 39, 105, 215, 221
topic, 13, 52, 85, 102–103, 116
  and discourse interaction, 127
  identifying topics, 127–128
  inexplicit nature of, 127
  *See also* discourse dynamics framework, linguistic metaphor
transcription, 99–101, 184–186
  as trace, 82–83
  *See also* intonation unit
trustworthiness, 11, 33, 38–39, 114–115, 120, 184–188, 222–223, 237, 251
Tuckwell, N., 234
Turkle, S., 234, 247
Turner, M., 46, 51, 70

Urios-Aparisi, E., 195

values, 7, 27, 39, 79–80, 93, 97, 115–118, 123, 137, 147, 152–154
vehicle, 3, 8, 79, 85, 103, 116
  development of, 89, 90–91
  literalization of, 90
  prepositions, 112

redeployment of, 89
vehicle boundary, 106, 108
very common verbs/nouns, 111–112
*See also* discourse dynamics framework, identification of metaphors, linguistic metaphor, metaphor analysis, metaphor shifting
vehicle groups/grouping, 12, 13, 118–126, 186–188
  discourse evidence for, 120
  evolution of groupings, 120
  flexibility of, 119, 120, 126
  inductive process, 118
  labelling groups, 124–125
  naming categories, 118
  using groupings from others' research, 125
  *See also* metaphor analysis
Vervaeke, J., 61, 66, 67, 75, 125
Villamil, O., 30
virtual autoethnography, 234
Vygotsky, L., 77, 232

Walker, K., 194
Wan, W., 30, 31
*war on terror*, 87
Wearn, A., 35
Webb, R., 199
Wenger, E., 232
Wheeler, B., 172
Wilkinson, C., 37
Wilson, D., 65

Yardley, L., 223

Zapata, G., 30–32

Lightning Source UK Ltd.
Milton Keynes UK
UKOW040815100812

197317UK00002B/6/P